Microsoft System Center Configuration Manager Cookbook

Second Edition

Over 60 applicable recipes to administer and manage System
Center Configuration Manager Current Branch

Samir Hammoudi
Chuluunsuren Damdinsuren
Brian Mason
Greg Ramsey

Packt>

BIRMINGHAM - MUMBAI

Microsoft System Center Configuration Manager Cookbook

Second Edition

First published: September 2012

Second edtion: November 2016

Production reference: 1161116

Published by Packt Publishing Ltd.
Livery Place
35 Livery Street
Birmingham
B3 2PB, UK.
ISBN 978-1-78588-120-6

www.packtpub.com

Credits

Authors
Samir Hammoudi
Chuluunsuren Damdinsuren
Brian Mason
Greg Ramsey

Copy Editor
Laxmi Subramanian

Reviewer
Matthew Hudson

Proofreader
Safis Editing

Commissioning Editor
Kartikey Pandey

Graphics
Kirk D'Penha

Acquisition Editor
Meeta Rajani

Indexer
Pratik Shirodkar

Technical Editors
Narsimha Pai
Nirant Carvalho

Production Coordinator
Shantanu N. Zagade

About the Authors

Samir Hammoudi is a Microsoft Full Time Employee (MSFT) working as a Sales Engineer (TSP) on Surface devices and Windows 10 in Tokyo, Japan. During the beginning of his career, he worked as a Senior ICT Consultant in Switzerland for 7 years offering his wide technical expertise on Microsoft technologies such as Active Directory, Exchange, Virtualization, and Windows client deployment and management. Looking for a new challenge, he then moved to Japan and joined Microsoft as a Premier Field Engineer (PFE) on System Center Configuration Manager, where he covered customers all around APAC region. Avid of learning new technologies, Samir is the holder of a wide range of Microsoft certifications as MCSE (Server and Private Cloud) and MCITP (Enterprise Admin, Messaging Admin, and Lync Server Admin). He regularly writes tech notes and articles in both his blogs, one written in English covering Microsoft Devices and Cloud technologies (aka.ms/beanexpert) and one written in Japanese covering mainly Microsoft Deployment Toolkit (aka.ms/mdtjp). Samir loves sharing information to empower the Microsoft IT pros community. He tries his best through his blogs to cover information that is missing from official Microsoft sites. Samir is passionate about sports (football in particular) and about technology in general. Always open to direct contact, he encourages anyone wanting to discuss about anything on Windows client technologies to head over to his blogs and contact him personally.

Chuluunsuren Damdinsuren is a Microsoft Full Time Employee (MSFT) working as a Premier Field Engineer (PFE) in client management area such as Active Directory, System Center Configuration Manager, and Remote Desktop Services for Microsoft Japan. He has an Engineering degree from Osaka University and an MS degree in Computer Science. His primary focus is to design, migrate, deploy, train, and troubleshoot System Center Configuration Manager and Active Directory. He has a couple of technical blogs, and various MSCA and MCSE certificates. He is a passionate fan of football and topcoder.

Brian Mason is a Systems Engineer at Wells Fargo where he manages over 350,000 resources with CM (note that any views expressed in this book are Brian's and not necessarily those of Wells Fargo). Brian is a 6-time Microsoft MVP for Configuration Manager (CM). He currently runs the Minnesota System Center User Group and its website where he blogs. He can be found answering forum questions on TechNet and myITforum.

Greg Ramsey is a Systems Engineer specializing in global systems management for Dell Services. He has a B.S. in Computer Sciences and Engineering from the Ohio State University and is a Microsoft Most Valuable Professional (MVP) for Microsoft System Center Configuration Manager. Greg co-authored SMS 2003 Recipes: A Problem Solution Approach (Apress, 2006) and Microsoft System Center Configuration Manager Unleashed (Sams, 2009). Greg is the co-founder of the Ohio SMS Users Group and the Central Texas Systems Management User Group.

About the Reviewer

Matthew Hudson has been involved in IT for over 25 years.He has focused on Enterprise Systems Management for more than a decade at various companies ranging from Higher Education to the Energy sector. Matthew is currently a Microsoft MVP in Enterprise Mobility.

www.PacktPub.com

For support files and downloads related to your book, please visit www.PacktPub.com.

Did you know that Packt offers eBook versions of every book published, with PDF and ePub files available? You can upgrade to the eBook version at www.PacktPub.com and as a print book customer, you are entitled to a discount on the eBook copy. Get in touch with us at service@packtpub.com for more details.

At www.PacktPub.com, you can also read a collection of free technical articles, sign up for a range of free newsletters and receive exclusive discounts and offers on Packt books and eBooks.

Mapt

https://www.packtpub.com/mapt

Get the most in-demand software skills with Mapt. Mapt gives you full access to all Packt books and video courses, as well as industry-leading tools to help you plan your personal development and advance your career.

Why subscribe?

- Fully searchable across every book published by Packt
- Copy and paste, print, and bookmark content
- On demand and accessible via a web browser

Table of Contents

Preface

Microsoft's System Center Configuration Manager Current Branch (CM CB) is arguably the most complex (and feature rich) offering of the System Center suite. CM administrators must be proficient in a variety of technologies in order to effectively design and operate a CM hierarchy. The list of technologies that CM touches is almost overwhelming, for example, SQL, IIS, MDT, WSUS, WMI, PXE, SSRS, workstation and server operating systems, networking, and more. It should come as no surprise then that CM admins have built themselves a strong network of support. Forums such as Microsoft TechNet and myITforum are daily filled with questions and answers. There are local user groups, online webcasts, and conferences held routinely for admins to learn and share their trials and tribulations.

We often hear of an Exchange or Active Directory admin suddenly getting the CM dropped in his lap from the boss. There is little time to sink or swim. By giving quick recipes to get things done, readers can get things going (or keep them running) to buy time to better learn the product. This book does not spend time going into why CM does things the way it does, nor does it go into deep details as admins too often don't have the time for that. There are also other Configuration Manager 2007/2012 (CM07/CM12) admins who don't want to spend time reading bible-sized books on CM CB. They know an old version of CM very well and just need a quick guide to get them up to speed. Therefore, this book is aimed at getting admins up to speed fast with CM CB.

This book will get the reader up to a working knowledge of the product. For example, we cover Operating System Deployment (OSD) far enough for the reader to create a Windows 10 image and deploy it. Real world finesse will come only with time, but that cannot begin until the reader picks up the terminology and fundamentals. This book should remove that feeling of being overwhelmed by putting the reader straight to work with step by step recipes. Once the reader has actually tried a recipe, the topic will seem less intimidating. By using these recipes, the reader will gain the fundamentals of site administration, reporting, software distribution and patching, and client management.

What this book covers

Chapter 1, *Designing a System Center Configuration Manager Infrastructure*, covers ways to reduce the drag on primary sites to help keep you on just one site if possible such as installing SQL to be as efficient as possible and how to offload roles.

Chapter 2, *Deploying Windows 10 with Operating System Deployment*, shows you how to create an image and deploy it, taking into consideration the need to manage drivers or migrate user data.

Chapter 3, *Deploying Applications and Software Updates*, covers applications, patching and upgrades, monitoring deployments, and use of the new Software Center and Application Catalog.

Chapter 4, *Managing Compliance Settings*, covers how to create configuration items, put them into baselines and deploy them, and then monitor computers for compliance to those baselines with e-mailed drift reports.

Chapter 5, *Managing Mobile Devices using Configuration Manager with Microsoft Intune*, details ways to manage mobile devices by taking advantage of the MDM solution called Microsoft Intune that can be integrated with CM to offer a unique single pane of glass to manage both desktop and mobile devices.

Chapter 6, *Managing Sites*, details ways to configure and manage sites, set up discovery tasks to find systems, and explains how to set up security roles and scopes for other admins.

Chapter 7, *Managing Clients*, covers installation and upgrade of the CM client on systems, how to manage and monitor health of that client, and how to manage power on those clients.

Chapter 8, *Managing Inventory*, details the set up and usage of the various inventory methods of CM as well as metering of software usage.

Chapter 9, *Managing Reports and Queries*, walks you through Reporting Services installation, building queries for reports, and editing and creating reports.

What you need for this book

Readers with experience in CM07 or CM12 will get up to speed sooner, but it isn't a requirement. However, experience is needed in the following areas:

- Installing server features
- Installing Windows operating systems, and installing programs (for example, what is an MSI?)
- Finding Windows event logs
- Navigating to an IP or UNC, HTTP versus HTTPS, and so on

You might also want to get a mobile device (Android or iOS) if you are interested in testing the mobile device management features offered by CM CB and Microsoft Intune.

Who this book is for

This book is for administrators who need to get up to speed quickly with CM CB. Readers are given how-to steps without all the fat and fluff. Need to get SQL and CM installed right away? This book has recipes for design considerations. Need to just get a Windows 10 deployment started right now? There is an entire chapter dedicated to that. Need to set up a security drift report for your boss? There is a chapter for that as well. All the main features of CM have recipes written as concisely as possible to give the reader a quick start.

Sections

In this book, you will find several headings that appear frequently (Getting ready, How to do it, How it works, There's more, and See also).

To give clear instructions on how to complete a recipe, we use these sections as follows:

Getting ready

This section tells you what to expect in the recipe, and describes how to set up any software or any preliminary settings required for the recipe.

How to do it...

This section contains the steps required to follow the recipe.

How it works...

This section usually consists of a detailed explanation of what happened in the previous section.

There's more...

This section consists of additional information about the recipe in order to make the reader more knowledgeable about the recipe.

See also

This section provides helpful links to other useful information for the recipe.

Conventions

In this book, you will find a number of text styles that distinguish between different kinds of information. Here are some examples of these styles and an explanation of their meaning.

Code words in text, database table names, folder names, filenames, file extensions, pathnames, dummy URLs, user input, and Twitter handles are shown as follows: "You could manually create your own reference build, Sysprep, and capture it to a .wim file."

A block of code is set as follows:

```
PCUSOURCE=\\Server\Share\SQLServicePackX
CUSOURCE=\\Server\Share\SQLCUX
```

Any command-line input or output is written as follows:

```
Setup.exe /CONFIGURATIONFILE=cmsqlconfig.ini
```

New terms and **important words** are shown in bold. Words that you see on the screen, for example, in menus or dialog boxes, appear in the text like this: "Change the properties of the **Rebuild Indexes** task to be enabled to **Weekly**."

Warnings or important notes appear in a box like this.

Tips and tricks appear like this.

Reader feedback

Feedback from our readers is always welcome. Let us know what you think about this book-what you liked or disliked. Reader feedback is important for us as it helps us develop titles that you will really get the most out of.

To send us general feedback, simply e-mail `feedback@packtpub.com`, and mention the book's title in the subject of your message.

If there is a topic that you have expertise in and you are interested in either writing or contributing to a book, see our author guide at `www.packtpub.com/authors`.

Customer support

Now that you are the proud owner of a Packt book, we have a number of things to help you to get the most from your purchase.

Errata

Although we have taken every care to ensure the accuracy of our content, mistakes do happen. If you find a mistake in one of our books-maybe a mistake in the text or the code-we would be grateful if you could report this to us. By doing so, you can save other readers from frustration and help us improve subsequent versions of this book. If you find any errata, please report them by visiting `http://www.packtpub.com/submit-errata`, selecting your book, clicking on the **Errata Submission Form** link, and entering the details of your errata. Once your errata are verified, your submission will be accepted and the errata will be uploaded to our website or added to any list of existing errata under the Errata section of that title.

To view the previously submitted errata, go to `https://www.packtpub.com/books/content/support`and enter the name of the book in the search field. The required information will appear under the **Errata** section.

Piracy

Piracy of copyrighted material on the Internet is an ongoing problem across all media. At Packt, we take the protection of our copyright and licenses very seriously. If you come across any illegal copies of our works in any form on the Internet, please provide us with the location address or website name immediately so that we can pursue a remedy.

Please contact us at `copyright@packtpub.com` with a link to the suspected pirated material.

We appreciate your help in protecting our authors and our ability to bring you valuable content.

Questions

If you have a problem with any aspect of this book, you can contact us at `questions@packtpub.com`, and we will do our best to address the problem.

1
Designing a System Center Configuration Manager Infrastructure

In this chapter, we will cover the following recipes:

- What's changed from System Center 2012 Configuration Manager?
- System Center Configuration Manager's new servicing models
- Keeping your CM deployment up-to date
- Infrastructure sizing considerations
- Dividing up site system roles
- Upgrading in-place from Configuration Manager 2012
- Installing SQL the right way
- Managing Internet-facing clients
- Using remote and workstation distribution points and BranchCache

Introduction

In this chapter, we will learn the new servicing model, and walk through the various setup scenarios and configurations for **System Center Configuration Manager Current Branch** (**SCCM CB**). Designing and keeping a **System Center Configuration Manager** (**SCCM**) infrastructure current by using best practices such as keeping SQL server on the site, offloading some roles as needed, and in-place upgrades from CM12.

What's changed from System Center 2012 Configuration Manager?

We will go through the new features, changes, and removed features in CM since CM 2012.

Getting ready

The following are the new features in CM since CM12:

- **In-console updates for Configuration Manager**: CM uses an in-console service method called Updates and Servicing that makes it easy to locate and install updates for CM.
- **Service Connection Point**: The Microsoft Intune connector is replaced by a new site system role named `Service Connection Point`. The service connection point is used as a point of contact for devices you manage with, upload usage and diagnostic data to the Microsoft cloud service, and makes updates that apply within the CM console.
- **Windows 10 Servicing**: You can view the dashboard which tracks all Windows 10 PCs in your environment, create servicing plans to ensure Windows 10 PCs are kept up to date, and also view alerts when Windows 10 clients are near to the end of a CB/CBB support cycle.

How to do it…

Whats new in CM Capabilities

This information is based on versions 1511 and 1602. You can find out if the change is made in 1602 or later by looking for the `version 1602 or later` tag. You can find the latest changes at `https://technet.microsoft.com/en-us/library/mt757350.aspx`.

- **Endpoint Protection anti-malware**:
  - **Real-time protection**: This blocks potentially unwanted applications at download and prior to installation
  - **Scan settings**: This scans mapped network drives when running a full scan
  - **Auto sample file submission settings**: This is used to manage the behavior

- **Exclusion settings**: This section of the policy is improved to allow device exclusions

- **Software updates**:
  - CM can differentiate a Windows 10 computer that connects to **Windows Update for Business** (**WUfB**) versus the computers connected to SUP
  - You can schedule, or run manually, the WSUS clean up task from the CM console
  - CM has the ability to manage Office 365 client updates by using the SUP (version 1602 or later)

- **Application management**:
  - This supports **Universal Windows Platform** (**UWP**) apps
  - The user-available apps now appear in Software Center
  - When you create an in-house iOS app you only need to specify the installer (`.ipa`) file
  - You can still enter the link directly, but you can now browse the store for the app directly from the CM console
  - CM now supports apps you purchase in volume from the Apple **Volume-Purchase Program** (**VPP**) (version 1602 or later)
  - Use CM app configuration policies to supply settings that might be required when the user runs an iOS app (version 1602 or later)

- **Operating system deployment**:
  - A new **task sequence** (**TS**) type is available to upgrade computers from Windows 7/8/8.1 to Windows 10
  - Windows PE Peer Cache is now available that runs a TS using Windows PE Peer Cache to obtain content from a local peer, instead of running it from a DP
  - You can now view the state, deploy the servicing plans, and get alerts of WaaS in your environment, to keep the Windows 10 current branch updated

- **Client deployment**:
  - You can test new versions of the CM client before upgrading the rest of the site with the new software

- **Site infrastructure**:
  - CM sites support the in-place upgrade of the site server's OS from Windows Server 2008 R2 to Windows Server 2012 R2 (version 1602 or later)
  - SQL Server AlwaysOn is supported for CM (version 1602 or later)

- CM supports Microsoft Passport for Work which is an alternative sign-in method to replace a password, smart card, or virtual smart card
- **Compliance settings**:
    - When you create a configuration item, only the settings relevant to the selected platform are available
    - It is now easier to choose the configuration item type in the create configuration item wizard and has a number of new settings
    - It provides support for managing settings on Mac OS X computers
    - You can now specify kiosk mode settings for Samsung KNOX devices. (version 1602 or later)
- **Conditional access**:
    - Conditional access to Exchange Online and SharePoint Online is supported for PCs managed by CM (version 1602 or later)
    - You can now restrict access to e-mail and 0365 services based on the report of the Health Attestation Service (version 1602 or later)
    - New compliance policy rules like automatic updates and passwords to unlock devices, have been added to support better security requirements (version 1602 or later)
    - Enrolled and compliant devices always have access to Exchange On-Premises (version 1602 or later)
- **Client management**:
    - You can now see whether a computer is online or not via its status (version 1602 or later)
    - A new option, **Sync Policy** has been added by navigating to the **Software Center** | **Options** | **Computer Maintenance** which refreshes its machine and user policy (version 1602 or later)
    - You can view the status of **Windows 10 Device Health Attestation** in the **CM** console (version 1602 or later)
- **Mobile device management with Microsoft Intune**:
    - Improved the number of devices a user can enroll
    - Specify terms and conditions users of the company portal must accept before they can enroll or use the app
    - Added a device enrollment manager role to help manage large numbers of devices
    - CM can help you manage iOS Activation Lock, a feature of the Find My iPhone app for iOS 7.1 and later devices (version 1602 or later)

- You can monitor terms and conditions deployments in the CM console (version 1602 or later)
- **On-premises Mobile Device Management:**
    - You can now manage mobile devices using on-premises CM infrastructure via a management interface that is built into the device OS

Removed features

There are two features that were removed from CM current branch's initial release in December 2015, and there will be no more support on these features. If your organization uses these features, you need to find alternatives or stay with CM12.

- **Out of Band Management**: With Configuration Manager, native support for AMT-based computers from within the CM console has been removed.
- **Network Access Protection**: CM has removed support for Network Access Protection. The feature has been deprecated in Windows Server 2012 R2 and is removed from Windows 10.

See also

- Refer to the TechNet documentation on CM changes at `https://technet.microsoft.com/en-us/library/mt622084.aspx`

System Center Configuration Manager's new servicing models

The new concept servicing model is one of the biggest changes in CM. We will learn what the servicing model is and how to do it in this chapter.

Getting Ready

Windows 10's new servicing models

Before we dive into the new CM servicing model, we first need to understand the new Windows 10 servicing model approach called **Windows as a Service (WaaS)**.

Microsoft regularly gets asked for advice on how to keep Windows devices secure, reliable, and compatible. Microsoft has a pretty strong point-of-view on this: Your devices will be more secure, more reliable, and more compatible if you are keeping up with the updates we regularly release.

In a mobile-first, cloud-first world, IT expects to have new value and new capabilities constantly flowing to them. Most users have smart phones and regularly accept the updates to their apps from the various app stores. The iOS and Android ecosystems also release updates to the OS on a regular cadence.

With this in mind, Microsoft is committed to continuously rolling out new capabilities to users around the world, but Windows is unique in that it is used in an incredibly broad set of scenarios, from a simple phone to some of the most complex and mission critical use scenarios in factories and hospitals. It is clear that one model does not fit all of these scenarios.

To strike a balance between the needed updates for such a wide range of device types, there are four servicing options (summarized in Table 1) you will want to completely understand.

Table 1. Windows 10 servicing options (WaaS)

Servicing Models	Key Benefits	Support Lifetime	Editions	Target Scenario
Windows Insider Program	Enables testing new features before release	N/A	Home, Pro, Enterprise, Education	IT Pros, Developers
Current Branch (CB)	Makes new features available to users immediately	Approximately 4 months	Home, Pro, Enterprise, Education	Consumers, limited number of Enterprise users
Current Branch for Business (CBB)	Provides additional testing time through Current Branch	Approximately 8 months	Pro, Enterprise, Education	Enterprise users

Long-Term Servicing Branch (LTSB)	Enables long-term low changing deployments like previous Windows versions	10 Years	Enterprise LTSB	ATM, Line machines, Factory control

How to do it…

How will CM support Windows 10?

As you read in the previous section, Windows 10 brings with it new options for deployment and servicing models. On the **System Center** side, it has to provide enterprise customers with the best management for Windows 10 with CM by helping you deploy, manage, and service Windows 10. Windows 10 comes in two basic types: a Current Branch/Current Branch for Business with fast version model, and the LTSB with a more traditional support model.

Therefore, Microsoft has released a new version of CM to provide full support for the deployment, upgrade, and management of Windows 10 in December 2015. The new CM (simply without calendar year) is called **Configuration Manager Current Branch** (**CMCB**), and designed to support the much faster pace of updates for Windows 10, by being updated periodically.

This new version will also simplify the CM upgrade experience itself. One of the core capabilities of this release is a brand new approach for updating the features and functionality of CM. Moving faster with CM will allow you to take advantage of the very latest feature innovations in Windows 10, as well as other operating systems such as Apple iOS and Android when using **mobile device management** (**MDM**) and **mobile application management** (**MAM**) capabilities.

The new features for CM are in-console Updates-and-Servicing processes that replace the need to learn about, locate, and download updates from external sources. This means no more service packs or cumulative update versions to track. Instead, when you use the CM current branch, you periodically install in-console updates to get a new version. New update versions release periodically and will include product updates and can also introduce new features you may choose to use (or not use) in your deployment.

Because CM will be updated frequently, will be denoted each particular version with a version number, for example 1511 for a version shipped in December 2015. Updates will be released for the current branch about three times a year. The first release of the current branch was 1511 in December 2015, followed by 1602 in March 2016. Each update version is supported for 12 months from its general availability release date.

Why is there another version called Configuration Manager LTSB 2016?

There will be a release named System Center Configuration Manager LTSB 2016 that aligns with the release of Windows Server 2016 and System Center 2016. With this version, as like previous versions 2007 and 2012, you do not have to update the Configuration Manager Site Servers like the current branch.

Table 2. Configuration Manager Servicing Options:

Servicing Options	Benefits	Support Lifetime	Intended Target Clients
CM CB	Fully supports any type of Windows 10	Approximately 12 months	Windows 10 CB/CBB, Windows 10
Configuration Manager LTSB 2016	You do not need to update frequently	10 Years	Windows 10 LTSB

Keeping your CM deployment up-to date

CM synchronizes with the Microsoft cloud service to get updates. You can then install from within the CM console. Only updates that apply to your infrastructure and version are downloaded and made available. This synchronization can be automatic, or manual depending on how you configure the service connection point for your hierarchy.You can choose either of the following methods for upgrading your CM Infrastructure.

You can choose either of the following methods for upgrading your CM Infrastructure:

- In **online mode**, the service connection point automatically connects to the Microsoft cloud service and downloads applicable updates
- In **offline mode**, you must manually use the Service Connection Tool to download and then import available updates into the service connection point

By default, CM checks for new updates every 24 hours. Beginning with version 1602 or later, you can also check for updates immediately by:

1. Navigating to **Administration** | **Cloud Services** | **Updates and Servicing**.
2. Clicking on **Check for Updates**.

> To view updates in the console, a user must be assigned a security role that includes the **Read** permission in the permission group **Site**, and the security scope **All**.

To configure the service connection point role:

1. Navigate to **Administration** | **Site Configuration** | **Servers and Site System Roles**.
2. Add **Service connection point role** by doing the following:
   - **New site system server**: On the **Home** tab in the **Create group**, click on **Create Site System Server** to start the **Create Site System Server** wizard.
   - **Existing site system server**: Click on the server on which you want to install the service connection point role. Then, on the **Home** tab, in the **Server group**, click on **Add Site System Roles** to start the **Add Site system Roles** wizard.
3. On the **System Role Selection** page, select **Service connection point**, and click on **Next**.
4. Complete the wizard.

> The service connection point site system role may only be installed on a central administration site or standalone primary site. The service connection point must have Internet access.

Getting ready

Before applying a CM update, there are three recommended actions you can execute in order to safely update CM:

1. Refer to the checklist made available by Microsoft:

   Refer to the checklist available at `https://technet.microsoft.com/en -us/library/mt691556.aspx` for updating from System Center Configuration Manager version 1511 to 1602.

2. Test the database upgrade:
   1. Obtain a set of source files from the `CD.Latest` folder of a site that runs the version you plan to update to from the lab environment. For example, if your site runs version 1501 and you want to update to 1602, you must get a `CD.Latest` folder from a site that has already updated to version 1602.
   2. Create a backup of the site database, and then restore it to an instance of a test SQL Server.
   3. Run Setup.exe from `CD.Latest`, for example, `SMSSETUP\BIN\X64\Setup.exe /TESTDBUPGRADE DBtest\CM_ABC`.
   4. Monitor `ConfigMgrSetup.log` in the root of the system drive.
   5. If the test upgrade fails, resolve any issues related to the site database upgrade failure.

3. Run the prerequisite checker:
   1. Navigate to **Administration** | **Cloud Services** | **Updates and Servicing**.
   2. Right-click on the update package you want to run the prerequisite check for.
   3. Choose **Run prerequisite** check. When you run the prerequisite check, content for the update replicates on child sites.
   4. To view the results, navigate to **Monitoring** | **Site Servicing Status** and look for the prerequisite status. You can also view the details from `ConfigMgrPrereq.log`.

How to do it...

Before installing a new CM update, be sure to have done the prerequisite checks described in the *Getting ready* section.

> **TIP**
> Child primary sites start the update automatically after the central administration site completes installation of the update. You can use Service Windows for site servers to control when a site installs updates.

When it comes to updating CM to a new version, you will have to consider updating the CM hierarchy in the following order:

1. The top-tier site (primary site or CAS if you have one). Follow these steps to apply the update to the top-tier site:
   1. From the top-tier site server, navigate to **Administration** | **Cloud Services** | **Updates and Servicing**.
   2. Select an available update and then click on **Install Update Pack**.

2. Update installation at secondary sites. After the parent primary site is updated, update the secondary site using the following steps:
   1. Navigate to **Administration** | **Site Configuration** | **Sites**.
   2. Select the site you want to update, and then on the **Home** tab, in the **Site group**, click on **Upgrade**.
   3. Click on **Yes**.

3. To monitor the status, select the secondary site server, and then on the **Home** tab, in the **Site group**, click on **Show Install Status**.

> You have to manually update secondary sites from the CM console after the primary parent site update is completed. Automatic update of secondary site servers is not supported. When you open the CM console after the site update, you are prompted to update the console.

4. Start update of CM clients. Perform the following steps to update clients:
    1. Navigate to **Administration | Site Configuration | Sites**.
    2. On the **Home** tab, in the **Sites group**, click on **Hierarchy Settings**.
    3. In the **Client Upgrade** tab, review the version and date of the production client.
    4. Click on **Upgrade all clients** in the hierarchy using the production client and click on **OK** in the confirmation dialog box.
    5. If you don't want client upgrades to apply to servers, click on **Do not upgrade servers**.
    6. Specify the number of days in which computers must upgrade the client after they receive the client policy.
    7. If you want the client installation package to be copied to prestaged distribution points, click on the **Automatically distribute** client installation package to distribution points.
    8. Click on **OK** to save the settings and close the **Hierarchy Settings Properties** dialog box.

How it works...

As part of the update installation, CM re-installs any affected components such as site system roles or the console, manages updates to clients based on the selections you made for client piloting, and basically there is no need to reboot site system servers as part of the update.

> When updates are installed, Configuration Manager also updates the `CD.Latest` folder which is used during a site recovery.

There's more...

From the CM console, it is also possible to verify any update installation status as well as monitor the update in progress.

To verify the status of updated packages, navigate to **Administration | Cloud Services | Updates and Servicing**. This node shows the installation status for all updated packages.

To monitor the CM update while it's applied, follow these steps:

1. Navigate to **Monitoring** | **Overview** | **Site Servicing Status**. You will find there the installation status of the CM update currently in progress.
2. You can view the CMUpdate.log file in
   <ConfigMgr_Installation_Directory>\Logs\.

After a CAS or primary site updates, each CM console that connects to that site must also update.

To start updating CM consoles:

1. Open the console, you are prompted to update a console, click on **OK**.
2. To verify the version, go to **About System Center Configuration Manager** at the top-left corner of the console where the new site and console versions are displayed.

See also

- Refer to the TechNet documentation on CM updates at https://technet.micros
  oft.com/en-us/library/mt607046.aspx

Infrastructure sizing considerations

In this section, we provide a quick reference on supported size and scale information and recommended hardware information. Basically, it depends on the scale of CM, make sure your planning hierarchy and hardware is good enough for CM requirements.

Supportable size and scale

You can verify the maximum supported size and scale information from the following tables:

Table 1. Sites

Site Type	Maximum Scale and Size
CAS	• Up to 25 child primary sites • 700k clients (50k clients for SQL Standard)
Primary	• Up to 250 child secondary sites • 150k clients
Secondary	• Does not support child sites • 15k clients

Table 2. Site Roles

Site Role Type	Maximum Scale and Size
Distribution Point	• A Primary/Secondary site supports up to 250 DPs • A Primary/Secondary site supports up to 2k pull-DPs • A Primary site hierarchy supports up to 5k DPs • Up to 10k packages and applications • 4k clients
Management point	• Primary site supports up to 15 MPs • Only single MP can be in secondary site • 25k clients
Software update point	• 25k clients (150k for Remote SUP)

Hardware recommendation

Microsoft has published detailed guidance on recommended hardware configurations, you can find it here: https://technet.microsoft.com/en-us/library/mt589500.aspx.

Table 3. Site Servers

Site Server Type	CPU Cores	Memory (GB)/for SQL (%)	Disk (GB)
Stand-alone primary with SQL	16	96/80	OS-32 (WS2012R2) CM-25~200 DB-100 per 25k clients TempDB – As needed Content- As needed
Stand-alone primary with remote SQL	8	16/-	–
Remote SQL for stand-alone primary	16	64/90	–
CAS with SQL	16	96/80	–
CAS with remote SQL	8	16/-	–
Remote SQL for CAS	16	96/90	–
Child primary with SQL	16	96/80	–
Child primary with remote SQL	8	16/-	–
Remote SQL for child primary	16	64/90	–
Secondary	8	16/-	–

Table 4. Remote site system servers

Site System Role	CPU cores	Memory (GB)	Disk (GB)
Management point	4	8	50
Distribution point	2	8	As needed
Application Catalog	4	16	50
Software update point	8	16	As needed
All other site system roles	4	8	50

See also

- Refer to the TechNet documentation on CM supported configurations at `https ://technet.microsoft.com/en-us/library/mt589499.aspx`

Dividing up site system roles

It is likely that most installations of CM consist of a single primary site with all roles loaded locally on the same server. Depending on the hardware used (RAM and disk IO chief among them), this will suffice for many organizations. As companies grow and the workload of CM starts to stress the hardware of a single server, administrators need to offload roles to other servers.

> While it was a best practice to offload SQL in CM07, we now advise keeping SQL on box in CM as SQL replication has replaced much of the file-based replication of CM07. CM is native x64 code, so there is no performance hit for a WOW64 translation like there was with CM07 on x64 servers. Underpowered VMs, however, might benefit from offloading SQL to more powerful servers.

Getting ready

Admins should move roles off as described in the following *How to do it...* section until the primary site starts to perform as expected. We will start with both **Distribution Point** (**DP**) and **Management Point** (**MP**). Unlike CM07, CM allows for more than one MP with no default MP to define. Offloading these two roles will do more to alleviate stress than any other steps. For this step, have another server ready where you can move these roles to.

How to do it...

1. Add the machine account of the primary site to the local admin's group of the server taking on the MP and DP role.
2. If you need to prevent content from copying to any particular drive on the new server, drop a file on the root of the drive named `no_sms_on_drive.sms`.
3. Navigate to **Administration** | **Site Configuration** | **Servers and Site System Roles**. From the **Home** tab on the ribbon, click on **Create a Site System Server**.
4. Enter the name of the new server, select the **primary site code**, and enter the `FQDN` of the new server.
5. Check the boxes for both **Distribution Point** and **Management Point**.
6. Check the box to allow CM to install the IIS role on the new server.
7. CM now gives the ability to force content on a DP to drive letters of your preference. Choose as needed.
8. CM has moved the PXE service point to the DP. Select this option only if you plan to image devices with an *F12* boot. Enable multicast only if needed; the rule of thumb in security is *less is better*; you reduce the surface area of attack and reduce the odds you have something to patch down the road.
9. CM can now verify the content of your packages on a DP, which reduces the chance of clients failing to install an application due to corrupt files. CM now allows you to associate DPs to boundary groups. Use this feature only if you're trying to protect the network, otherwise leave this alone as it introduces another possible point of failure in a distribution you may have to troubleshoot one day.
10. For the MP settings, use the defaults for now; you can always set up SQL replication to the MP at a later time to reduce additional load.
11. Complete the wizard and then read `sitecomp.log` and `distmgrr.log` on the primary server and `MPSetup.log` on the new server to verify a successful installation.

12. Test the new MP by stopping the **SMSAgentHost** service on the primary, and then verify that clients are contacting the new MP (check `mpfdm.log` on the new MP).
13. Test the new DP by distributing content to it.

With a working MP and DP on another server, these roles can now be removed from the primary site. Follow these steps to remove the roles:

1. Navigate to **Administration** | **Site Configuration** | **Servers and Site System Roles** and select your primary site in the right-hand pane.
2. In the bottom pane, select both **Management Point** and **Distribution Point** (use *Ctrl + click)* and then click on **Remove Role** from the ribbon.
3. If you see a warning that this is the last management point for the site, click on **No** and go back to testing the new MP as the site is not aware that it is working.

How it works...

Once all IIS roles have been offloaded, IIS can be removed from the primary site. This strengthens security of the server and frees up resources for the remaining duties of the site. As you offload roles, the server has less to do as resources are freed up.

There's more...

Beyond IIS-based roles, there are still several items that can cause stress to the primary site server, which you can offload to other servers.

Offloading the SUP

With the MP and DP offloaded, the bulk of the client traffic to the primary site has been removed. The SUP role should be offloaded next as it's another point where clients can directly hit your primary site. To do this simply follow these steps:

1. Install the latest version of **WSUS** on the MP/DP server (that already has IIS installed) and be sure to cancel the configuration wizard when it starts (CM will configure it instead). Also, be sure to select the option **Use this server as the active software update point**.

2. Navigate to **Administration** | **Site Configuration** | **Servers and Site System Roles**, select the MP/DP server, and add the software update point role. Verify that the setup encountered no errors by checking SUPSetup.log, then look out for errors in WSUSCtrl.log and wcm.log.

3. With the new SUP working, that role can now be removed from the primary site. From the admin console, select the **Primary server** and remove the **Software update role**.

4. Uninstall WSUS from the primary site server, but be sure to leave the WSUS admin console installed as its files are needed to manage the SUP.

Offloading Endpoint Protection

If you are using Endpoint Protection in your company, you can move this role next, but note that there will be no change to the server load. To do this simply follow these steps:

1. Select the MP/DP/SUP server in the admin console and add the **Endpoint Protection Point** role.

2. Verify that the setup encountered no errors by checking EPSetup.log, then watch for errors in EPCtlMgr.log. Often, this server will have to be rebooted before it can become functional and that will show in EPSetup.log.

3. From the **admin** console, select the primary server and remove the **Endpoint Protection Point** role.

Offloading SQL Reporting Services

The **SQL Reporting Service Point** can cause stress if people are repeatedly running reports that are hard for your primary to query. The smart move there is to simply set such reports to cache for a certain amount of time (an hour, a day, and so on) so that no matter how often the report is run, the cached data is used instead of fresh queries to the primary site's database. Additionally, reporting services for SQL 2008 and above no longer require IIS, so offloading the role doesn't help towards the ability to remove IIS. Should you still wish to offload that role anyway, (perhaps just as a rule you might decide that no other roles be allowed on a primary) select a server with SQL Reporting Services installed (IIS is not necessary).

Follow these steps to offload SQL Reporting Services Point role:

1. Navigate to **Administration** | **Site Configuration** | **Servers and Site System Roles**, select the **Create Site System Server** from the **Home** tab in the ribbon. Enter the FQDN of the server and choose the CAS if you have one or choose the primary server.

2. Select the **Reporting services point** as the role, verify the settings by clicking on the **Verify** button, and enter a domain account that you have granted the smsschm_users role in SSMS (generally, the same account used when SRS was created on the primary site).

3. Complete the wizard and verify that the new site is working by running a report from the **Monitoring** | **Reporting** node in the console and choosing the new server (not the primary site).

4. Navigate to **Administration** | **Site Configuration** | **Servers and Site System Roles**, choose your primary site and remove the **Reporting services point** role.

5. Log on to the primary site, click on the **Start** button and type SQL Server Installation Center (64-bit) and hit Enter. Run the installation wizard and remove the reporting services role by unchecking it, thereby completing the wizard.

The remaining roles should cause no discernible stress to the primary. But there is one additional step you can take to reduce the impact of the MP role on your server and that is to create a transnational replica between the primary site and the MP. With such a replica, the MP can answer all client requests without querying the primary site. This also allows clients to remain functional if the primary site is down for maintenance or patching (assuming you've offloaded other roles needed like DP, SUP, and so on).

By creating this replica, there is a benefit in that if other roles are offloaded from the primary site, the primary site could go down for patching or maintenance while software distribution and patching could continue.

See also

- How to set up a publication of this replica is already documented quite well by Microsoft at https://technet.microsoft.com/en-us/library/mt608546.aspx

Upgrading in-place from Configuration Manager 2012

You can perform an in-place upgrade to CM from a CM12 hierarchy. Before starting the upgrade, you must prepare sites, which requires you to remove specific configurations, and then follow the upgrade sequence from top to bottom level.

Getting ready

Microsoft has published a checklist for upgrade preparation. You can refer the information from here `https://technet.microsoft.com/en-us/library/mt627853.aspx`.

The following are some of important items to note:

- Ensure that the site system environment meets the supported configurations that are required for upgrading to CM
- Review the server OS versions
- Review the required prerequisites for the site system server (especially, ADK Windows 10)
- Install all critical updates for OS
- Run Setup Prerequisite Checker
- Create a backup of the site database at the CAS and primary sites

How to do it...

Before you start the CM hierarchy upgrade, read the *Getting ready* section.

To upgrade the CM hierarchy, you upgrade the top-tier site of the hierarchy (CAS or standalone primary site). After the upgrade of the top-tier site is completed, you can upgrade child primary sites in any order that you want. After you upgrade all primary sites, you can upgrade a child secondary site.

Starting the upgrade installation at the CAS or primary site

Follow these steps to install the upgrade to the CAS or primary site:

1. Make sure the user has the following security rights:
   - Local Administrator rights on the site server computer.
   - Local Administrator rights on the remote site database server for the site, if it is remote.
2. Open Explorer and browse to `<ConfigMgSourceMedia>\SMSSETUP\BIN\X64`.
3. Double-click on `Setup.exe`. The **Configuration Manager Setup** wizard opens.
4. On the **Before You Begin** page, click on **Next**.
5. On the **Getting Started** page, select **Upgrade this Configuration Manager site**, and then click on **Next**.
6. On the **Product Key** page, click on **Next**.
7. On the **Microsoft Software License Terms** page, read and accept the license terms, then click on **Next**.
8. On the **Prerequisite Licenses** page, read and accept the license terms, then click on **Next**.
9. On the **Prerequisite Downloads** page, specify download the latest files or use previously downloaded files, and then click on **Next**.
10. On the **Server Language Selection** page, check required languages, then click on **Next**.
11. On the **Client Language Selection** page, check required languages, then click on **Next**.
12. On the **Settings Summary** page, click on **Next** to start **Prerequisite Checker**.
13. On the **Prerequisite Installation Check** page, make sure there are no problems listed, then click on **Next**.
14. On the **Upgrade** page, you can see the progress status. When setup completes the installation, close the wizard.

Starting the upgrade installation at a secondary site

To upgrade a secondary site by the following steps:

1. Make sure the user has the following security rights:
     - Local Administrator rights on the secondary site computer
     - Infrastructure Administrator or a Full Administrator security role on the parent primary site
     - **System administrator** (**SA**) rights on the site database of the secondary site
2. Navigate to **Administration** | **Site Configuration** | **Sites**.
3. Select the secondary site; on the **Home** tab in the **Site group**, click on **Upgrade**.
4. Click on **Yes** to confirm the decision.
5. The secondary site upgrade progresses in the background.

Starting the upgrade installation of clients

Perform the following steps to update clients:

1. Navigate to **Administration** | **Site Configuration** | **Sites**.
2. On the **Home** tab, in the **Sites group**, click on **Hierarchy Settings**.
3. In the **Client Upgrade** tab, review the version and date of the production client.
4. Click on **Upgrade all clients** in the hierarchy using the production client and click on **OK** in the confirmation dialog box.
5. If you don't want client upgrades to apply to servers, click on **Do not upgrade servers**.
6. Specify the number of days in which computers must upgrade the client after they receive the client policy.
7. If you want the client installation package to be copied to prestaged distribution points, click on **Automatically distribute** client installation package to distribute points.
8. Click on **OK** to save the settings and close the **Hierarchy Settings Properties** dialog box.

How it works...

When you upgrade to CM, the site performs a site reset, which includes a re-installation of all site system roles, and if the site is the top-tier site, it updates the client installation package on each DP in the hierarchy. The site also updates the default boot images to use the new Windows PE version which is included with the Windows Assessment and Deployment Kit 10. If the site is a primary site, it updates the client upgrade package for that site.

There's more...

From the CM console, it is possible to verify the upgrade status of any secondary site.

To verify the upgrade status:

1. In the **CM** console, select the **secondary site server**.
2. On the **Home** tab in the **Site** group, click on **Show Install Status**.

You must manually upgrade each standalone consoles, after CM upgrade.
To start updating CM consoles:

1. Open the console, you are prompted to update a console, click on **OK**.
2. To verify the version, go to **About System Center Configuration Manager** at the top-left corner of the console where the new site and console versions are displayed.

See also

- Refer to the information at `https://technet.microsoft.com/en-us/library/mt627853.aspx` for Upgrading System Center Configuration Manager

Installing SQL the right way

How well SQL is installed before CM can have a dramatic effect on how people perceive CM to be as a product. Common complaints heard are *CM is slow*, *The console is slow*, and *It can't keep up with these many clients*. A well thought out installation will go unnoticed where the reverse can cause downright agony for admins.

Getting ready

Get the latest supported version of SQL, the latest supported service pack, and the latest version of the cumulative update files. An already slipstreamed set of files from Microsoft will make things easier if available. The enterprise version has many benefits such as online re-indexing of tables, support for more than 50,000 clients and more, but the decision of which edition to use usually comes down to cost, as the enterprise edition is far more expensive than the standard version.

The more memory SQL has access to, the better it will run. The more disks and controllers it can use, the better it will run. SQL doesn't perform well in a virtual machine on virtual disks. This can be done in a lab or even on a laptop as a lab, but for production, memory and disks will define the CM experience.

How to do it...

Consider the following disk layout optimized for an enterprise-class primary site or CAS:

Disk	Controller	Number of Drives	Drive letter	Partitions
0	0	4	C	OS
1	1	4	T	TempDB
2	1	4	X	TxLogs
3	1	6	R	SQLDB1
4	2	6	S	SQLDB2
5	2	8	D	Data\Backup

External controllers 1 and 2 get as much RAM as you can afford (1 GB optimally). Each gets one hot, spare drive. All controllers are formatted with RAID 10. SQL activity is split across two controllers. RAID cache settings should be set to **Write Back, no Read Ahead**.

From the previous table, you can peel away the number of drives as costs constrain your budget in the following order:

1. The OS could be on a simple mirror.
2. `TempDB` and `TxLogs` could be on a single drive.
3. The SQL files could be on the same drive.
4. The SQL files could be mixed with `TempDB`.
5. The SQL files `Data\Backup` and `TempDB` could be on the same drive.
6. Move `TxLogs` to `C:` and all other data on the second drive.
7. Everything sits on one drive (small lab scenario).

How it works...

With the best layout of disks you can afford and the most memory you can afford, SQL will be able to stand under the stress CM puts on it. If using SAN, multiple dedicated LUNs are best, if available. Notice `TxLogs` were the last to be compromised as nothing can be committed to SQL until first written to `TxLogs`. Even with plenty of RAM, data must still be written to disk, which makes `TxLogs` an important point in any design.

There's more...

Drive layout is the key to smooth SQL operations. But that's just the start. A few more easy steps will keep your installation bug free and optimized for CM use.

Installing SQL with an unattended file

After the preparation of the drives, SQL can be installed using an unattended file, which has the additional benefit of being reused for a reinstall, or being used on similar primary sites. An example of an unattended file is included in this chapter. It includes two sections of note:

```
PCUSOURCE=\\Server\Share\SQLServicePackX
CUSOURCE=\\Server\Share\SQLCUX
```

The location of any service pack not already slipstreamed should be used for the PCUSOURCE and the location of the latest cumulative update should be used for CUSOURCE. If service packs have already been slipstreamed into the setup files, simply comment them out.

To `callout` the unattended file, simply use a command similar to the following:

```
Setup.exe /CONFIGURATIONFILE=cmsqlconfig.ini
```

Edit the unattended file as needed to match your drive layout. It is currently set to use R, S, T, and X drives so read carefully. The file works only for SQL 2008 R2, but SQL 2008 and SQL 2012 are similar enough that some simple editing can make them work. The key here is that you can read the file to see how to properly lay out the files and options in advance.

Setting some limits

SQL will be happy to eat all the memory on a server leaving nothing for the OS, base applications, or CM. So you need to limit it. Simply open **SQL Server Management Studio** (**SMSS**) and right-click on your server to view properties, and navigate to **Memory**. Because CM is all x64, leave AWE alone. But you do want to enter a maximum server memory here. Leave the OS with 2 GB, your base apps could vary, but 1-2 GB should suffice, and leave CM with 4 GB. Add all that and subtract it from the server's total memory and enter that number here. Note that a CAS requires 8 GB minimum to be dedicated to SQL (anyone choosing to use a CAS is likely to use 16 GB or more anyway).

Transaction logs have been known to grow to consume the entire drive and when that happens, everything stops as nothing can be committed to SQL until first written to the transaction log. A fair limit would be 15 percent less than the entire free space of the drive. Refer to the *SQL file layout section*, (step 5) for where to do this.

SQL file layout

With SQL installed, it now has to be configured to make the best use of the processors on the server. Use more than one file for the SQL database. The rule of thumb is to use as many files as there are physical processing cores.

1. From the Microsoft **SQL Server Management Studio** (**SMSS**) right-click on your **CM database** and choose **Properties**. Go to **Files** and then click on the **Add** button.
2. If you had eight cores and two drives for the SQL database (R and S), you would add four files to R and three more to S (assuming you initially installed SQL to S).

3. Set the initial size of each file to one-eighth the size of what you expect your entire database size to be.

4. Set **Autogrowth** to 1000 MB.

5. Set **Autogrowth of the transaction log** to 1000 MB. Additionally, restrict the growth of the file to a size that is smaller than the free space on the drive on which it resides.

6. Click on **OK** to commit the changes; no need for reboot.

Helping SQL

CM has a maintenance task to rebuild indexes, which is disabled by default. Over time, SQL will slow down as the indexes grow stale.

1. From the CM admin console, navigate to **Administration** | **Site Configuration** | **Sites** and click on **Site Maintenance** in the ribbon.

2. Change the properties of the **Rebuild Indexes** task to be enabled to **Weekly**.

3. Choose a time of day where CM isn't busy. The default of 1 a.m. on Sunday is probably a good choice.

4. Repeat for all primary sites (and the CAS if you have one).

Additionally, if you have no need to keep data around for 3 months, then help keep the database size smaller by shortening the clean-up tasks from 90 days to something you can live with (perhaps 21 days or 30 days).

Lastly, verify that the recovery model for the CM database is from **Full** to **Simple**. Because CM runs backup itself, only its point in time backup can be used to recover the database so you will never recover to some point in time with a full backup. This also keeps the transaction log from having to be backed up. This setting can be found in SMSS by right-clicking on the database, navigating to **Options** and selecting **Simple for the Recovery model**.

See also

- Install SQL Server 2012 Using a Configuration File at `https://technet.microso ft.com/en-us/library/dd239405(v=sql.110).aspx`
- Install SQL Server 2016 Using a Configuration File at `https://msdn.microsoft. com/en-us/library/dd239405.aspx`

Managing Internet-facing clients

Depending on the environment, you may have clients that:

- Regularly move between the Internet and the intranet
- Are home computers and never connect to the intranet

Managing clients that are not always connected to the internal network can be a challenge. If remote computers use **Virtual Private Networking** (**VPN**) to connect to the corporate network on a regular basis, Internet-facing support may not be required. But if we know that clients may use some type of remote desktop to connect to the corporate network, or maybe they don't have to connect to the corporate network at all to do their job, then Internet-facing support should be considered to ensure proper patch and asset management.

CM has two client communication methods: HTTPS only and **HTTPS or HTTP**. One CM site can support both HTTPS and HTTP communication if required.

Getting ready

Public Key Infrastructure (**PKI**) certificates are required for Internet-based client communication. Engage with the team that owns PKI in your infrastructure. If a PKI infrastructure doesn't currently exist, follow Microsoft's step-by-step example of deploying PKI `https://technet.microsoft.com/en-us/library/mt627852.aspx`. Once you have all valid certificates, proceed to the next section.

How to do it...

To enable Internet-facing clients, perform the following steps:

1. Navigate to **Administration** | **Site Configuration** | **Sites**, and select the desired site to support Internet-based clients. Right-click on the site and select **Properties**.
2. From the **Client Computer Communication** tab, select either **HTTPS** only if you only want to support HTTPS, or **HTTPS** or **HTTP** as required.
3. Enable the checkbox to **Use PKI client certificate**, and then click on the **Modify** button to select the client certification selection criteria, as well as the store name, and then click on **OK**.
4. Click on the **Set** button to specify the **Trusted Root Certification Authorities**, and then select the starburst to browse to a new certificate file.

5. Select **OK** to save changes to **Site Properties**.
6. From the **Servers and Site System Roles** node, select the desired site in the top pane. Select the desired roles from the bottom pane (**Management Point**, **Distribution Point**, **Software Update Point**, as well as **Application catalog Point**, if required).
7. Specify **HTTPS** for client communication types.
8. As long as the new site systems are accessible from the Internet at this point, the infrastructure configuration is complete. Follow the client installation instructions given at `https://technet.microsoft.com/en-us/library/mt489016.aspx;` to install the CM client properly.

How it works...

CM allows clients assigned to the same primary site to use either HTTP or HTTPS communication. If a client has the PKI cert, it can be set to use HTTP for the intranet and HTTPS for the Internet.

See also

- Refer to the document PKI certificate requirements for System Center Configuration Manager at `https://technet.microsoft.com/en-us/library/mt613191.aspx`
- Refer to the Plan for managing Internet-based clients in System Center Configuration Manager document at `https://technet.microsoft.com/en-us/library/mt629422.aspx`

Using remote and workstation distribution points and BranchCache

When CM administrators ask us, *What are the most resource-intensive components of CM?*, we usually start with the obligatory *It depends*, and then quickly follow up with distribution points. Distribution points are the file shares and websites that clients use for installing software, security patches, operating system deployments, and more. So depending on the content we plan to deploy, we may need more distribution points than any other server.

Similar to CM12, it supports a single instance store, adding consistency checks with the distribution point role, and adding a sender for throttling. Troubleshooting and deploying a distribution point to a workstation is very similar to troubleshooting and deploying a distribution point to a server.

From CM12, it also has integrated **BranchCache**, which allows us to reduce the amount of traffic that occurs between each network client and the distribution point for downloading content. For example, when a supported system needs to download content, it will first check to see if any system on its local network already has the content (based on file hash), and if so, it will download from a peer. If not, it will download from the distribution point, and then store the content so that it can be shared among other peers on the same network in the future.

Getting ready

We described the process of installing a distribution point in the *Dividing up site system roles* recipe, so we will use this section to help you determine how to choose which type of distribution point(s) you need.

How to do it…

To determine the best distribution point for your needs, ask the following questions:

- How many clients will use the distribution point?
- Will **Preboot Execution Environment** (**PXE**), also known as network-based boot, be required?
- Must the distribution point support BranchCache?
- Is the distribution point connected to the site server over a slow or fast network link?

- Do you plan to use any third-party add-on tools or WAN accelerators for remote locations?
- Do you require redundancy, in the event that a distribution point is offline or a DP fails?

Review the following table to help determine the proper DPs for your environment:

CM Feature	Workstation DP	Server DP
Supports PXE	No	Yes
Supports multicast	No	Yes
Supports BranchCache	No	Yes
Maximum concurrent connections	20	Unlimited
Supports bandwidth throttling	Yes	Yes
Supports single instance store	Yes	Yes
Supports content validation	Yes	Yes
Supports boundary groups	Yes	Yes
Supports additional site roles (MP, Web Svc Pt, and so on)	No	Yes

How it works...

You cannot distribute software or software updates to clients without DPs. The decision on how many to place, where to place them, whether or not to throttle them and if so, how much, are all considerations that affect the ability of clients to get software in an efficient manner. Don't just throttle a DP because you can now. Do so only because you need to alleviate a possible network bottleneck.

There's more...

As we can see from the previous table, bandwidth throttling is available on DPs either on a workstation or a server. This new feature alone may allow you to reduce the need for secondary sites in remote locations. Refer to the following sections for more discussion about maximizing content efficiency with CM.

When to choose BranchCache

BranchCache is practically free, so be sure to spend some time evaluating it for your needs. If your environment meets the requirements for BranchCache, you should consider enabling it at least at remote sites to reduce bandwidth utilization, possibly reducing the need for CM infrastructure in those remote locations.

BranchCache is supported on the following operating systems:

- Windows 10 Enterprise and Education Editions (or newer)
- Windows 8.1 Enterprise Edition (or newer)
- Windows 7 Enterprise and Ultimate Editions (or newer)
- Windows Vista Enterprise with at least service pack 2 and BITS 4.0

The configuration for the server component of BranchCache is only supported on Server 2008 R2 (and newer Server OS). CM DPs must reside on a server with the BranchCache feature enabled for clients to leverage BranchCache. Also, CM requires BranchCache to be configured in distributed mode.

Some WAN accelerator configurations may interfere with BranchCache, so be sure to review the BranchCache documentation as well as test in your environment. Follow the instructions referenced in the *See also* section of this recipe for configuring BranchCache. After configuring the CM DPs, we can use GPO to configure BranchCache on client systems.

When to choose a workstation distribution point

Workstation DPs can be a great addition to your CM hierarchy, and significantly reduce the need for server-class hardware in smaller locations. The following table briefly describes the limitations to a workstation DP:

CM Feature	Limitations
Supports PXE	Workstation operating system does not support this WDS server feature
Supports multicast	Workstation operating system does not support this WDS server feature
Supports BranchCache	Workstation operating system does not support the server feature required for BranchCache configuration on a DP.
Max concurrent connections	Workstation has a maximum of 20 concurrent connections. This may put larger locations of clients into a *waiting for content* situation, until enough connections become available.
Supports additional site roles (MP, Web Svc Pt, and so on)	Workstation operating system does not support additional roles for a CM site.

Operating System Deployment (**OSD**) is probably the most affected as far as limitations on a workstation operating system go, as PXE and multicast are not supported. We can still use bare-metal builds, as well as OS deployment from Software Center, and successfully build systems.

When to choose a server-class distribution point

For a full-featured DP, choose to install the DP on a server operating system. All the features described previously in this chapter are fully supported. As mentioned previously, we might find that we can simply install a DP at a remote location, instead of a full secondary site.

See also

- Refer to BranchCache at `https://technet.microsoft.com/en-us/library/mt613461.aspx`
- Refer to the document Manage content and content infrastructure for System Center Configuration Manager at `https://technet.microsoft.com/en-us/library/mt607024.aspx`

2
Deploying Windows 10 with Operating System Deployment

In this chapter, we will cover the following recipes:

- Creating an OSD test environment
- Leveraging the build and capture process
- Migrating user state
- Managing drivers
- Customizing the build process with prestart hooks
- Patching your reference build
- Using the new Windows 10 in-place upgrade task sequence
- Leveraging the Microsoft Deployment Toolkit with CM OSD

Introduction

Operating System Deployment (OSD) in **Configuration Manager (CM)** is a key feature of the product. Many admins report that their primary reason for implementing CM was just to leverage OSD, and frankly, we can't blame them. The **Task Sequence (TS)**, which the CM uses to drive the OSD process, is very flexible and powerful, as you will learn in this chapter.

OSD is a complex and powerful feature of CM. Entire books and careers are built around it. Our aim in this chapter is just to get the reader started with the basics; the art and finesse will come with time.

While the title of this chapter mentions Windows 10, all recipes should equally apply to Windows 7 and 8/8.1 (or Server 2008 R2/2012 R2). Mass storage challenges are present with both servers and workstations.

Creating an OSD test environment

The first step in creating a successful OSD is to have a useful test environment that you can connect to remotely and rebuild quickly. You need a **Virtual Machine** (**VM**). VMs allow you to quickly perform testing cycles with OSD. Enter MICROSOFT HYPER-V.

This may come as a surprise to many, but Microsoft Hyper-V Server 2012 R2 is actually a free product. Microsoft Hyper-V Server is a free download from Microsoft. You can obtain the latest version of Hyper-V Server on https://www.microsoft.com/en-us/evalcenter /evaluate-hyper-v-server-2012-r2.

Or if you have an available license for Windows Server 2012 or R2, you can simply install the OS on your server, and enable the Hyper-V role. If you are using a Windows 10 computer, the Hyper-V feature can also be added for free. We'll see how to use the free Hyper-V offering later to make a VM, but the option for the Hyper-V role is similar.

Getting ready

Install Microsoft Hyper-V Server 2012 R2 on a server (preferred) or workstation system. Once Hyper-V is installed, it will appear similar to Windows Server Core, in that you will not have a graphical user interface to log in to. Depending on your hardware, you may need to add network drivers to the Hyper-V server using drvload.exe (http://technet.micros oft.com/en-us/library/dd744511(v=WS.10).aspx) or pnputil.exe(http://technet.mi crosoft.com/en-us/library/ff800798(v=WS.10).aspx).

Ensure your Hyper-V server is on a DHCP network that can resolve to the FQDN of the **Management Point** (**MP**) and **Distribution Point** (**DP**). Install the **Remote Server Administrator Toolkit** (**RSAT**) on a Windows workstation, and then install the Hyper-V component.

How to do it...

1. Launch **Hyper-V Manager** from a Windows 10 system, and connect to your Hyper-V server.

2. Use **Virtual Network Manager** to create a new virtual network. For **Connection type**, select **External**, and select the actual NIC card in the system, and enable the **Allow management operating system to share this network adapter** checkbox. Click on **OK** to close the **Virtual Network Manager** configuration utility.

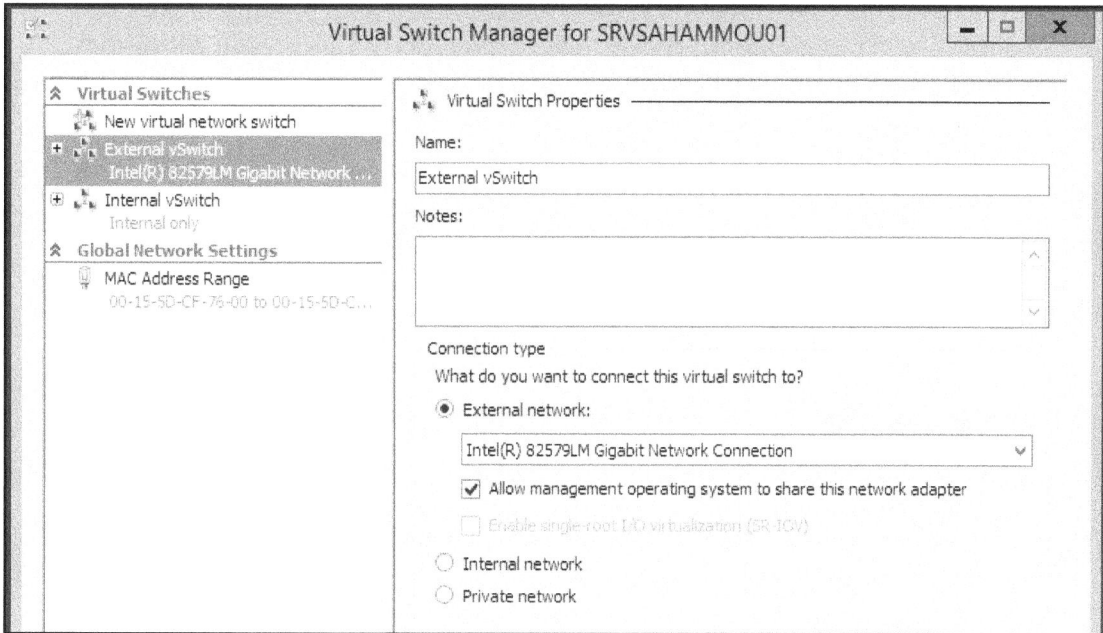

3. Right-click on the server and go to **New** | **Virtual Machine**. Provide an appropriate name and location to store the virtual machine.
4. Select **Generation 1** for that virtual machine.
5. Assign a default memory of at least **1024 MB**. It's not recommended to use Dynamic Memory for that reference computer VM.
6. To configure networking, specify the connection to be your Local Area Connection NIC.
7. Specify whether to use an existing virtual hard disk or create a new virtual hard disk.
8. Leave the default **Installation Options**, and then select **Finish** to complete the **New Virtual Machine** wizard.

9. Before powering on the new VM, right-click on the VM and view **settings**. If you plan to build the system using PXE, it's necessary to add a **Legacy Network Adapter** from the **Add Hardware** action and remove the standard network adapter.

You have successfully created a test VM for OS Deployment testing. You can now mount an ISO file and boot that VM from it. Testing OS deployment in a VM will significantly reduce the time required for test and re-test.

How it works...

VMs are essential to building, capturing, and deploying images. Hyper-V is a tool you can quickly bring up to get you started. The VMs you create with it can be used for creating and testing OS deployments.

There's more...

Testing OS deployment in a VM simplifies the testing process. Depending on your operating system version, you can either install the Hyper-V components natively from the OS, or you can install RSAT, and then enable the Hyper-V console. You can completely create and test your reference image (discussed in the *Leveraging the build and capture process* recipe. You can also perform significant testing for your production build in a VM.

The reference image in a VM

In the next recipe, you will create a reference build. This is simply the base image that will be used in your production's build process. Your reference build should contain no additional drivers at all if possible, the goal is to keep them modular so that you can update both drivers and applications as necessary. By keeping the drivers separate, you can leverage CM to surgically inject the necessary drivers into the driver store at production build time. Your goal is to have one image per OS architecture, and dynamically apply drivers and other hardware-specific applications during the production OS deployment.

It is recommended that companies update their reference images on a regular interval, this could be every quarter or bi-annually, depending on the image changes. Refer to the *Patching your reference build* recipe for an easier method to apply Windows patches. Performing the entire process in a standard VM provides a very repeatable and reusable process.

The production build in a VM

Many OS deployments will eventually be deployed to physical hardware, so testing will need to occur on the physical hardware. Perform initial testing of your production build in a VM. This allows the admin to quickly perform several test iterations of the image and application deployment during the OSD process.

Network, mass storage, and video drivers must be fully tested after image deployment. In addition to drivers, you may have software-based hard drive encryption, Bluetooth applications, and other utilities that are tied to the hardware. Keep these in mind, and test these on real hardware when possible.

Leveraging the build and capture process

The build and capture process is often described as the process to create a reference image. You will create a build and capture task sequence that will deploy the operating system, install any additional standard applications, OS customization, and software updates and then perform an OS capture to create a WIM file (the reference image). The goal is for this process to be 100 percent automated, so that you can recreate the reference build at any time with little effort.

The build and capture process is not a requirement for using OS Deployment in CM. You could manually create your own reference build, Sysprep, and capture it to a `.wim` file. But as you will see next, using the build and capture process in CM will allow you to take advantage of software updates and other applications that are already in CM. This will provide a completely unattended process to prepare a reference build which can be updated easily at regular intervals.

Getting ready

You must first decide what applications you need to install into your reference build. There are two basic schools of thought on reference builds, thick image and thin image, each is based on a corporate or personal choices.

A thin image is a reference build that contains minimal software. During your production task sequence, you can apply the image, and then install any additional software during the task sequence. A thick image is an image that contains just about everything you need for a standard build in your environment. Some may consider it the 90 percent rule. If 90 percent of users have a common application then it should be part of the reference build. There are advantages to each school.

For example, when Adobe Reader requires an update, you may not need to update the thin image, as Adobe Reader is being installed later in your production task sequence. But when Adobe Reader is in the reference build, you must re-create (sometimes referred to as **re-spin**) your reference builds to ensure you are installing up-to-date software.

On the other hand, you will generally find that a production OS deployment TS with a thicker reference build will complete faster than a production OS deployment TS with a thin reference build. For example, installing Microsoft Office during a production build will take a considerable amount of time. If Microsoft Office is a part of the reference build, Office is already installed in the image, and downloading the larger sized `.wim` file is generally faster than downloading hundreds of smaller installation files too.

The key to success is to have an easily repeatable and automated reference build process. The more automated this process is, the easier it is to quickly create builds on a quarterly or monthly basis.

Before you create the TS, locate your licensed Windows 10 installation media, downloaded from the Volume Licensing Service Center, in `.iso` format. Use an ISO extraction tool (such as `www.7-zip.org`) to extract the contents of the `.iso` file to a share that the CM site server has appropriate access to, and follow these steps to create a **Operating System Images** package:

1. Navigate to **Software Library | Operating Systems | Operating System Images**, and select **Add Operating System Image** from the ribbon.
2. On the **Data Source** page of the wizard, enter the UNC path of the `install.wim` file located in the OS media (under the **sources** folder) you extracted previously.
3. On the **General** page, enter a friendly name, version, and comment.
4. Continue the wizard to completion.
5. Distribute the new OS Image package to your local DP. As this process is only to create the reference build, you only need to send it to a DP local to your test VM.

How to do it...

Follow these steps to create a build and capture task sequence:

1. Navigate to **Software Library\Operating Systems**, right-click on **Task Sequences** and select **Create Task Sequence**.
2. On the **Create a new Task Sequence** page, select **Build and capture a reference operating system image**.

3. On the **Task Sequence Information** page, enter a TS Name, description, and select the required boot image. Select the default boot image that matches the architecture of the OS you plan to build. For example, if the OS installer is Windows 10 x64, select **Boot image (x64)**. This is the default boot image. As this is a reference build and will only be built on a VM, there is no need for a custom boot image or additional drivers.

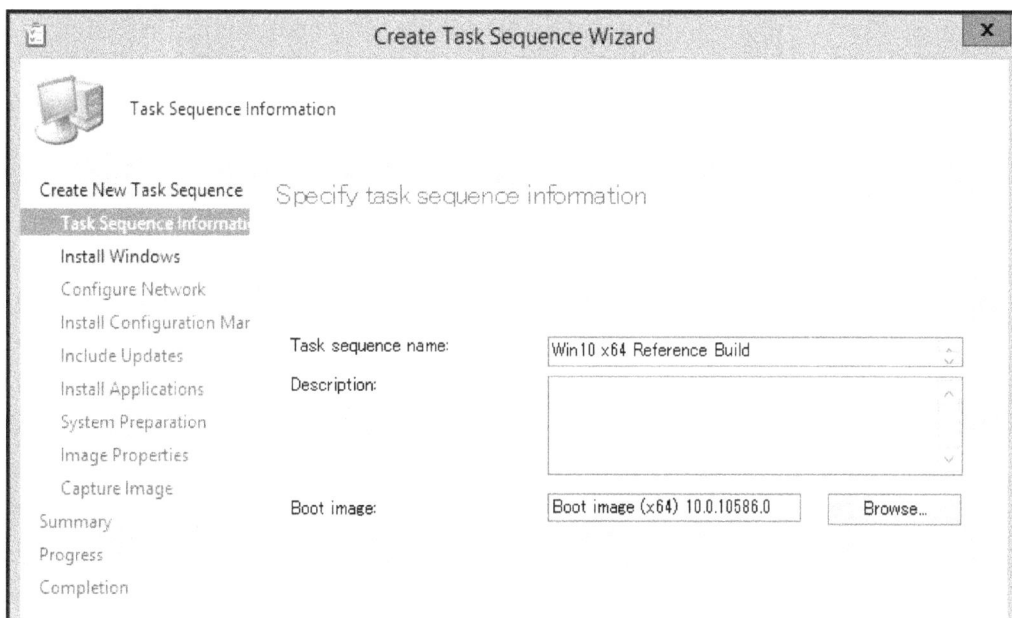

4. On the **Install Windows** page select the OS Image package that you imported previously. Verify that your licensed edition is selected in the **Edition** drop-down box. Some OS media may contain more than one edition of Windows.
5. Enter the **Multiple Activation Key** (**MAK**) if you have one, otherwise leave the product key blank and activate later with **Key Management Service** (**KMS**). Enable the radio button to **Always use the same administrator password**.

> This password will only be valid for the reference build, so you will probably only use it when you're troubleshooting the build and capture process. When you deploy the captured image in a production task sequence, you will specify a new password (or elect to disable the admin account) at that time.

6. On the **Configure Network** page, leave the default to **Join a workgroup**, and enter a temporary workgroup name.

7. On the **Install Configuration Manager** page, select the **Configuration Manager Client Package**. This package is in the root of the `Packages` node by default, and is automatically created by CM during site installation. Add any additional installation properties you need (you will find details about client installation properties in the TechNet documentation at `https://technet.microsoft.com /en-us/library/mt489016.aspx`). In order to install patches during OSD, you do need to specify the `SMSMP=<myMP server>` parameter in the command-line installation. Here is an example of parameters admins commonly set for client installation: `/mp:SMSMP01 /logon SMSSITECODE=S01 FSP=SMSFSP01 SMSMP=SMSMP01` . For details about each parameter, please refer to the previous TechNet documentation.

8. On the **Install Updates** page, select whether to install only mandatory, mandatory and option, or no updates.

> Note that the system must be in a collection that is being targeted with the updates (either mandatory or optional) for update installation to occur.

9. On the **Install Applications** page, click on the starburst to select one or more applications to install. The application must be able to run as the system account with no user interaction. Dependent applications will be installed if applicable. Also choose whether to continue installing applications even if one application in the list fails.

10. On the **System Preparation** page, you will see that it is disabled. The reason is because `Sysprep` is now native to all operating systems starting from Windows Vista and Server 2008.

11. Add any custom info you need on the **Image Properties** page. This information will be captured in the metadata of the image.

12. On the **Capture Image** page, specify a UNC Path, as well as credentials that can create/copy files to that path.

13. Click on the **Summary** button and finish the wizard.

How it works...

Select the new TS and choose **Properties** from the ribbon. Review the **General** and **Advanced** tabs so that you know how to change the boot image or rename the task sequence in the future.

Next, select the new TS and choose **Edit** from the ribbon. Now you can see all the TS steps that were created during the wizard. If you have additional steps you need to run during the TS, you can select the **Add** button from the **Task Sequence Editor**. For example, under **Add | General**, you see options such as **Run Command Line** and **Install Package** (for package/programs). If you are new to CM task sequences, start small and verify things are working properly, then copy your working task sequence, and then begin to add additional required steps.

Also notice that by following the wizard, you will have an **Install Updates** step before the **Install Applications** step. Depending on the applications you chose to install, you may want to switch the order of these steps. For example, if you install Microsoft Office during the task sequence, it is recommended to run the **Install Updates** step after the Office installation, to ensure all targeted Office patches are installed to your reference build.

> Before running the build and capture task sequence, there's one feature which has been introduced in Windows 10 that you have to disable in order to successfully Sysprep your image before you capture it. This feature is called **Consumer Experience**. That is the feature which will automatically download some recommended modern apps like *Candy Crush* that you would find in the Start menu on any Windows 10 machine. The real problem with that feature is that if any of these recommended modern apps get installed, then Sysprep will fail.

There's more...

After creating the task sequence, you need to send content to a DP. As this is a reference build you only need to send content to the DP that will be used to build and capture your reference image. Select the desired task sequence and choose **Distribute Content** from the ribbon. As you walk through the wizard you will see that all associated content for the task sequence will be distributed. Choose the desired DP and complete the wizard.

Verify that the **Network Access Account** has been configured. Verify by navigating to **Administration** | **Overview** | **Site Configuration**. Choose **Sites** and navigate to **Configure Site Components** | **Software Distribution** from the ribbon. View the **Network Access Account** tab. You should use a low-rights account configuration that will be used to connect to DPs; a member of domain users only is generally sufficient. The **Network Access Account** is a very important account; it is used during the OS deployment when the computer is still not a member of a domain and needs access to the DP.

Move to the **Monitoring** tab and navigate to **Distribution Status** | **Content** to view the status for each package.

Creating bootable media

As mentioned previously, the standard boot image should suffice for a reference build using a VM. You do want to modify the default boot image by viewing the boot image properties, and on the **Customization** tab, select **Enable Command Support**. When you click on **OK** you will see the **Distribution Point Update Required** dialog. Select **Yes** to update the distribution points for the boot disk and complete the wizard. During this process, CM will mount the `boot.wim` file, apply any modifications (for this example, enable command support), unmount the `.wim` file and commit changes, and then send to DPs.

Enabling command support will allow you to troubleshoot OS deployment easier, and will be discussed in the next section.

After the DP is updated, create the `.iso` using the following steps:

1. Select the **Task Sequences** node, and then choose **Create Task Sequence Media** from the ribbon.
2. On the **Select Media Type** page, choose **Bootable media**.

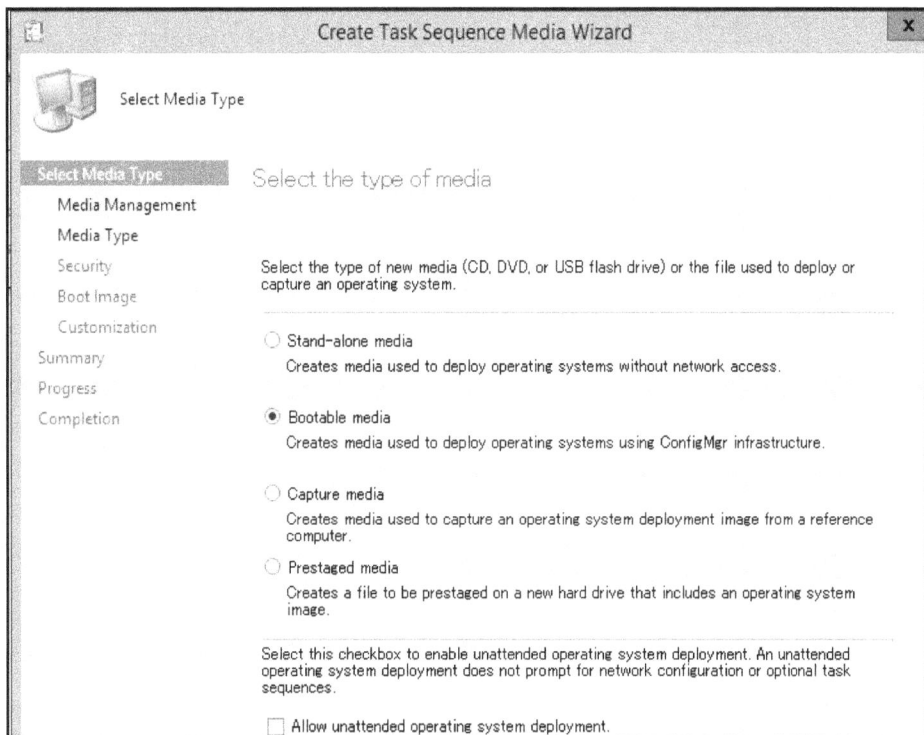

3. On the **Media Management** page, choose **Dynamic media**, if you have more than one primary site.

4. On the **Media Type** page, choose **CD/DVD** set, and enter a valid path and filename for the **Media file**. Specify `.iso` as the file extension. The ISO file created can be later burnt to a USB or a DVD drive.

5. On the **Security** page, choose whether to allow unknown computer support and whether to protect boot media with a password.

6. On the **Boot Image** page, choose the desired boot image, as well as the DP that will be used as the boot image source to create the `.iso` file. Also click on **Add** to add the required MP(s) for the reference build.

7. Leave the **Customization** page as default.

8. View the **Summary** page, and complete the wizard. You will use this boot image in the next section.

Deploying the task sequence to a device collection

Create a collection, and add **Unknown Systems** to the collection if required (be very careful not to select **All Systems** here!). If you do not add **Unknown Systems** to the collection, you must import the computer to a collection. To import a computer, select **Devices** from the left menu, and then choose **Import Computer Information** from the ribbon. To import, you will need the MAC address or the SMBIOS GUID of the systems. Be sure to add the system to the proper collection during import, so that the reference build task sequence will be available to it.

Perform the following steps to deploy the task sequence:

1. Navigate to **Software Library** | **Overview** | **Operating Systems** | **Task sequences**, select the desired TS and choose **Deploy** from the ribbon.
2. Choose the desired target collection. Note that you cannot change the deployment name; it will be automatically generated based on the TS name.
3. On the **Deployment Settings** page, choose whether the install is **Available** or **Required**. For this example, choose **Available.** You will also notice a menu called **Make available to the following** as shown here. Choose whether this task sequence will be available to CM clients, from the boot media and/or PXE.

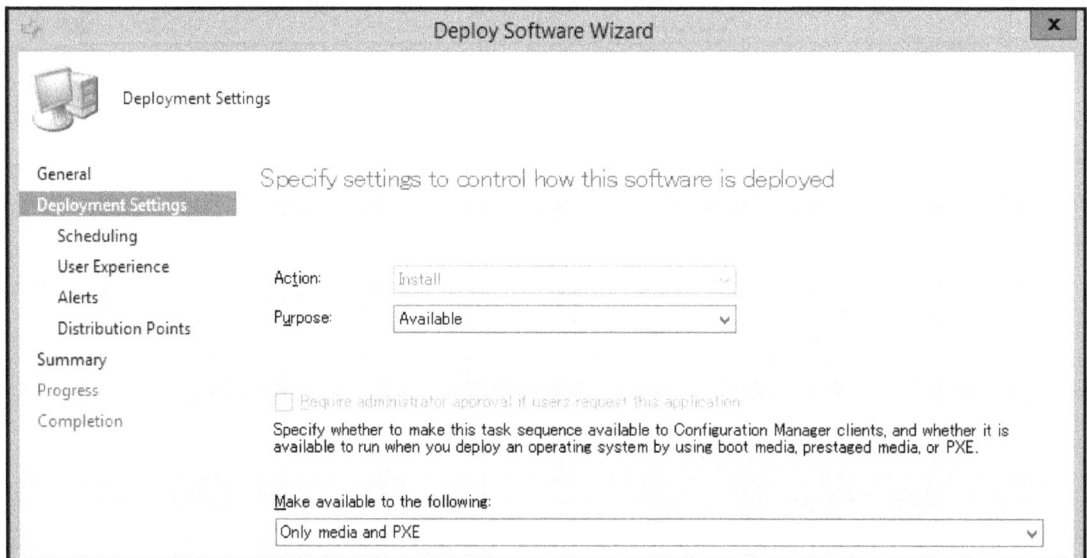

4. Skip the **Scheduling** tab, as this deployment will be an optional deployment. The **Scheduling** tab lets you select whenever a deployment is available or a deadline for it.

5. Leave the defaults for the **User Experience** page. Also leave defaults for the **Alerts** page.

6. On the **Distribution Points** tab, choose whether to download content when needed, or download all content before the TS begins. You can also choose the client actions to prefer when no DP is available, and to allow clients to fallback to a source location (for example, primary site) for content.

7. View the summary page, and complete the **Deploy Software Wizard**.

Starting the build process and troubleshooting information

Now that you've confirmed all content is on the DP, and you have a bootable `.iso`, you're ready to start building your test system. In Hyper-V, connect to the test VM created earlier in this chapter. Navigate to **Media** | **DVD Drive** | **Insert Disk** and browse to the `.iso` file created previously.

Power on the VM. If this is a brand new VM, the boot media will automatically start. If this is a VM that already has a formatted disk, you will need to quickly press a key to boot to media. Next you will see a welcome screen, clicking on **Next** will display a list of optional deployments. Select the build and capture TS to continue.

A basic build and capture may run for 30 minutes or more, depending on network speed, VM performance, and the number and type of applications and security updates to apply. The key is that this process will be fully automated. You may spend some time working the kinks out to get everything working properly, but once you do, maintaining a reference build will take very little time out of your day, and allow you to quickly update the build as required.

If you encounter failures during the build and capture process, take a look at the monitoring status for the task sequence. Also, as you enabled command support for the boot media, you can press *F8* to open a command prompt during the TS to view the logs. After pressing *F8*, run `CMTrace.exe` from the current directory to launch the Configuration Manager Trace Utility. This tool will help you read CM logs. The location of these logs depends on the deployment phase where the OSD failed. Here are the three possible locations of the log files:

- If the TS is currently in the WinPE phase, view `SMSTS.log` in `x:\windows\temp\smstslog\`
- If the TS is currently in the Windows phase and the CM agent is not yet installed, view `SMSTS.log` in `c:\_smstasksequence\logs\smstslog\`

- If the TS is currently in the Windows phase and the CM agent has been installed, view `SMSTS.log` in `c:\windows\ccm\logs\smstslog\`

Once the capture is complete, you can add the `.wim` file as an OS Image into CM. This chapter does not walk you through the process of creating your production TS-the process is almost identical to the steps you have completed for a build and capture TS. The rest of the chapter will focus on specific steps within your production TS.

See also

- You will find many demos and walk-throughs for OS deployment at: `https://aka.ms/configmgrcbsg/`
- TechNet documentation on Client Installation Properties: `https://technet.micr osoft.com/en-us/library/mt489016.aspx`
- Refer to the TechNet documentation for OS deployment at: `https://technet.mi crosoft.com/en-us/library/mt627945.aspx`

Migrating user state

The **User State Migration Tool** (**USMT**) is used to transfer user state and data during OS deployment. You can save user state to the local disk (when performing an in-place upgrade) or to a CM State Migration Point (when migrating a user to a different computer.)

Getting ready

You must have a package for USMT source files. Create a new package and specify the source location for USMT. USMT is contained in the **Windows Assessment and Deployment Kit for Windows 10** (Windows ADK). The default location for USMT installation files is `C:\Program Files (x86)\Windows Kits\10\Assessment and Deployment Kit\User State Migration Tool`. Be sure when you create the package, the source folder shows only the x86 and x64 subfolders in the root of your package source.

You must use USMT version 10.0 in order to migrate user data from Windows Vista/7/8.1/10 to Windows 10. You can download it from `https://developer.microsoft.com/en-us/windows/hardware/windows-assessment-deployment-kit`. USMT does not support any of the Windows Server operating systems or any of the starter editions for Windows Vista or Windows 7.

Using USMT, you can migrate a 32-bit operating system to a 64-bit operating system. However, you cannot migrate a 64-bit operating system to a 32-bit operating system.

How to do it...

1. When you create a new task sequence with the **Install an existing image package** option, you will be prompted for the USMT package. By default, you will only have the option to save user settings on a **State Migration Point** (**SMP**). If you want to store user state locally instead of an SMP, you must remove the **Partition and format the target computer before installing the operating system** option from the **Install Windows** page in **Create Task Sequence Wizard**.

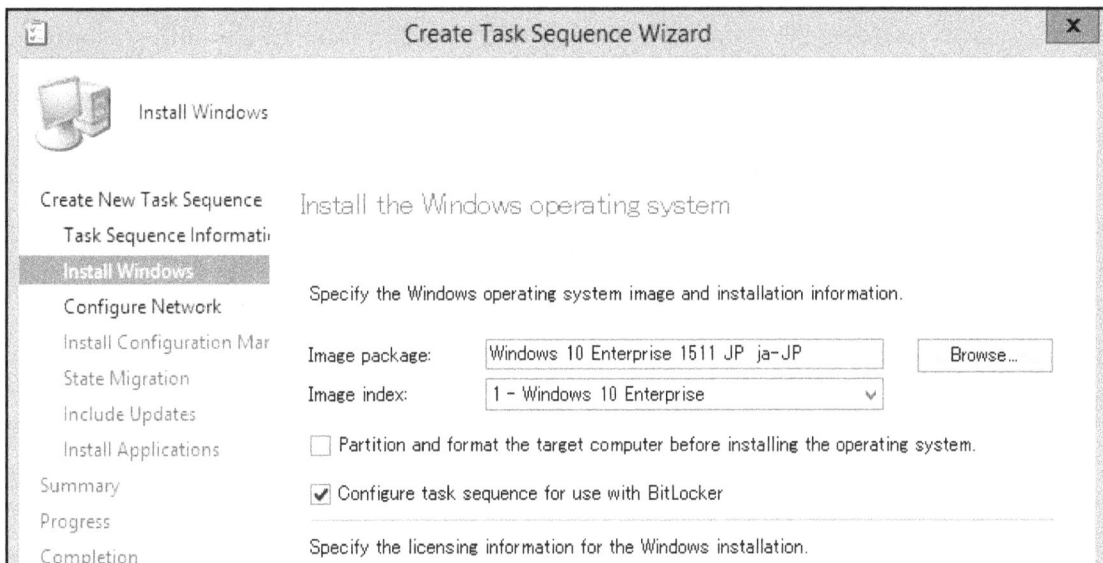

Create Task Sequence Wizard	x

Install Windows

Create New Task Sequence
  Task Sequence Informati
  Install Windows
  Configure Network
  Install Configuration Mar
  State Migration
  Include Updates
  Install Applications
Summary
Progress
Completion

Install the Windows operating system

Specify the Windows operating system image and installation information.

Image package: `Windows 10 Enterprise 1511 JP ja-JP` Browse...

Image index: `1 - Windows 10 Enterprise` ∨

☐ Partition and format the target computer before installing the operating system.

☑ Configure task sequence for use with BitLocker

Specify the licensing information for the Windows installation.

2. Edit the TS you just created and review the **Capture User Files and Settings** group, as well as the **Restore User Files and Settings** group. If you selected the defaults to use a SMP, you will see additional steps to request and release the user state. If you selected to store locally, you'll see that CM will manage the location on the local disk to save to the TS variable `%_SMSTSUserStatePath%`. As you spend more time with task sequences, you'll find that just about everything you select in the GUI is managed by a TS variable, which gives you a very flexible and powerful TS process.

3. Next, review the **Capture User Files and Settings** step. By default all user profiles and applications supported by the version of USMT will be captured. You can specify custom configuration files to instruct USMT to capture additional files and settings. Review the USMT XML Reference site at `https://technet.mic rosoft.com/en-us/itpro/windows/deploy/usmt-include-files-and-setting s`. This site describes the default applications and settings that are captured, as well as how to customize. If you create custom configuration files, copy them into both the `x86` and `x64` directories of the USMT package, and then add each filename by selecting the **Customize how user profiles are captured** option.

4. You may consider skipping files that use **Encrypting File System** (**EFS**). By default, USMT will fail if an encrypted file is found. If you don't skip EFS files, you need to perform extra steps, as described in the USMT online documentation site at `https://technet.microsoft.com/en-us/itpro/windows/deploy/usmt-migrate-efs-files-and-certificates`.

5. You also see the option to **Capture locally by using links instead of by copying files**. This feature is also known as **hard links**. It will perform user state capture and restore much faster than the traditional copy to state store. **Capture in off-line mode** is also an option. Should you decide to capture in off-line mode, you'll need to move the USMT section to just after the **Restart in Windows PE** step (in the **Install Operating System** group). The default location for user state capture only runs in Windows (not WinPE).

How it works...

Based on the options you configure in the TS step, CM will build the appropriate run command line for USMT.

There's more…

As new versions of USMT are released, you may find additional features and options that aren't available in the CM USMT configuration options. Have no fear, as the CM team created a variable to allow you to append command-line options for USMT. Just before the capture, create a step to set a TS variable, and give the name `OSDMigrateAdditionalCaptureOptions`, and then set the value to the additional command-line options for USMT. The `OSDMigrateAdditionalCaptureOptions` variable will be appended to the end of the CM-generated ScanState command line.

See also

- Off-line migration: `https://technet.microsoft.com/en-us/itpro/windows/deploy/offline-migration-reference`.
- Hard-link migration: `https://technet.microsoft.com/en-us/itpro/windows/deploy/usmt-hard-link-migration-store`.
- Capture User State Task Sequence Action Variables: `http://technet.microsoft.com/en-us/library/0b3df5ab-dce7-4dcf-a49e-3bf046798076#BKMK_CaptureUserState`.

Managing drivers

Driver management is often considered one of the more challenging configurations in OS Deployment. CM does a great job of simplifying the process. In this recipe, we will discuss the process to import drivers as well as different strategies for applying them during a task sequence.

> Using the driver management function in CM, it is very important to understand exactly what the implications are of any choice done during drivers' import into CM. It is also critical to organize drivers correctly.

First, a few terms to ensure everyone is speaking the same language.

- **Driver:** This is also known as *raw driver*, which usually is a `.inf` file accompanied with `.dll`, `.cat`, and other files referenced in the `.inf` file for the driver.
- **Driver package**: This is a CM package that contains drivers. This is different from a standard package. Driver packages are located under the **Operating Systems** node.
- **Driver category**: Categories can be assigned during or after import of one or more drivers. You can use driver categories with the **Auto Apply Drivers** TS step.
- **Apply Driver Package**: This is one of the two ways to install drivers during a task sequence. When you **Apply Driver Package**, all drivers contained in the driver package are injected to the driver store. This TS step works for network-based, prestaged, and standalone build processes.
- **Auto Apply Drivers**: This is a more dynamic process to install drivers during OS Deployment. By default, the Auto Apply Drivers TS step will query the target system for **Plug and Play** (**PNP**) information, and then query CM for drivers that match by PNP ID. Then the client would download the appropriate drivers and inject them to the driver store. This TS step works for both network-based and prestaged build processes.
- **Network-based build**: This includes any OS deployment process that requires access to the MP and a DP. Builds can start from bootable media, PXE, or prestaged media.
- **Prestaged media build**: A specific type of network-based build, prestaged media requires access to MP and DP during OS deployment, but with prestaged media, you can stage the OS `.wim` file on the system to remove the need to download and apply the `.wim` file during the OS deployment process. The primary example for this is to leverage prestaged media when you order hardware directly from the hardware vendor. The vendor can apply the prestaged media `.wim` file to the system, which will automatically configure the system to boot to WinPE. This process will simulate the network-based build, but will skip the **Apply Operating System** step, as that occurred during the manufacture of the hardware.

- **Standalone media build**: This is also known as **full media build**, or remote media build. You can use a standalone media build to build a system without any access to your CM infrastructure. This is an ideal build process for a remote employee, or remote locations that do not have DPs available on the LAN. This build is normally created on a USB device or one (or more) DVD `.iso` file(s).
- **Driver pack**: This is a set of drivers for a model or family of models. Computer manufacturers such as Dell and HP have created driver packs to simplify OS Deployment.

Now that you understand the terms, you must think about which processes are applicable to your environment. For example, if you want to allow systems to be built without any connection to the CM infrastructure, you must use a standalone media build. If you want to be able to update drivers without the need to completely re-create the standalone build, then you should leverage a network-based build.

Getting ready

To import drivers, you must have a network path to the drivers you choose to import. These drivers must also contain the extracted drivers, so that you can see `.inf`, `.dll`, `.cam`, and so on. Often, the driver is downloaded from the hardware manufacturer in a `.zip` or `.exe` file, so you must extract the drivers to a location first. Check with your hardware vendor to see if a driver pack is available for the desired system model(s). A driver pack will significantly reduce the time required to identify, download, and extract each driver to a logical path.

How to do it...

1. In the CM console, navigate to **Software Library** | **Operating System** | **Drivers**. You might want to verify that the root Drivers node has no drivers in it. You cannot import drivers to a specific folder; you import drivers to the base root node, and then move drivers to the proper location.
2. Select **Import Driver** from the ribbon.
3. Choose to import all drivers from a **Universal Naming Convention** (UNC) path, or select and specify a specific `.inf` file to import.

4. On the **Locate Driver** page, choose the proper setting for your environment for **Specify the option for duplicate drivers**. You can choose to import and overwrite or append existing categories, or not change existing categories:

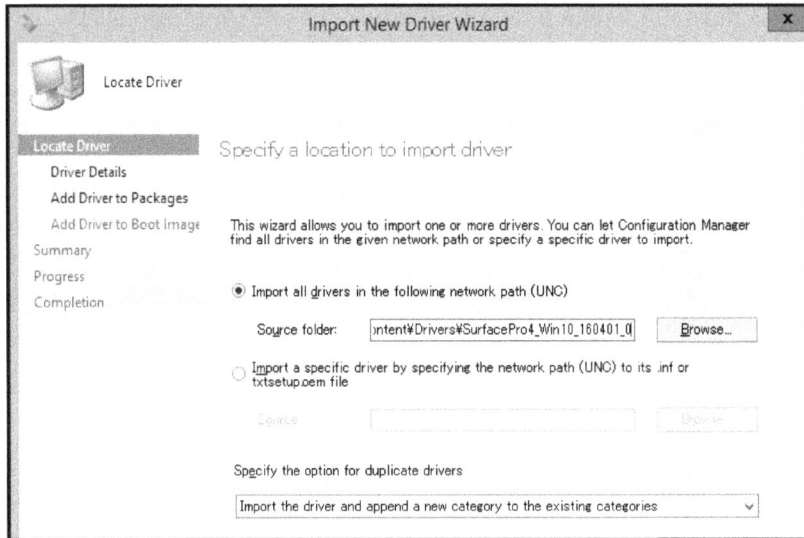

5. On the **Driver Details** page, select the desired drivers to import. Also, select any categories you desire to associate with this set of drivers. Choose category names wisely to leverage category names with the **Auto Apply Drivers** TS step.

A good practice when importing drivers is to set the device model name as the category. For instance, when importing drivers for Microsoft Surface Pro 4, create a category named *Microsoft Surface Pro 4* to tag the imported drivers. Doing so will simplify identifying which driver has been imported for which device model. Also when using the **Auto Apply Drivers** TS step, you will be able to easily select that appropriate category to deploy all the drivers tagged for that device model. It is also a good practice to add the OS version and architecture to the category name.

6. On the **Add Driver to Packages** page, select any driver package you wish to install the drivers to. This is optional at this point. You can import without adding to a driver package, but keep in mind that you can't actually leverage a driver until it's on a DP, which requires it to be in a driver package. You can also choose to update DPs when finished.

Another good practice is to create a driver package per device model. Doing so will simplify driver package management and will give you several smaller driver packages instead of a very big one containing all the drivers. When deploying or updating a smaller driver package to DP, it will transfer much faster and will save quite a lot of bandwidth.

7. On the **Add Driver to Boot Images** page, choose whether to add the imported drivers to a boot image. A common mistake on this step is to add the wrong drivers to the boot image. Be conservative when adding drivers to boot images. Less is more when adding drivers to boot images-ensure you need them before you add them.

Even if installing Windows 7, the boot image drivers should correspond to the version of WinPE. So even if installing Windows 7 x64, and your boot image is x86, you need to install the Windows 10 x86 version of the drivers to WinPE.

WinPE 10 already contains quite a lot of generic drivers, which might be enough to deploy Windows 10 to your device. A good practice is to first try to deploy the OS without injecting any drivers into the boot image. If a driver is missing during the boot phase, it will be either a network or a storage driver. Add the needed drivers to the boot image only when OS deployment cannot proceed with the base WinPE boot image.

8. Complete the wizard to import drivers.
9. Select the drivers in the root of the drivers node, and move them to any desired subfolder.

How it works...

CM imports the drivers and stores the info in the root of the **Drivers** node. You may want to consider organizing drivers as you import them, as drivers can only be imported to the root of the **Drivers** node, a suggested practice would be to move drivers to subfolders after you import them.

You may see the occasional failure to import a driver. When you see the failure, inspect the referenced .inf file to see if it's actually a driver. Some vendors have used .inf files that aren't driver installation files, and these will appear as errors if you attempt to import them. They can be safely ignored.

There's more…

Drivers must be in a driver package and on a DP to be used in OS Deployment. Depending on how you plan to install drivers to the OS, you may see significant value in adding drivers to a driver package during import. The next sections will describe the two methods for installing drivers during a TS: **Auto Apply Drivers** and **Apply Driver Package**. Review each method to determine which is best for your environment.

Auto Apply Drivers

Use **Auto Apply Drivers** for a more dynamic approach to injecting drivers during OS Deployment. This step dynamically injects the best driver into the driver store, based on PNP ID. This TS step does require connectivity to the MP during OS Deployment, so it will be ignored with standalone media. You can control which drivers are applied with this step by leveraging driver categories and WMI conditional statements. This TS step will only install applicable drivers identified through PNP, and filtered by category if enabled.

Applying Driver Package

If you want to inject drivers for devices such as printers and scanners that are not yet attached to the system, consider using this step. Also, if you need to leverage standalone media, you will need to use this step. Many administrators are more comfortable with this step, because you create a driver package, apply it, and know that all the drivers in the driver store will be injected. This step allows you to know with certainty which drivers are injected into the driver store. Also keep in mind that hardware vendors may not always support the latest driver with a system that shipped two years ago. The **Auto Apply Drivers** step will automatically install the "best" driver for the system, based on PNP, creation date, and driver signing. So **Auto Apply Drivers** could potentially get you into a situation where they are unsupported by your hardware vendor. Work with your vendor to ensure you know supported versus nonsupported tasks.

Customizing with WMI conditional statements

A TS can be a very powerful tool. WMI conditional statements can take a TS to a whole new level. A perfect example of this is if you use driver packages to manage drivers, and you have a specific driver package for each notebook model in your environment. You can simply create multiple apply drivers steps, and on each driver package in the TS, navigate to the **Options** tab, and verify that you have added a condition. For this example, add a WMI condition on the **Options** tab of the TS step. Enter the following query:

```
Select * From Win32_ComputerSystem Where Model Like '%Optiplex%'
```

This WQL will only show systems with a model name that contains **Optiplex**. Also be sure to select the **Test Query** button to validate syntax. You can add this type of conditional on any task sequence step or group to control if that step/group will run.

See also

- Import additional drivers from a USB Drive during the OS deployment: `http://g regramsey.wordpress.com/2012/02/15/how-to-inject-drivers-from-usb-du ring-a-configmgr-operating-system-task-sequence/`
- More information about TS variables and conditional statements: `http://techne t.microsoft.com/en-us/library/gg712685.aspx`

Customizing the build process with prestart hooks

Prestart hooks (previously known in CM07 as pre-execution hooks) are used to allow the admin to perform additional steps prior to the start of the TS, such as capturing the username and prompting the user to input data. Prestart hooks can be used at the beginning of the TS to prompt the user for information, or programmatically determine information that applies to the OS deployment process. For example, you could prompt the user to select a location, or additional components to install during the TS. You could also query a web service or a database to determine the role of a server to deploy.

CM07 enables you to create prestart hooks by mounting a boot image, and add a `.ini` file with instructions to launch the desired script or executable. While that process is still available, CM provides two additional methods to configure prestart hooks from the admin console:

- On the boot image properties
- During the media (USB or ISO) creation process

Prestart hooks have been used to create task sequence variables, provide a user interface for OS deployment, to allow the user to select options, set variables such as computer name, clean the disk drive, as well as many other tasks that need to be performed prior to installing a new OS. Prestart hooks only work in Windows PE and are triggered prior to the TS start. Specifically, prestart hooks launch after selecting the **Next** button on the welcome screen and before the window that allows you to select a task sequence.

Getting ready

You must create a prestart hook that can run in WinPE. Check the current version of WinPE used in your CM environment to see which languages or commands are available. Here is an example VBScript to prompt the end user to enter a computer name as a prestart hook:

```
ComputerName = inputbox("Enter Computer Name")
Set oTSEnv = CreateObject("Microsoft.SMS.TSEnvironment")
oTSEnv("OSDComputerName") = ComputerName
```

You can see in this script that the user is prompted to enter a username, and then set the `OSDComputerName` variable to the value captured in the `ComputerName` variable. Save this script to `SetComputerName.vbs`, to an UNC Path, as you will use it in the next section.

This script requires the TS environment. If you attempt to run it manually, you will encounter a failure.

As far as prestart hooks are concerned, PowerShell as well HTA are supported. For both languages, the implementation will be the exact same way for the VBScript method described in the next section. It simply means that you need to save the PowerShell or HTA script file to an UNC Path and specify the command line to run it.

You will find a well explained example of PowerShell and HTA implementation in the prestart hook in the following blog: `https://blogs.msdn.microsoft.com/steverac` `/2015/04/22/power-belongs-to-youthe-osd-prestart-command/`.

How to do it...

Now that you have a VBScript, perform the following steps to create a prestart hook that's associated to boot media:

1. In the CM console, navigate to **Software Library | Operating System | Boot Images**. Select the desired boot image and then select **Properties** from the ribbon.
2. Select the **Customization** tab from the boot image property dialog.
3. Enable the **Enable prestart command** checkbox.
4. For the command-line property, enter `cscript //nologo X:\SMS\PKG\SMS10000\SetComputerName.vbs`.
5. Select the **Include files for the prestart command** option.

6. Click on the **Browse** button and navigate to the UNC path that contains `SetComputerName.vbs`:

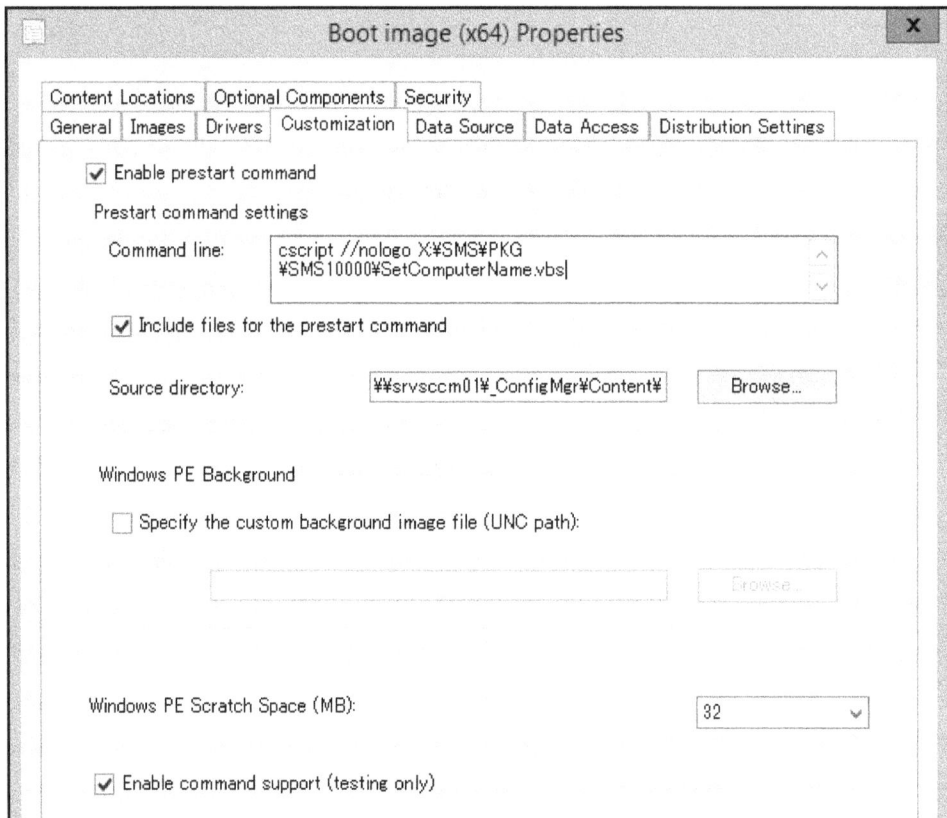

7. Double-check the settings on this page, and then click on **OK**. You will be prompted to update DPs. Click on **Yes**.

How it works...

View `smsts.log` (as described in the *Leveraging the build and capture process* recipe earlier in this chapter) to see the information as to how this process works. When you boot TS media, the prestart script will run immediately before the welcome screen (unless you configured a password for the PXE boot in CM; in that case the prestart script will run after the welcome screen). The TS variable, **OSDComputerName**, will be set to the name entered into the textbox.

When you follow the previously mentioned steps , you are prompted to update DPs. When you update DPs, CM performs a similar process that occurs when you add drivers to a boot `.wim`. CM will mount the `.wim`, make the required changes, unmount it, and commit the changes. CM will then update DPs. Once that process is successful, you can create media. This process will also work with media booted from PXE boot.

You may have noticed the static configuration for the prestart path as `X:\SMS\PKG\SMS10000`. This is a standard path that will always be used with prestart hooks that are created with bootable media. Depending on the code that you're running, you may be able to avoid the hardcoded path and run `cmd.exe /c cscript //nologo SetComputerName.vbs`, but if you encounter path issues with other dependencies on the script, revert to the static `X:\SMS\PKG\SMS10000` path.

There's more...

An alternate method to create a prestart hook is to add the information during the process of creating bootable media. This process does not support boot from PXE (as this hook is stored in `.iso`, not `.wim`). While this process provides more flexibility in that you can customize the boot media each time you create it, it does require access to the content and the ability to enter command lines and arguments each time bootable media is created, which leads to more opportunities for human error. When possible, use the previous method to enable the prestart command in `boot.wim`. If you still have a need to create specific media at ISO-creation time, follow these steps:

1. Create a package that contains the source required for the prestart command, and send to at least one DP.
2. Follow the process in the *Creating Bootable Media* section from the *Leveraging the build and capture process* recipe described earlier in this chapter.
3. On the **Customization** page, select the **Enable prestart** checkbox to enable the prestart command.
4. Enter the command, prepend `cmd.exe /c` to the beginning of it to ensure the command environment is fully loaded and available, for example, `cmd.exe /c cscript //nologo importcomputer.vbs`.
5. Select the prestart command package and DP created in the first step.
6. Complete the wizard.

Notice in this process you used `cmd.exe /c` before the desired prestart command. If you take a look at the contents of the created `.iso`, you will see that the package source defined for the prestart command is in the `\SMS\PKG\` folder. In the previous example, it was contained within the actual `.wim` file on `.iso`. As this process does not stage the prestart hook in the `.wim` file, this process is not supported with PXE (use the first process described in this recipe to support PXE).

See also

- Preselect a preferred OS deployment TS using a prestart script: `http://blogs.te chnet.com/b/inside_osd/archive/2010/06/07/v-next-beta-1-feature-sele ct-preferred-deployment-from-pre-execution-hook.aspx` (this link is related to CM12 but it is still valid for CM Current Branch)
- How to Create Bootable Media: `https://technet.microsoft.com/en-us/libra ry/mt627921.aspx`

Patching your reference build

Patch your reference build at regular intervals. The recipe in this chapter that describes building a reference machine stresses the need to have a fully automated process if possible. A fully automated process allows you to quickly run a build and capture to update the reference build. There is another useful feature in CM that may allow you to increase the interval between running a build and capture process called **Schedule Updates**. This feature allows you to apply Windows updates to an offline image. Before CM12, you could perform these steps manually using DISM commands to inject patches into the `.wim` image. CM allows you to initiate the steps from the console, and schedule them at a time that is convenient.

Getting ready

To leverage offline updates, you must have the desired Windows updates downloaded and deployed using software updates. You don't have to target a specific collection, but CM will show only updates that can be installed offline and that are deployed.

How to do it...

Follow these steps to apply the applicable offline updates to an operating system image:

1. In the CM console, navigate to **Software Library | Operating System | Operating System | Operating System Images**. Select the desired image and then select **Schedule Updates** from the ribbon.

2. The **Choose Updates** page will show all the available updates for the image. Verify that the selection for **Windows Architecture** matches the architecture of the image.

> The first time the Schedule Updates process is run on an image all the available updates will be displayed, even if you already incorporated them into your reference build. The updates process will then identify updates that are already applied and will not display them in the future.

3. On the **Set Schedule** page, choose whether to run immediately, or schedule a time to perform the updates process.

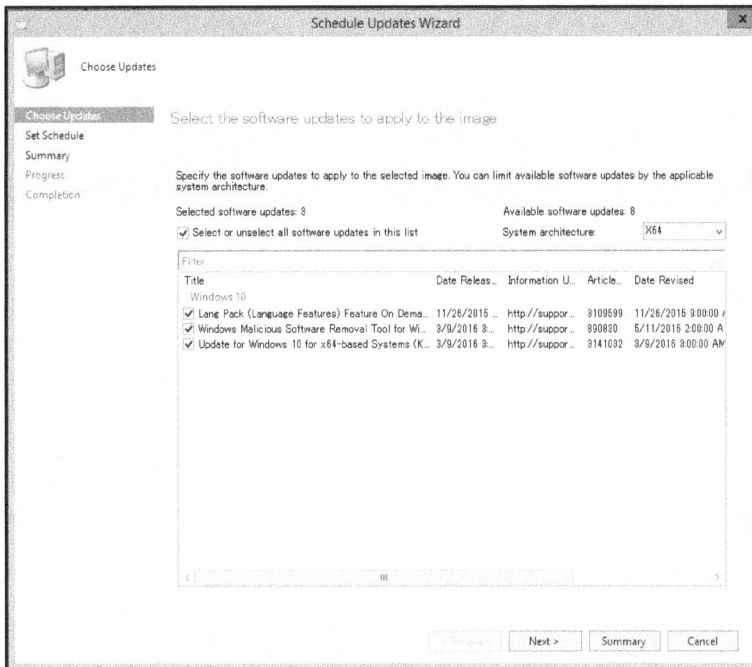

4. Follow the wizard to completion.

How it works...

If you elected for the process to run immediately, view `OfflineServicingMgr.log` on the site server. You will see that CM copies the `.wim` file from the source path to the local disk, mounts the image, and then attempts to apply each update.

After all updates have been applied, you can view the status tab for the OS Image to review the status of each patch (Installed, Not Required, and Unknown). Once you have reviewed status, update the DPs with the patched image.

> You must update distribution points manually.

See also

- Apply Updates to an Image Using DISM to understand the manual process: `http://msdn.microsoft.com/en-us/library/ff794819(v=winembedded.60).aspx` (this article also applies to Windows 10)

Using the new Windows 10 in-place upgrade task sequence

To support the Windows 10 in-place upgrade process from Windows 7 or Windows 8/8.1, ConfigMgr Current Branch introduced a new type of TS called **Upgrade an operating system from upgrade package**. And for this same purpose, CM has renamed the previously named **Operating System Installers** to **Operating System Upgrade Packages**. The name has changed but the content remains the same as before. Unlike the **Operating System Image** where you only need to import the `install.wim` file, in **Operating System Upgrade Package**, you have to import the whole content of the Windows 10 installation media ISO file.

> During an in-place upgrade to Windows 10, the upgrade process is run using the **Windows Setup Program** `setup.exe` included in the Windows 10 installation media. That's the reason why you need to import all the files included in a Windows 10 installation media and not only `install.wim`.

The in-place upgrade TS is very simple. You will have to specify the OS upgrade package and just specify if software updates and applications will have to be deployed during the TS execution.

Getting ready

Before you create the TS, locate your licensed Windows 10 installation media (downloaded from the Volume Licensing Service Center) in `.iso` format. Use an ISO extraction tool (such as `www.7-zip.org`) to extract the contents of the `.iso` file to a share that the CM site server has appropriate access to, and follow these steps to create a **Operating System Upgrade** package:

1. Navigate to **Software Library | Operating Systems | Operating System Upgrade Packages**, and select **Add Operating System Upgrade Package** from the ribbon.
2. On the **Data Source** page of the wizard, enter the UNC path to the OS media you extracted previously.
3. On the **General** page, enter a friendly name, version, and comment.
4. Continue the wizard to completion.
5. Distribute the new OS Image package to your local DP. As this process is only to create the reference build, you only need to send it to a DP local to your test VM.

How to do it...

Create the Upgrade TS.

Follow these steps to create a Build and Capture task sequence:

1. Navigate to **Software Library | Operating Systems**, right-click on **Task Sequences** and select **Create Task Sequence**.

2. On the **Create a new Task Sequence** page, select **Upgrade an operating system from upgrade package**.

3. On the **Task Sequence Information** page, enter a TS Name, description.

4. On the **Upgrade the Windows Operating System** page, select the Upgrade package imported previously:

   1. Verify that your licensed edition is selected in the **Edition** drop-down box. Some OS media may contain more than one edition of Windows.

   2. Enter the **Multiple Activation Key** (**MAK**) if you have one, otherwise leave the product key blank and activate later with **Key Management Service (KMS):**

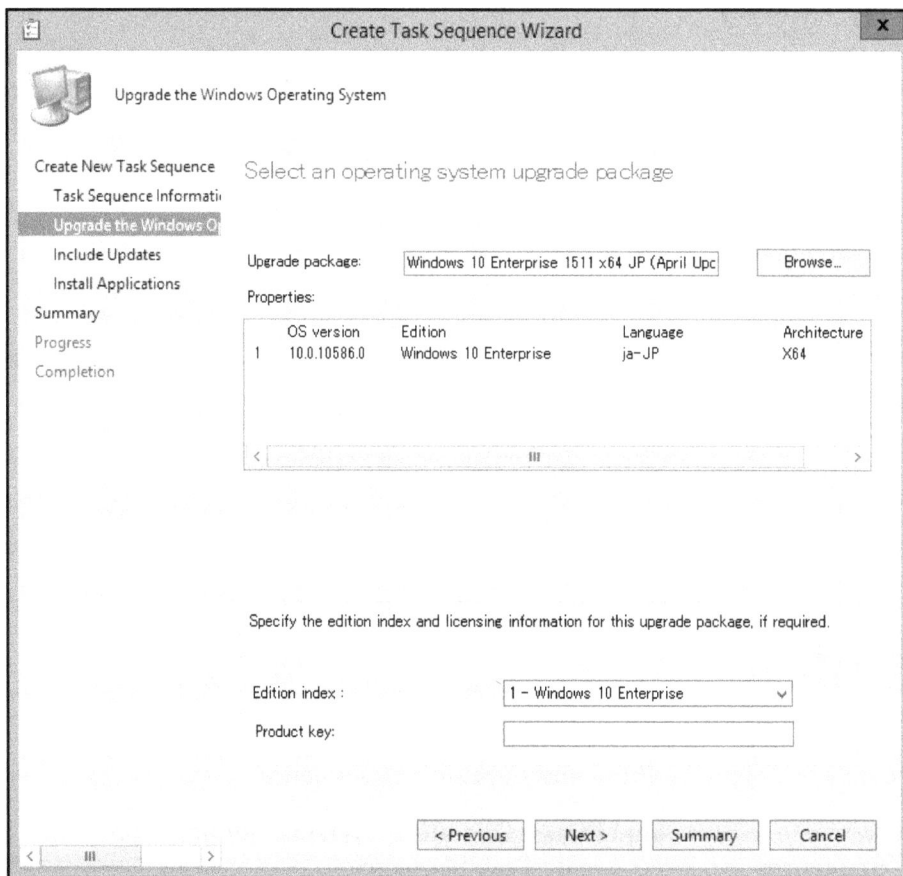

5. On the **Include Updates** and **Install Applications** pages, select whether to install software updates and/or applications after the in-place upgrade has taken place.

6. Click on the **Summary** button and finish the wizard.

> After you have created the upgrade TS, you can add additional steps to uninstall applications with known compatibility issues, or add postprocessing actions after the computer is restarted and the upgrade to Windows 10 is successful. Add these additional steps in the **Post-Processing** group.

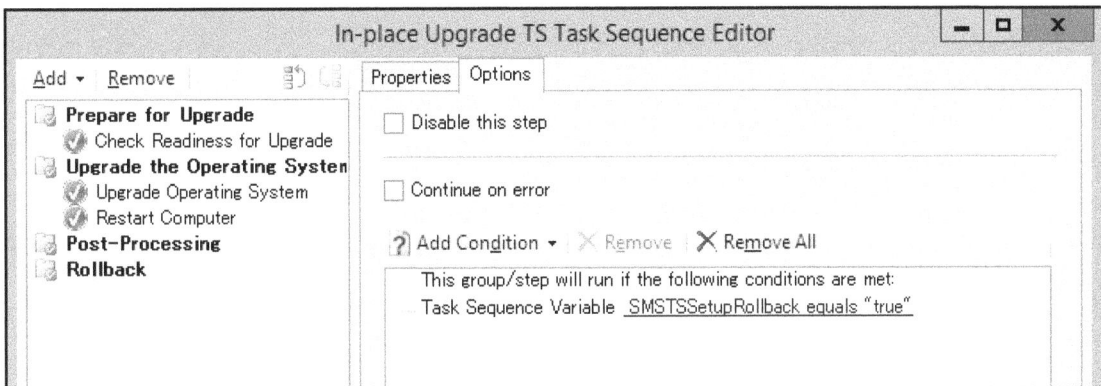

> An upgrade TS can have two expected results. Either the upgrade was successful and the TS ended by running actions configured in the **Post-Processing** group or; the upgrade failed and it has rolled back the client computer to the OS it came from. In the latter case, any actions configured in the **Rollback** group will be executed.

Deploying the upgrade TS to a device collection containing Windows 7/8/8.1 clients

Unlike the other types of TS, the upgrade TS has to be run from a running Operating System (Windows 7/8/8.1). Thus, when deploying such a TS, the option to **Make available to the following** is grayed out and preset to **Only Configuration Manager Clients**, as shown in the following screenshot:

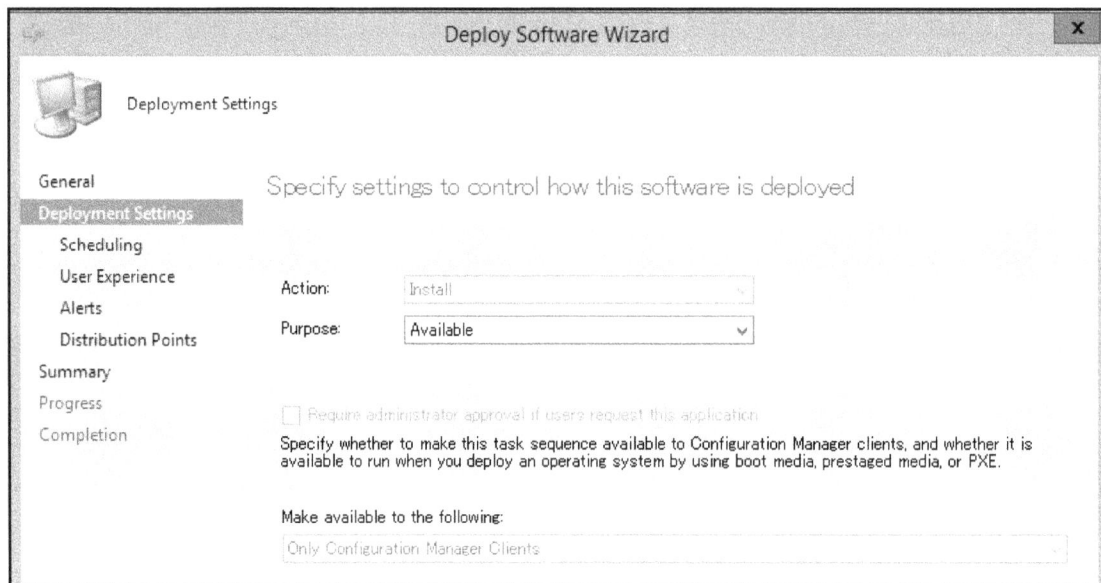

If you don't already have a device collection containing the Windows 7/8/8.1 clients to upgrade, follow these steps described in the *Managing collections* section in Chapter 6, *Managing Sites*.

> To create a device collection only containing Windows 7 machines, use the following WQL query: select
> SMS_R_System.NetbiosName,SMS_R_System.OperatingSystemName
> andVersion from SMS_R_System where
> SMS_R_System.OperatingSystemNameandVersion like
> "%Workstation 6.1%"

How it works...

When the upgrade TS begins, it automatically initiates the in-place upgrade process by invoking the Windows setup program Setup.exe with the necessary command-line parameters to perform an automated upgrade, which preserves all data, settings, applications, and drivers.

There's more...

When deploying an operating system through the network, we can leverage a new feature that has been introduced in CM Current Branch to reduce wide area network (WAN) traffic by enabling Windows PE clients to obtain content from a local peer instead of downloading content from a DP. This feature called **Windows PE Peer Cache** helps minimize WAN traffic in branch office scenarios where there is no local distribution point. In that configuration, you will have **Peer Cache clients** and **Peer Cache sources**.

Be aware that Windows PE Peer Cache only works in Windows PE. If you start the TS from the operating system context, such as from **Software Center** on the client, Windows PE Peer Cache is not used.

A TS configured to use Windows PE Peer Cache can get the following content objects while running in Windows PE:

- Operating system image
- Driver package
- Packages and Programs (When the client continues to run the task sequence in the full operating system, the client gets this content from a peer cache source if the task sequence was originally configured for peer cache when running in Windows PE.)
- Additional boot images

> Applications and Software Updates will never be transferred using Peer Cache.

For details about how to configure Windows PE Peer Cache, refer to the official online documentation at `https://msdn.microsoft.com/en-us/library/mt613173.aspx`.

Leveraging the Microsoft Deployment Toolkit with CM OSD

If you're not familiar with the **Microsoft Deployment Toolkit** (**MDT**) yet, now is the time to take a look. MDT can be used as a complete OS deployment solution, and can also be used to add functionality to CM OSD. MDT integration with CM is definitely a "better together" story. Here are a few of the features that you get by integrating MDT with CM:

- **User-driven Installation** (**UDI**): This is a rich end-user experience to assist with the OS Deployment process. UDI can allow users to walk through a wizard to select optional installations, capture/restore user state, provide user-friendly deployment status information, and more.
- **Boot Disk configuration**: This allows the admin to configure additional features at boot disk creation (such as ADO and HTA).
- **DaRT Integration**: Using DaRT integration with the MDT-created boot disk (for CM) will allow you to remotely connect to a system during OSD, in WinPE.
- **MDT Monitoring**: Integrating CM with MDT allows the admin to follow OS deployment status in real time.
- **Additional Task Sequence variables**: These are variables such as `IsOnBattery`, `IsVM`, `VMHost`, `isLaptop`, `isDesktop`, and others to help you make decisions during a TS.
- **Additional TS Steps**: These are steps such as installing language packs, installing and configuring Windows components (for both server and workstation), installing updates offline, validating minimum requirements, capture and restore local group membership information

Getting ready
In addition to the features mentioned earlier, MDT also has its own wizard for creating different types of task sequences (standard, replace scenario, server, and UDI), all of which are smartly built in a way to capture and store logs and user state in case of failure. Even if you have no plans to leverage the features of MDT, install it in a lab and review the task sequences that can be created in order to learn best practices. Getting ready To install MDT toolkit integration, download the most recent installation files from http://www.microsoft.com/mdt.

How to do it...

Perform the following steps on the system from where you run the ConfigMgr admin console:

1. Install the MDT Toolkit.
2. From the MDT Toolkit group on the **start** menu, select the **Configure ConfigMgr Integration** option. Use the Shift key to right-click and launch it with **Run as administrator**.

3. Select the **Install the MDT extensions for Configuration Manager** option.
4. Verify the option to install for CM, as well as the FQDN and site code for the site server:

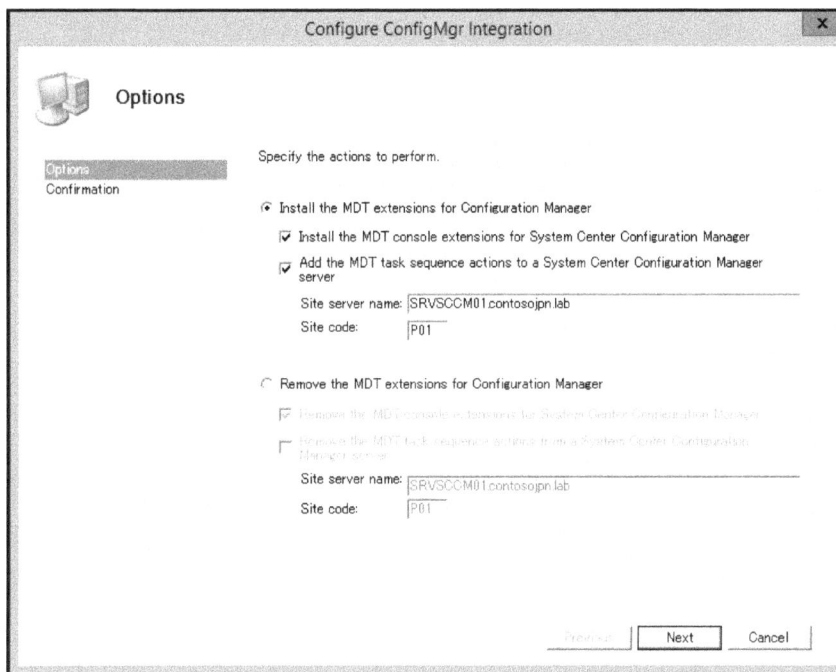

5. Follow the wizard to completion.

How it works...

This process adds additional WMI namespaces to CM to support the additional features from MDT. You perform this step one time on the site server(s) and CAS. You install the actual MDT installer on any system that will use the admin console with OSD.

There's more...

In addition to all the great features for MDT with CM, you will also find detailed walk-through documents in the MDT documentation for CM. These walk-throughs are a great help for getting the novice and intermediate OSD admin started.

See also

- MDT home page: `http://www.microsoft.com/mdt`
- DaRT Integration: `http://blogs.technet.com/b/mniehaus/archive/2011/11/28/mdt-2012-new-feature-dart-integration.aspx`

3
Deploying Applications and Software Updates

In this chapter, we will cover following recipes:

- Creating applications and deployment types
- Deploying Store Apps – Windows, iOS, and Android
- Creating Mobile Application Management Policy
- Managing Software Center and Application Catalog
- Reducing collection dependencies with conditional rules and global conditions
- Converting classic packages to applications
- Creating and deploying Virtual Applications – App-V
- Superseding applications
- Monitoring content and deployment status
- Preparing for software updates
- Creating and monitoring software updates
- Leveraging Automatic Deployment Rules – ADRs
- Deploying custom updates
- Leveraging Windows 10 Servicing to deploy features upgrades

Introduction

The three most common uses for CM are patching, software distribution, and OS deployment. This chapter will cover software distribution as well as the software update management methods.

CM can still make use of `Packages/Programs` and `Applications/Deployment Types` like previous versions. `Packages/Programs` function stays same, `Applications/Deployment Types` function has a few minor changes and extensions. You can see the changed points at `https://technet.microsoft.com/en-us/library/mt 622084.aspx`.

Software updates have received a tune-up in CM – you create an upgrades deployment plan for Windows 10, and can WSUS clean up the task from CM console.

Creating applications and deployment types

When we deploy applications, we have significantly more granular control of how they are installed, as well as confirmation that the application is truly installed (instead of just a success or fail return code). However, with additional functionality, we sometimes encounter additional complexity. Follow this recipe to drive through the application creation process, as well as the *There's more…* sections to understand the power of the application.

Applications in CM are state-based, which means that CM will determine if an application is installed (or not) on a regular basis. In CM, application state is verified on a weekly basis (and can be modified in the **Client Agent Settings** configuration). So before you can create an application, you should know how to determine if an application is installed. The following are a few examples of how you may determine application installation status:

- File information (whether the file exists, the file version, the file date, and so on)
- Folder information (whether folder exists)
- Registry information (whether the registry key-value exists, the specific registry value)
- Windows Installer product code
- Script-based detection (run a custom VBScript, PowerShell, or JScript to determine whether an application is installed)

Once you have this information, you are ready to proceed to create an application.

Getting ready

The first application we create is one of the easiest. Start here and work your way towards more complex applications.

> An application that uses an **Application Virtualization** (**App-V**) package is the easiest to import (as well as maintain) in CM. Next, a Windows Installer (.msi) based application is preferred.

We are going to create and deploy a very simple application: **7-ZIP**. This will show you how to make multiple deployment types for an application. Before proceeding, have the latest versions (both the x86 and x64) downloaded using the following link:

```
https://sourceforge.net/projects/sevenzip
```

Copy them to a share where CM can access them like SCCM-EngSource$7-zipMSI.

> Note that either the service account CM is running under, or the machine account of the primary (or CAS if you have one) must have read access to that share.

How to do it...

The **Create Application Wizard** allows us to easily create a new application. When you select the .msi file, CM automatically uses the product code of the selected MSI for the application detection rule.

Create a new application and a deployment type for an x86 install by performing the following steps:

1. Navigate to **Software Library** | **Application Management** | **Applications** and click on **Create Application** in the ribbon.
2. Under **General**, click on **Browse**, and then select the application's x86 .msi (for our example, sccm-engSource$7-zipMSI7z920.msi). Click on **Open** and then on **Next** to begin the creation process. Ignore any warning about the publisher not being verified.
3. Under **Import Information**, click on **Next**.

4. Populate the **General Information** tab, the screenshot of which is as follows:

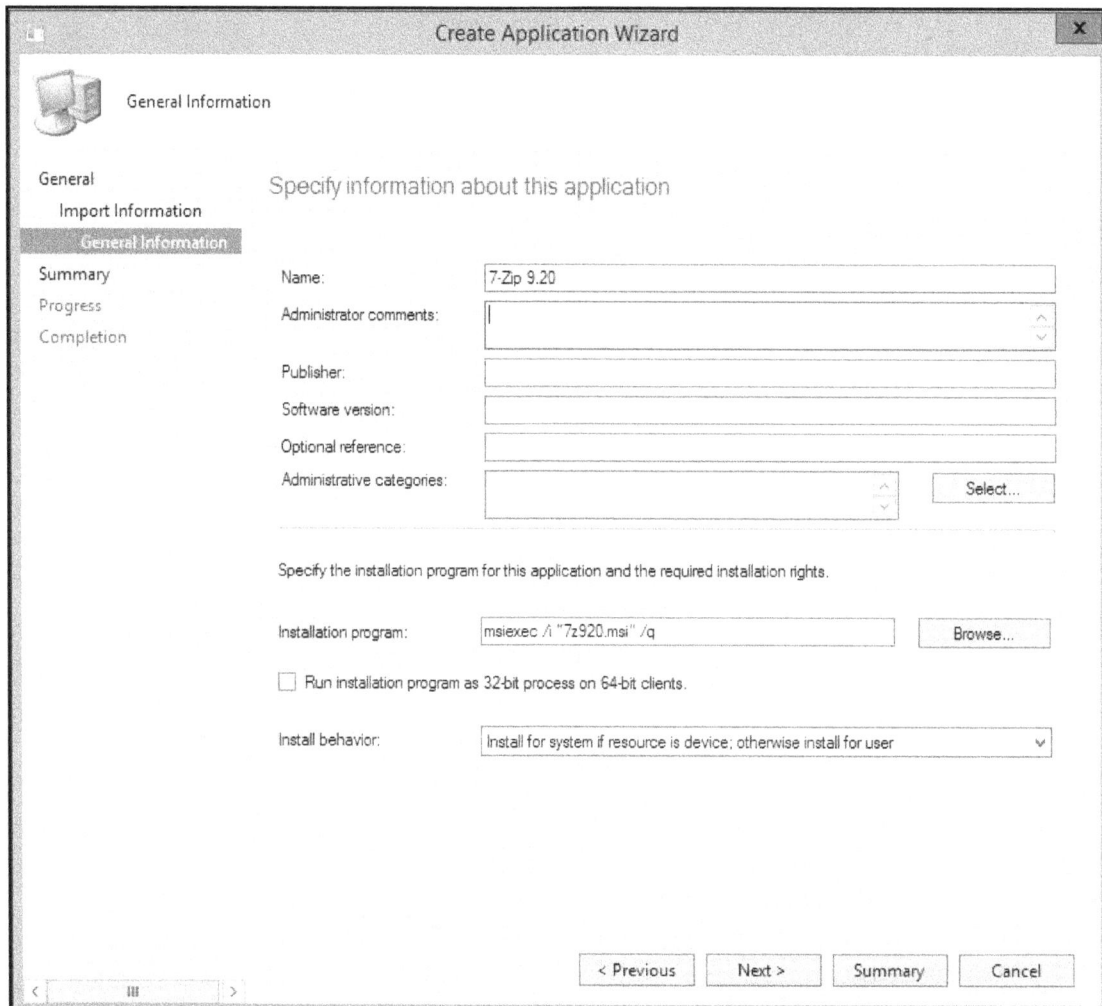

Notice that the **Installation program** contains the default command lines for a standard Windows Installer program. Modify the command line as required.

5. Optionally, you can add **Administrative categories** by clicking on **Select**.
6. Finally, click on **Next** twice and then click on **Close** to complete the **Create Application Wizard**.

How it works...

Although we successfully created an application, there are several more options that are available to us to improve the user experience, as well as define proper targeting of the application. This section will examine all the options that are available to us for the 7-Zip application we just created.

Navigate to **Software Library** | **Application Management** | **Applications**. Then right-click and select **Properties** for the 7-Zip application. A discussion about the various tabs under **7-Zip properties** is as follows:

- The **General Information** tab:

This tab provides information for the administrator. Add information to this tab to share with CM colleagues. The field **Optional reference** can be used to capture trouble ticket or work order numbers, or anything else used in your organization.

TIP

None of the information on the **General Information** tab is available to the end user in Software Center or **Application Catalog**.

- The **Application Catalog** tab:

7-Zip 9.20 Properties   ☒

| Security |
| General Information | Application Catalog | References | Distribution Settings | Deployment Types | Content Locations | Supersedence |

Specify information about how you want to display this application to users when they browse the Application Catalog. To provide information in a specific language, select the language before you enter a description.

Selected language: English (United States) default   ⌄   Add/Remove...

Localized application name: 7-Zip 9.20

User categories: Edit...

User documentation: Browse...

Link text:

Privacy URL:

Localized description:

Keywords:

Icon: ▢   Browse...

☐ Display this as a featured app and highlight it in the company portal

                                        OK   Cancel   Apply

This tab contains all properties to enhance the user experience when software is available through either the Software Center (for machine-targeted software) or the Application Catalog (for user-targeted software).

- Select **Add/Remove** to add local language (based on users regional settings):
    - **Localized application name** will be the name that appears to the user in Software Center and Application Catalog
    - **User Categories** define the categories that appear in Application Catalog
    - **User documentation** can be an uploaded file, or a link to a web page
    - **Link Text** offers a description of the link used in **User Documentation**
    - **Localized Description** and **Keywords** are searchable through both Application Catalog and Software Center
    - **Icon** is only used with the Application Catalog. Import an icon to help users locate familiar applications
- The **References** tab is used to display applications that depend on this application, as well as any application that the current application needs.
- The **Distribution Settings** tab handles how content is managed.
- The **Deployment Types** tab shows one item by default when we run the wizard to import a Windows Installer application. With our example application (7-Zip), there are two Windows Installer applications available, one for x86 and one for x64 operating systems. But CM imported only the x86 version so far.

There's more...

We can create some **deployment types** (**DTs**) and deliver their content to DPs.

Creating deployment types

We will now modify the existing **Deployment Type** (**DT**) so that it will only install on x86 and create a new deployment type to support x64 installations.

From the **Deployment Types** tab of the 7-Zip application's properties, select **Edit** to edit the DT. Review and modify the DT properties to confirm the proper configuration. Commonly modified defaults are as follows:

- **Content**: Modify distribution settings to all clients to fall back to unprotected distribution points, and changing the default of **Do not download content** for when a client is connected within a slow or unreliable network boundary to **Download content from distribution point and run locally**.

- **Programs**: Modify the Windows Installer installation command line if necessary. Also, notice the **Uninstall Program** option – by default, this is available with an MSI deployment type, and will allow users to uninstall the (non-mandatory) application from Software Center. Verify that the uninstall command is functional, and modify as necessary, or remove the uninstall command line to prevent the uninstall functionality from Software Center.

- **Detection Method**: This information is used to confirm the installation state of the application and (by default) will be checked weekly, according to client agent settings.

It is important to verify proper detection method. The detection method is used to verify whether the application is installed. Invalid methods may cause undesired results, such as automatic re-installations of a product or improper supersedence rules. Review more about supersedence rules later in this chapter.

- **Requirements**: By default, you have no requirement rules defined. Since there are no requirements, this DT will install for any targeted system. For this example, you have a separate installation for x86 and x64 platforms, so add a requirement rule for x86 platforms by following these steps:

  1. From the **Requirements** tab, click on **Add.**
  2. Select **Device** as the category, and then select **Operating System** as the condition.
  3. Check the boxes for all Windows 32-bit operating systems, for example, **All Windows 7 (32-bit):**

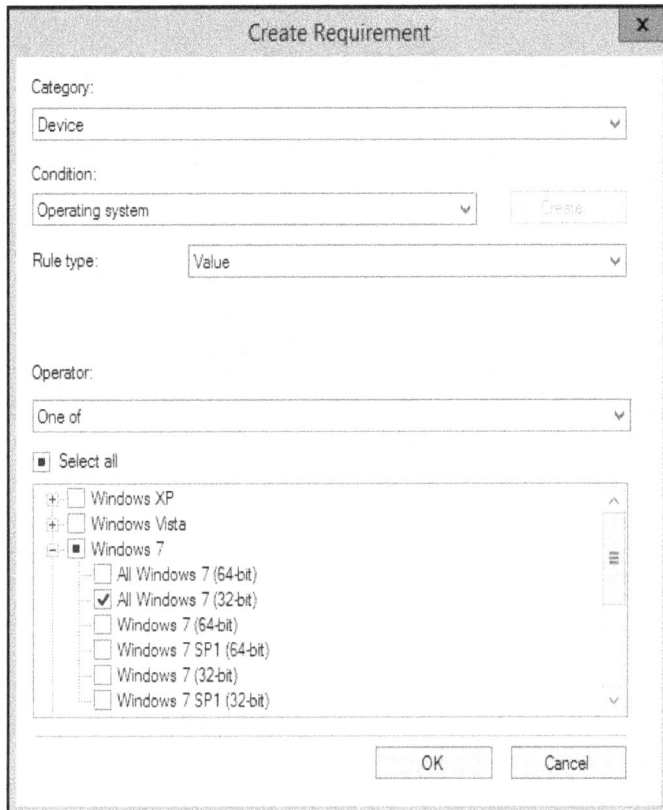

4. Click on **OK** to complete the deployment type.

- **Return Codes**: If the installation returns any nonstandard exit codes, add those codes here, as well as whether the code means success or failure.
- **Dependencies**: We can add dependencies (such as .NET framework) if required – this provides a similar experience as "run another program first" with Packages, but with applications, the process is a bit smarter.
- Switch to the **General** tab, and add x86 to the end of the **Name** to show admins that this DT is just for x86 systems. After all the changes are completed, click on **OK** to save the Deployment Type configuration.

Perform the following steps to create a second deployment type (for x64 platform):

1. Click on **Add** from the **Deployment Types** tab to start the **Create Deployment Type Wizard**.

2. Click on **Browse** to select the x64 MSI (for example, `sccm-engsource$7-zipMSI7z920-x64.msi`). Click on Open and then click on **Next** twice. Ignore any warning about the publisher not being verified.

3. Under **General | General Information**, add `x64` to the end of the name. Click on **Next**.

4. For **Requirements**, click on **Add**. Choose **Operating System** for **Condition**.

5. Check the boxes for all Windows 32-bit operating systems, for example, **All Windows 7 (64-bit)**. Click on **OK**, then on **Summary**, then on **Next** and finally on **Close** to end the **Create Deployment Type Wizard**.

6. Notice there are two deployment types (x86 and x64), **Priority 1**, and **Priority 2**. This is the order in which the deployment types will be evaluated. CM will execute using the first deployment type that qualifies for the system.

7. Click on **OK** to close (and save) the modified application.

8. Click on the **Deployment Types** tab in the bottom right-hand pane of the console to verify that 2 DTs show; one per OS type.

Specifying application settings

The process followed in this recipe so far has been for a simple Windows Installer-based installation (a `.msi` file). We also find a simple wizard for App Virtualization and Windows Mobile Cabinet (`.cab`) files. For all other applications, choose to **Manually specify the application information** in the **Create Application Wizard**. Many steps in the "Manual" process are the same, so you should be familiar with them after creating a Windows Installer based application. The manual process will walk you through to the **Create Deployment Type Wizard**, where you will specify the content source location, as well as install and uninstall command lines.

The most challenging step to creating a manual configuration is the detection rule(s). As mentioned previously, applications are state-based, and will regularly verify if the application is installed. Spend time to ensure the detection rules are precise to avoid any surprises.

Classic package versus application
Now that we have walked through the process of creating an application, you may be wondering when to use classic package and program, compared to an application. As always, the answer is "It depends".

Remember that when we deploy an application, it must be able to determine installation state based on detection rules. If we wanted to deploy something simple, like a `netsh` command to modify networking configuration, we would probably want to use a classic package/program. Most utility-type scripts will remain packages, while true applications should move to an application installation.

You can continue to use classic package and programs for software installation, but you will not be able to take advantage of the granularity with deployment types and requirement rules offered by applications. Also, as shown using our 7-Zip installation, you deploy one application for x86 and x64, and at install time, CM determines the best DT to use.

Distribute an application to your DPs

Creating a package or application doesn't get it to the DPs. We have to do that manually. Let's send 7-Zip to the DPs now by following these steps:

1. Navigate to **Software Library** | **Application Management** | **Application** and right-click on **7-Zip** in the right-hand pane.
2. Select **Distribute Content**. Click on **Next** twice.
3. Under **Content Distribution**, click on **Add** and select either **Distribution Point** or **Distribution Point Group**.

The former allows you to pick DPs one by one while the latter chooses a group. Groups have an advantage, in that, any new DPs added to them will get this application automatically:

1. Assuming you have one DP, click on **Add**, select **Distribution Point**, check the box for your DP, and click on **OK**.
2. Click on **Next** twice and then click on **Close**.

Deploying an application to workstations

Now that you have your application with at least one deployment type and it has been distributed to your DPs, you can make a deployment. We're going to deploy 7-Zip to the All Workstations collection.

1. Navigate to **Software Library** | **Application Management** | **Application** and then right-click on **7-Zip** in the right-hand pane.
2. Select **Deploy**.
3. Under **General**, click on the bottom **Browse** button, choose **Device Collections** in the left-hand pane and select **All Workstations** in the right-hand pane. Click on **OK**.
4. If you skipped the previous step to distribute the 7-Zip `msi` files to the DPs, you can do so now. Otherwise, just click on **Next**.
5. Under **Deployment Settings**, change **Purpose** to **Required** (for this exercise, we're assuming all machines in a lab must have 7-Zip). Feel free to leave it as **Available** instead if you wish, but users will have to go to Software Center to get it. Click on **Next**.
6. Under **Scheduling**, select a time or just leave the defaults. Beware that if you set a time, it defaults to UTC instead of local time. You can select **Client Local time** instead under **Time based on**. Click on **Next**.
7. Under **User Experience**, select **Hide in Software Center and all notifications** (unless you didn't make **Purpose** to **Required** in step 5). Click on **Next**.
8. Under **Alerts**, you can optionally set up any alerts you wish to appear in the console. Click on **Next**.
9. Under **Summary**, click on **Next**.
10. Under **Completion**, click on **Close**.

You can monitor this deployment by clicking on the **Deployments** tab in the bottom right-hand pane of the console.

See also

- How to create applications in CM at `https://technet.microsoft.com/en-us/library/mt595707.aspx`

Deploying Store Apps – Windows, iOS, Android

In this section, we will see how to create and deploy store apps on different platforms such as Windows, iOS, and Android. For iOS and Android, you will need to configure Intune subscription, you can reference the steps from `Chapter 5`, *Managing Mobile Devices using Configuration Manager with Microsoft Intune*.

Getting ready

To enable Platform enrollment:

1. Navigate to **Administration** | **Cloud Services** | **Microsoft Intune Subscription**.
2. Under **Home** | **Subscription** | **Configure Platforms**, navigate to **Android/Windows/iOS**.
3. Select the **Enable Android enrollment/Enable Windows enrollment/Enable iOS and MAC OS X (MDM) enrollment** checkbox.
4. Click on **OK**.

Before creating the store apps, you have to prepare the source files for side-loading deployments.

Device Type	Supported Files	Supported Actions
Windows	`*.appx`, `*.appxbundle`	Available, Required, Uninstall
iOS	`*.ipa` (don't need to specify `.plist` file)	Available, Required (required user consent), Uninstall
Android	`*.apk`	Available, Required (required user consent), Uninstall (required user consent)

> Windows 10 devices don't require a sideloading key to install line of business apps. However, the registry key **HKLM Software Policies Microsoft Windows Appx AllowAllTrustedApps** must have a value of to 1 to enable sideloading.

> To enable iOS app deployments, you should configure iOS certApple Push Service by following steps provided at `https://technet.microsoft.com/en-us/library/mt629418.aspx`.

How to do it...

In this section, we will take a look at the following techniques:

- Deploy Apps directly from Stores – Deep Link
- Deploy Apps by Side-Loading

Deploy Apps directly from Stores – Deep Link

To create store app by deep link:

1. Navigate to **Software Library** | **Application Management** | **Applications** and click on **Create Application** in the ribbon.
2. Under **General**, select the target type of app, and click on **Browse**:
   - **Windows app package (in the Windows Store)** for Windows
   - **App Package for iOS from App Store** for iOS
   - **App Package for Android on Google Play** for Android

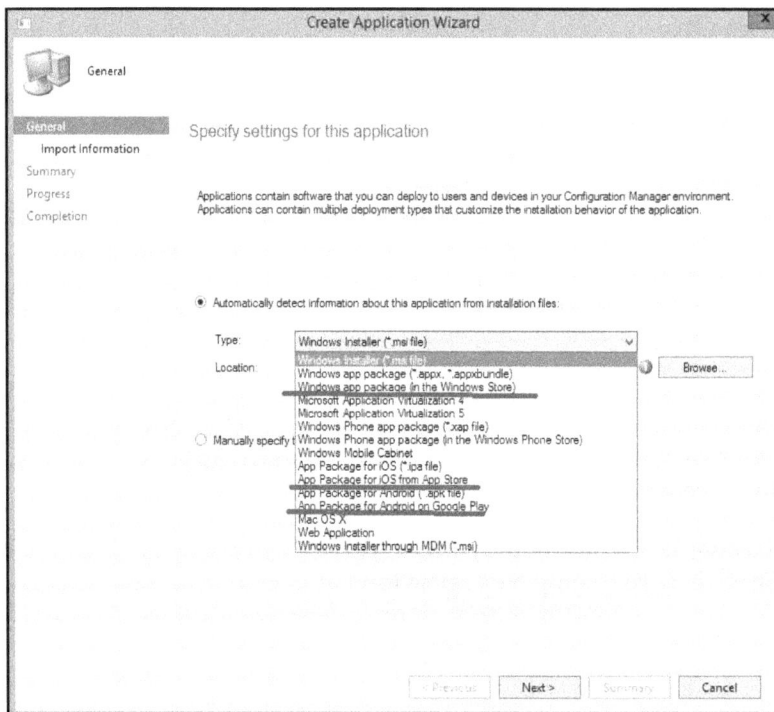

3. Under App navigator wizard, use the search box, and select the target app, then click on **OK**:

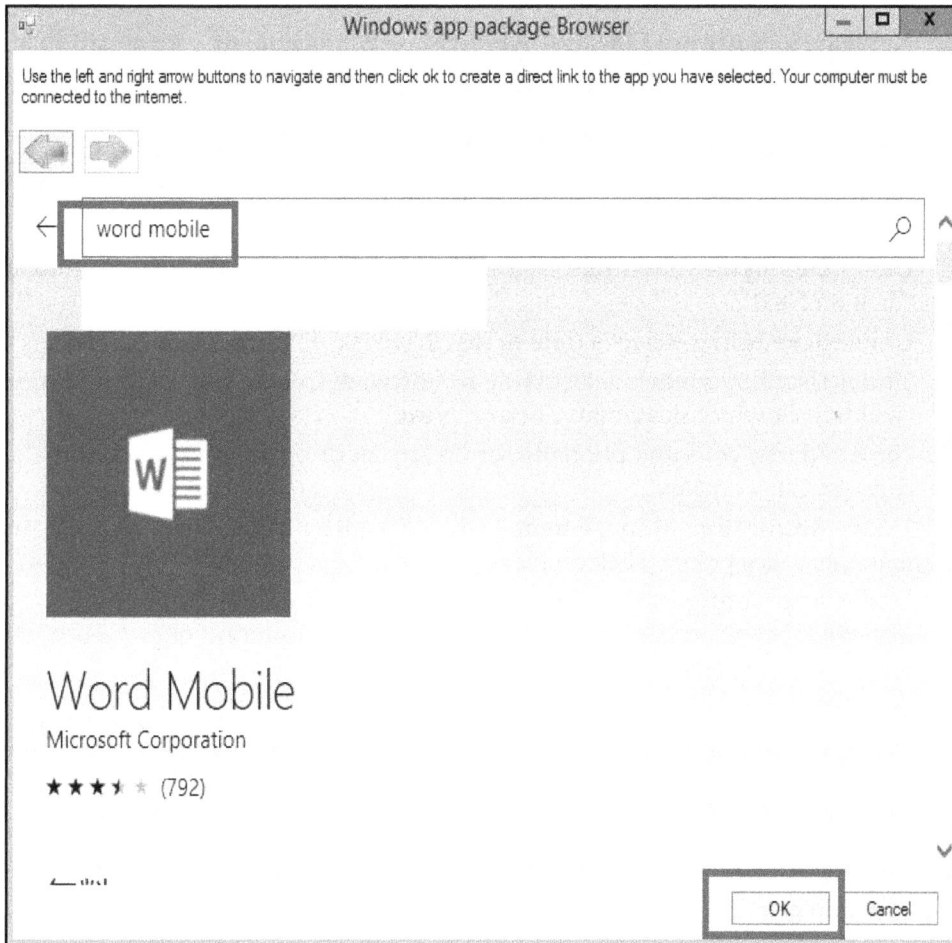

4. Again under **General**, now you can see the **Location** field is filled by app link, click on **Next**.
5. Under **Import Information**, make sure the app information is correct, then click on **Next**.
6. Under **General Information**, fill the input fields (Name, Comments, Publisher, and so on…) as needed, click on **Next**.

7. Under **Summary**, click on **Next**.
8. Under **Completion**, click on **Close**.

Now, you are ready for deployment of store apps. Follow these steps for deployment:

1. Navigate to **Software Library** | **Application Management** | **Application** and then right-click on the target app in the right-hand pane.
2. Select **Deploy**.
3. Under **General**, click on the bottom **Browse** button, choose **User Collections** in the left-hand pane and select **All Users** in the right-hand pane. Click on **OK**.
4. Under **Content**, click on **Next**.
5. Under **Deployment Settings**, change **Purpose** to **Required** if you want to force. Click on **Next**.
6. Under **Scheduling**, select a time or just leave the defaults. Click on **Next**.
7. Under **User Experience**, select **Hide in Software Center and all notifications** (will not show notifications). Click on **Next**.
8. Under **Alerts**, you can optionally set up any alerts you wish to appear in the console. Click on **Next**.
9. Under **Application Management** (only for Android/iOS), select an application management's policy, click on **Next**.
10. Under **App Configuration Policies** (only for iOS, read details at **There is more...**), click on **New** and select an App Configuration Policy (you leave it blank), click on **Next**.
11. Under **Summary**, click on **Next**.
12. Under **Completion**, click on **Close**.

Deploy Apps by Side-Loading

To create store app by side-Loading:

1. Navigate to **Software Library** | **Application Management**, click on **Applications**.
2. Under **Home** | **Create**, click on **Create Application**.
3. Under **General**, select **Automatically detect information about this application from installation files**. In the **Type** drop-down list, select the supported file type:
   - **Windows app package (*.appx, *.appxbundle)** for Windows
   - **App Package for iOS (*.ipa)** for iOS

- **App Package for Android (*.apk)** for Android

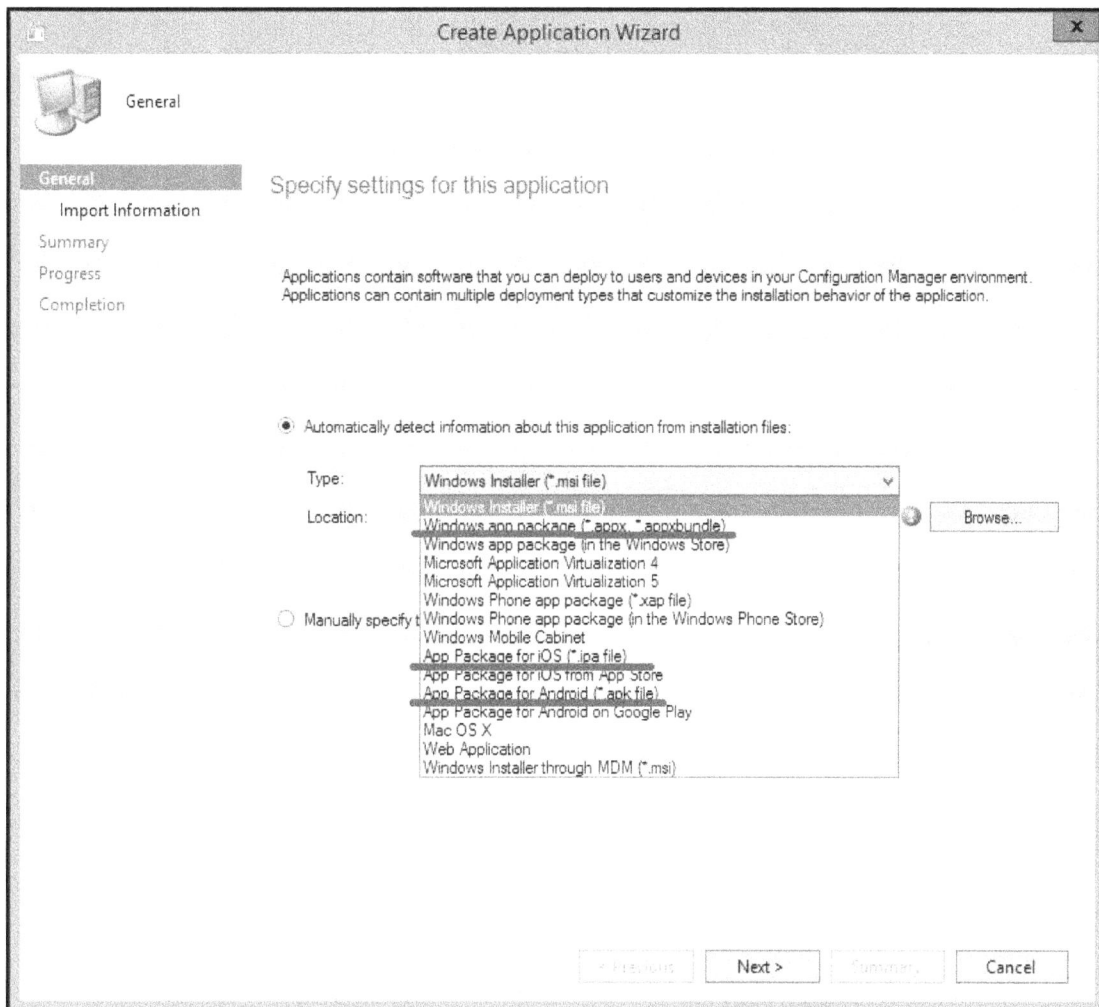

4. Click on **Browse** to select the app package, click on **Next**.
5. Under **Import Information**, make sure the app information is correct, then click on **Next**.
6. Under **General Information**, fill the input fields (Name, Comments, Publisher and so on) as needed, click on **Next**.
7. Under **Summary**, click on **Next**.
8. Under **Completion**, click on **Close**.

To deploy the app, please follow these steps:

1. Navigate to **Software Library** | **Application Management** | **Application** and then right-click on the target app in the right-hand pane.
2. Select **Deploy**.
3. Under **General**, click on the bottom **Browse** button, choose **User Collections** in the left-hand pane and select **All Users** in the right-hand pane. Click on **OK**.
4. Under **Content**, click on **Next**.
5. Under **Deployment Settings**, change **Purpose** to **Required** if you want to force. Click on **Next**.
6. Under **Scheduling**, select a time or just leave the defaults. Click on **Next**.
7. Under **User Experience**, select **Hide in Software Center and all notifications** (will not show notifications). Click on **Next**.
8. Under **Alerts**, you can optionally set up any alerts you wish to appear in the console. Click on **Next**.
9. Under **Summary**, click on **Next**.
10. Under **Completion**, click on **Close**.

How it works...

CM can track the last application deployment state for users and devices. For example, you can view the compliance state of the deployment and the deployment purpose in the CM console, as well as all software deployments by using the Monitoring workspace in the CM console.

Application deployments are regularly re-evaluated by CM every 7 days by default. If a deployed application is uninstalled by the user, at the next evaluation cycle, CM detects that the application is not present and reinstalls it.

An application was not installed on a device because it failed to meet the requirements. Later, a change is made to the device and it now meets the requirements. CM detects this change and the application is installed.

There's more...

Use app configuration policies can supply settings that might be required when the user runs an iOS app first time (Example: Port, Language, Security, Branding settings). The settings are then supplied automatically, and the user needs to take no action.

To create app configuration policy:

1. Navigate to **Software Library | Application Management**, click on **App Configuration Policies**.
2. On the **Home | App Configuration Policies**, click on **Create new Application Configuration Policy**.
3. Under **General**, specify the **Name**, **Description**, and **Category** information.
4. Under **iOS Policy**, choose how you will specify the policy:
    - **Specify name and value pairs**: The option for property list files that do not use nesting.
    - **Browse to a property list file**: The option if you already have an app configuration XML file, or for more complex nested files.
5. Click on **Next**.
6. **Complete** the wizard.

You can find detailed information and sample XML files at here `https://technet.microso ft.com/en-us/library/mt627960.aspx`.

The Windows Store for Business is where you can find and purchase Windows apps for your organization, individually or in volume. By connecting the store to CM, you can synchronize the list of apps you've purchased with CM, view these in the CM console, and deploy them like you would any other app. You can read details at `https://technet.micr osoft.com/en-us/library/mt740630.aspx`.

The iOS app store give you the ability to purchase multiple licenses for an app you want to run in your company. This helps you reduce the administrative overhead of tracking multiple purchased copies of apps. CM helps you deploy and manage iOS apps you purchased through the program by importing the license information from the app store and tracking how many of the licenses you have used. You can read details at `https://tec hnet.microsoft.com/en-us/library/mt627954.aspx`.

See also

- Refer to the following TechNet documentation for more information about creating and deploying: `https://technet.microsoft.com/en-us/librar y/mt627959.aspx`

Creating Mobile Application Management Policy

CM **Application Management** (**MAM**) Policies let you configure the security settings of apps to meet your company's security requirements. You can create and configure MAM policies under **Software Library** | **Application Management** | **Application Management Policies** as shown in the following screenshot:

Mobile application management policies support devices running Android 4 and later as well as devices running iOS 7 and later.

Getting ready

To apply a MAM policy to an app, the app must incorporate the Microsoft Intune App SDK that sometimes called **managed app**. There are three types of apps that you can associate MAM policy:

- Use a native store managed app
- Use a wrapped app by Intune App Wrapping Tool
- Write your own app using the Intune App SDK

To get the link to a managed app from the store. For example, the link of MS Word for iPad app is `https://itunes.apple.com/us/app/microsoft-word-for-ipad/id586447913?mt=8`.
The list of managed apps: `https://www.microsoft.com/en-us/cloud-platform/microsoft-intune-partners=`.

To create a wrapped app, use the following references:

- iOS App wrapper tools: `https://technet.microsoft.com/en-us/library/dn878028.aspx`
- Android App wrapper tools: `https://technet.microsoft.com/en-us/library/mt147413.aspx`

How to do it...

1. Navigate to **Software Library** | **Application Management**, click on **Application Management Policies**.
2. In the **Home** | **Create**, click on **Create Application Management Policy**.
3. Under **General**, enter the **name**, **description**, then click on **Next**.
4. Under **Policy Type**, select the **platform** and the **policy type**, then click on **Next**.
    - **General**: The General app policy, such as restricting cut, copy, and paste operations within a limited app.
    - **Managed Browser**: Configure whether to allow or block the managed browser from opening a list of URLs.

5. Under **iOS Policy** or **Android Policy** page, configure the values as required, and then click on **Next**.

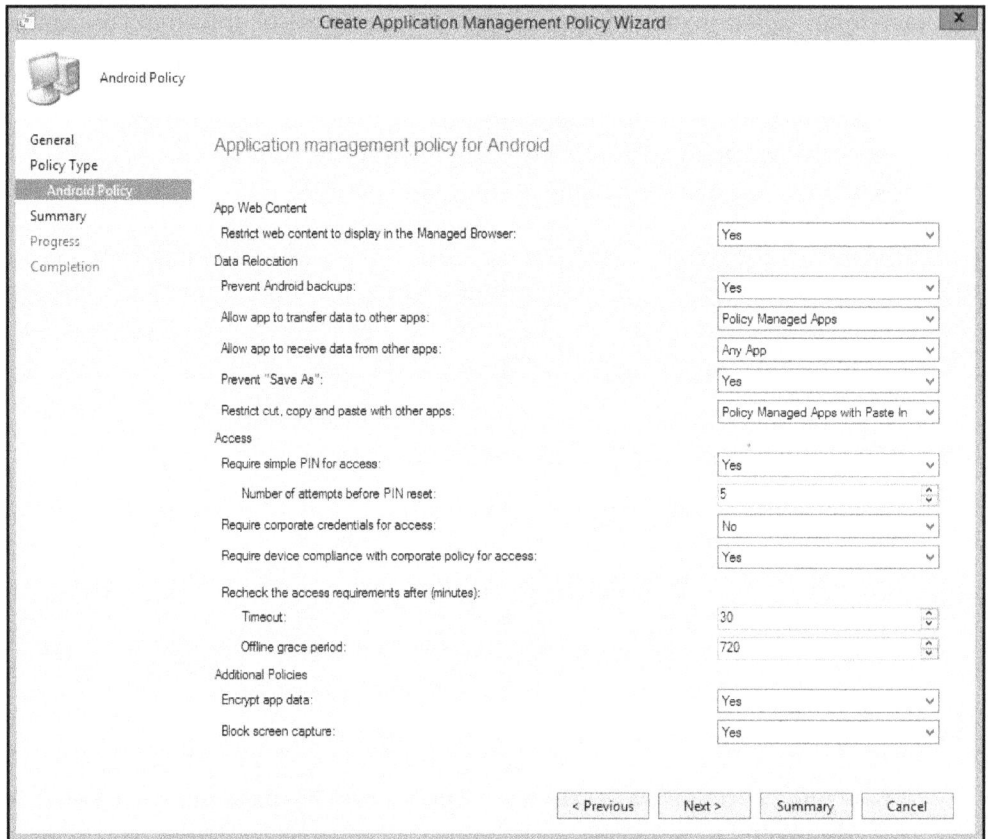

6. Close the wizard.

When you are creating a deployment type, CM will recognize that an app management policy must be linked to this deployment type if the app is needed it.

How it works...

If the app is already deployed, then the deployment for the new deployment type will fail until this association is made. You can make the association in **Properties** for the application, on the **Application Management** tab.

There's more...

You can deploy the **Intune Managed Browser** (a web browsing application) linked with a **Managed Browser Policy** which can configure an allow list or a block list that restricts the websites that users of the managed browser can visit. You can also apply MAM policies to the app, such as controlling the use of cut, copy, and paste, preventing screen captures and also ensuring that links to content that users click only open in other managed apps as shown in the following screenshot.

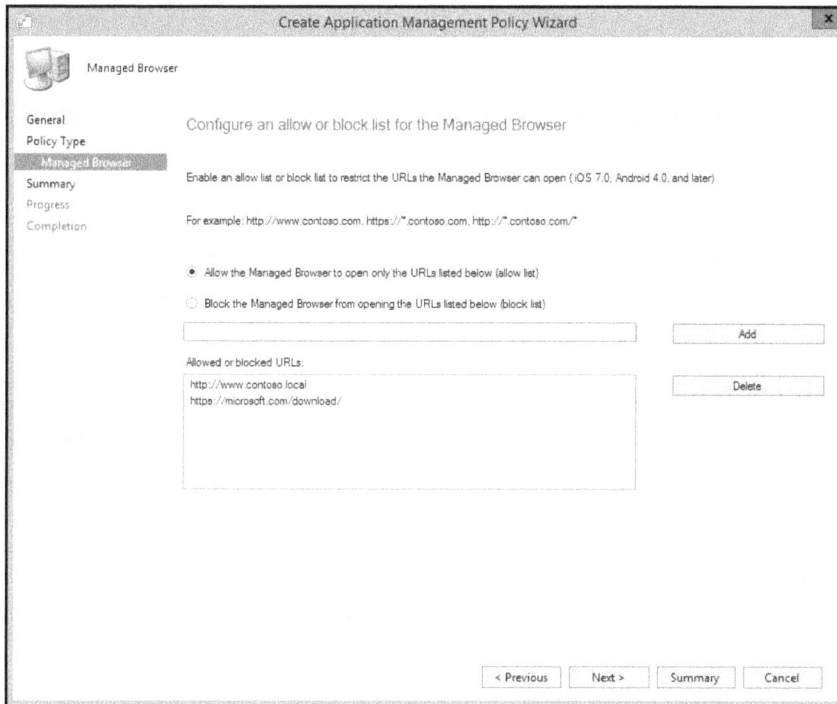

You can create managed browser policies for the following device types that run Android 4 and later as well as devices that run iOS 7 and later.

To create managed browser policy, follow these steps:

1. Navigate to **Software Library | Application Management**, click on **Application Management Policies**.
2. Under **Home | Create**, click on **Create Application Management Policy**.
3. Under **General**, enter the **name** and **description** for the policy, and then click on **Next**.
4. Under **Policy Type**, select the platform, select Managed Browser for the policy type, and then click on **Next**.
5. Under **Managed Browser**, select one of the following options:
   - **Allow the managed browser to open only the URLs listed here**
   - **Block the managed browser from opening the URLs listed here**

> **TIP**
>
> You cannot include both allowed and blocked URLs in the same managed browser policy.

6. Close the wizard.

Now, you can create a software deployment type for the managed browser app, and you must associate both a General and Managed Browser policy. More information and samples at here `https://technet.microsoft.com/en-us/library/mt488780.aspx`.

See also

- For more information about MAM refer to `https://technet.microsoft.com/en-us/library/mt627956.aspx`

Managing Software Center and Application Catalog

In CM12, if you plan to target software to users, you will use the Application Catalog, or If you plan to target software to devices (computers, mobile devices, and so on), you will use Software Center. Also Software Center was used to schedule software installations, configure remote control, power management settings. Users could connect to the Application Catalog to browse for and request software.

In CM, a new version of Software Center is now available that allows you to browse for applications without having to use the Application Catalog. However, the Application Catalog website point and Application Catalog web service point site system roles are still required for user-available apps to appear in the new Software Center.

Now, you have two options:

- The old Software Center and the Application Catalog – this is the default option. Users use the CM12 like client UI.
- The new Software Center – you have to enable it. User-available apps now appear in the Applications tab. The Application Catalog can still be accessed from Installation Status tab.

The New Software Center:

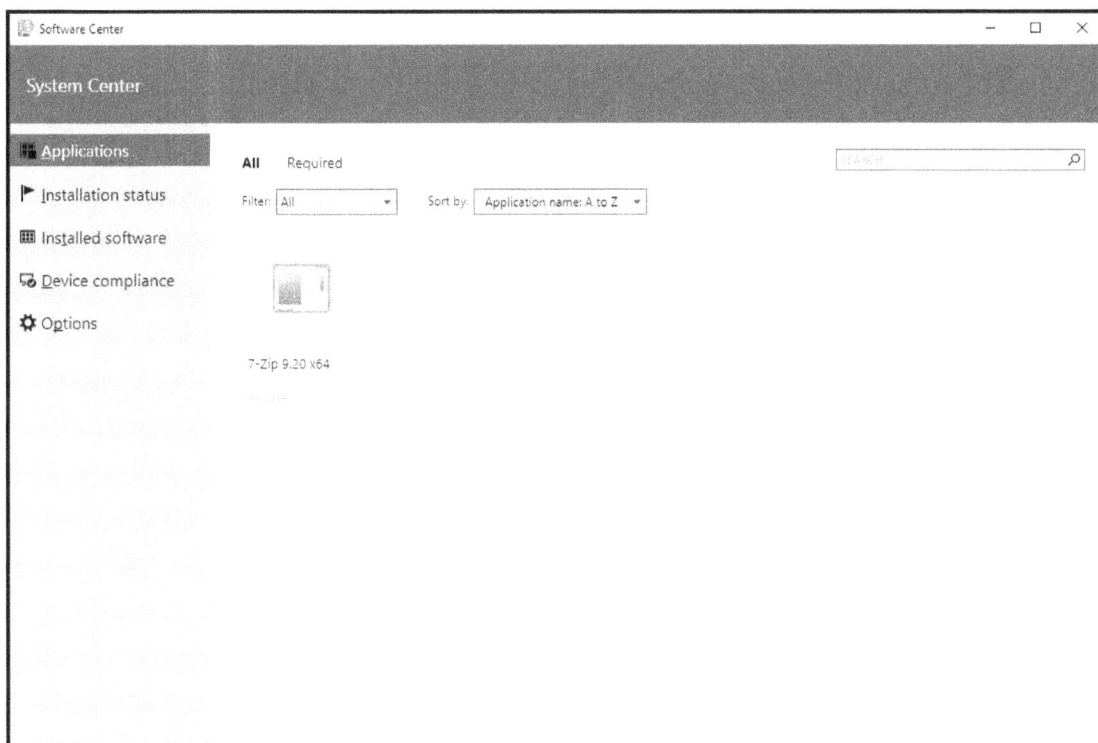

How to do it...

To enable the new Software Center:

1. Navigate to **Administration** | **Client Settings** | **Default Client Settings**.
2. On the **Home** tab, click on **Properties**.
3. From **Computer Agent**, set **Use new Software Center** to **Yes**.
4. Click on **OK** to close the **Default Client Settings** dialog box.

Use the following table to determine if you will need the new Software Center or old one in your environment:

CM Feature	Application Catalog	Software Center	(New) Software Center
User targeting	Yes	No	Yes
Device targeting	No	Yes	Yes
Supports task sequence deployment	No	Yes	Yes
Supports SW updates	No	Yes	Yes
Supports custom updates (SCUP)	No	Yes	Yes
Displays custom icons for available software	Yes	No	Yes
Supports software that requires admin approval	Yes	No	Yes (Redirects to App Catalog)
Displays all targeted software regardless of requirement rules	Yes	No	Yes

In addition to the preceding features, the following CM user-enabled configuration settings are available at the described location:

Configuration Item	Application Catalog	Software Center	(New) Software Center
Specify normal work hours	–	X	X
Opt out of power management	–	X	X
Software Center schedules for computer maintenance	–	X	X
Configure remote control	–	X	X
Configure user device affinity	X	–	–
Sync Policy	–	–	X

There's more...

One key difference between Software Center and Application Catalog is when requirement rules are evaluated. For example, if we take the 7-Zip application, and configure a DT requirement rule to only run on Windows 7 x64 systems. Consider the following scenarios:

1. We deploy the application as **Available** to **All Systems** collection.
    - Application Catalog will not display the deployment
    - Software Center will only display the deployment on systems that meet the requirement rule (in our example, Windows 7 x64 systems)

2. We deploy the application as **Available** to **All Users** collection.

- **Application Catalog** will display the deployment on for every user that connects to the Application Catalog. When a user elects to run the installation, CM will evaluate the requirements and then make a determination for installation. If no deployment types are available for the installation (meaning the requirement rules of the deployment type(s) do not match the running system), the user will receive an error stating that **This computer does not meet the minimum requirements for this application and cannot be installed**, as shown in the following screenshot:

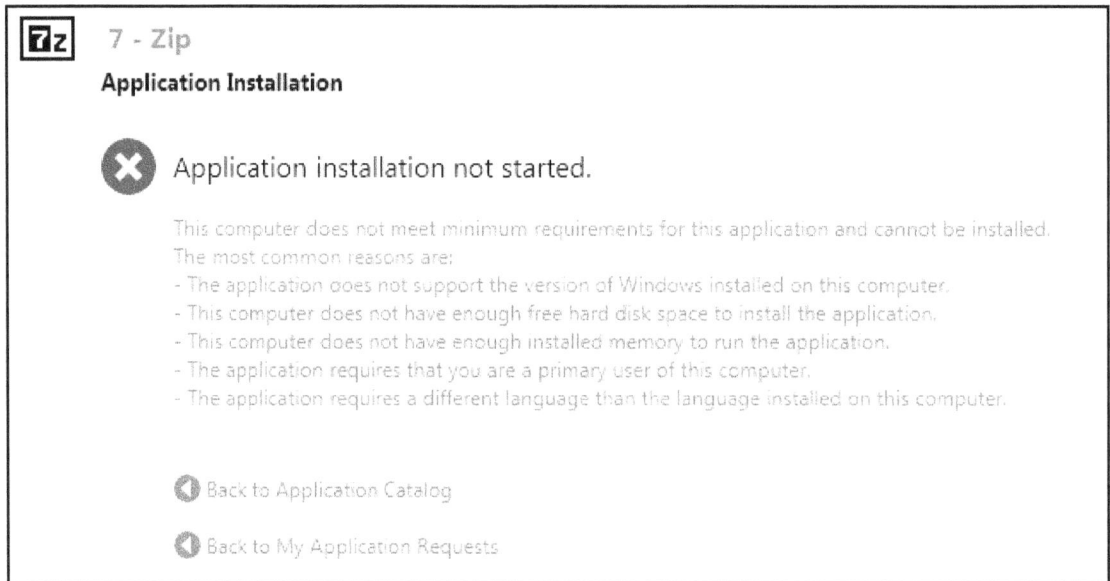

Software Center will not display the deployment.

As we can see, there are positive reasons for leveraging Software Center, as well as Application Catalog. Depending on the desired user experience, we may find more value in one or the other, or decide to use both.

See also

- For more information from Microsoft about application management refer to `htt ps://technet.microsoft.com/en-us/library/mt595706.aspx`

Reducing collection dependencies with conditional rules and global conditions

The new application model in CM12, or later, introduces the strategy of allowing clients to determine if they should run an application instead of carving out a specific collection for the distribution. Instead of waiting for inventory and collection of refresh cycles on the server, deployments of smart applications are evaluated in real time by each client.

Getting ready

We will create an application that will run `cmd.exe /C` if a machine has at least 4 GB of RAM on board. `cmd.exe /C` is a simple command used for testing software deployments. The command launched a command prompt window for an instant, and then exits. We will make use of global conditions and rules to make an application that is far smarter than the old style packages.

How to do it…

1. Navigate to **Software Library** | **Applications**. Click on **Create Application** in the ribbon to start the wizard.
2. Under **General**, choose **Manually specify the application information**.
3. Under **General** | **General**, enter `Client 4GB Test` for the **name**.
4. Under **General** | **Deployment Types**, add a script (opens yet another wizard) deployment type and name it `Close a cmd box if 4 GB or more`.
5. Under **General** | **Content**, type `cmd.exe /C` for the installation program.
6. A detection rule must exist. MSI-based apps and their versions, registry keys, and files and folders can all be set as detection methods for an application. We'll set it to look for **Windows** | **Fonts** folder, which is always there.
7. Under **General** | **Detection Method**, select **Add Clause** and then select **File System with Folder type**, the path of `%windir%`, and **Fonts** for the folder name.
8. Under **General** | **User Experience**, choose **Install for system, Whether or not a user is logged**, and **Hidden**.
9. Under **Requirements**, change the operator to **Greater than or equal to** and enter `4096` for a value.

You have just chosen to use one of the 20 default global conditions that come with CM. You can create your own and save them under **Software Library** | **Application Management** | **Global Conditions**.

10. Finish the wizards with the defaults, which will show the new **Client 4 GB Test application** in the list of applications in CM.

How it works...

When deployed, clients will evaluate the conditions set on the application just like they evaluate the need for software updates on their own. Just like you don't create a collection for every possible software update, you won't have to make one for each application. The `cmd.exe /c` is used for demonstration purposes. You can add this global condition (and many others) to the 7-Zip application created earlier in this chapter.

There's more...

Before sending any application, it's vital to test it and pilot it first. CM offers an additional way to pilot that CM07 did not have; a **Simulated Deployment**.

Testing the application using a Simulated Deployment

A collection created in advance offers the admin the opportunity to see how many clients would be targeted. A Simulated Deployment can offer that same information with no risk of anything ever actually installing. With a Simulated Deployment, nothing ever really installs.

Right-click on this application and choose **Simulate Deployment** to launch the **Simulate Application Deployment Wizard**.

Choose any collection you wish to test against. Choosing **All Systems** is perfectly safe.

Because this application does nothing more than launch a command window and then exit, it's already safe to send to any system. But choosing a simulated deployment over a standard deployment means that clients will only report that they would launch a command box if they had 4 GB or more of RAM.

Leave the action as **Install** and finish the wizard. Clients will evaluate against this application upon their next policy check from the MP. The check is not unlike a configuration item test via Settings Management.

All of the same console deployment status and SRS reports will work as if the simulation had been a normal deployment.

Any application can be sent as a simulated deployment at any time. A simulated deployment might save you when you expected an application to install to 50 machines and your report shows 5000 machines would have. It offers another chance to go over settings and conditions on applications themselves.

Converting classic packages to applications

The **Migration Wizard** in CM is fairly straightforward, and will help us migrate almost all objects from CM07 to CM. Now that we have migrated classic packages, it's time to take advantage of the new Application Model for deploying software. The *Creating Applications and deployment types* recipe walked through the process – we could simply follow that same process to recreate each of the classic packages into applications. This would be a bit of a time consuming manual process. To streamline this process, Microsoft created the **Package Conversion Manager** (**PCM**, a throw-back acronym to the Package Command Manager of SMS 1.2). We will walk through the analysis and conversion process in this recipe.

> PCM is not supported in CM 12 SP2 or later, however, we have found a workaround, do test it well and use it at your own risk: `http://blog.conf igmgrftw.com/package-conversion-manager-and-configmgr-r2-sp1-o r-sp2/`.

Getting ready

PCM is a separate installation. Download it from Microsoft, and install on the CM admin console to be used for package conversion.

How to do it...

Follow these steps to analyze and convert classic packages to the new Application Model:

1. Navigate to **Software Library** | **Application Management** | **Packages** and right-click on the title bar to add the **Last Analyzed/Converted** and **Readiness** columns.

2. Select one or more packages, and click on **Analyze Package** from the ribbon. (the package analyzer will run for a few moments, and then refresh the display to show **Readiness** state):

Library ▸ Overview ▸ Application Management ▸ Packages ▸ Adobe ▸				
Adobe 7 items				

Icon	Name	Programs	Manufacturer	Last Analyzed / Converted	Readiness
	Acrobat X Pro	1	Adobe	10/11/2011 1:45 PM	Automatic
	Acrobat X Standard	1	Adobe	10/11/2011 6:14 PM	Manual
	Air	5	Adobe	10/11/2011 4:48 PM	Manual
	AIR	5	Adobe	10/11/2011 6:14 PM	Manual
	Flash Player	10	Adobe	12/31/1979 6:00 PM	Unknown
	Reader Font Pack	9	Adobe	12/31/1979 6:00 PM	Unknown
	Reader Font Packs	5	Adobe	12/31/1979 6:00 PM	Unknown

3. Selected packages will now show one of the following Readiness states:
   - **Automatic**: The package can be automatically converted to an application. Typically, Windows Installer-based applications with one program can be automatically converted. We can multiselect automatic packages and convert them without additional effort.
   - **Fix and Convert**: The package requires additional effort before it can be converted. We can only fix one package at a time.
   - **Manual**: This may imply that the package should remain a package. Review the package properties, and walk through the manual wizard to understand the underlying problem.
   - **Unknown**: The package has not been analyzed.

4. Select all with a **Readiness** state of **Automatic**, and select **Convert Package** from the ribbon to begin the conversion process. When the conversion has finished, review the converted package(s) in the root of the application node.

5. From the **Packages** node, select a package with a **Readiness** state of **Manual** or **Fix and Convert**, and then select **Fix and Convert** from the ribbon:

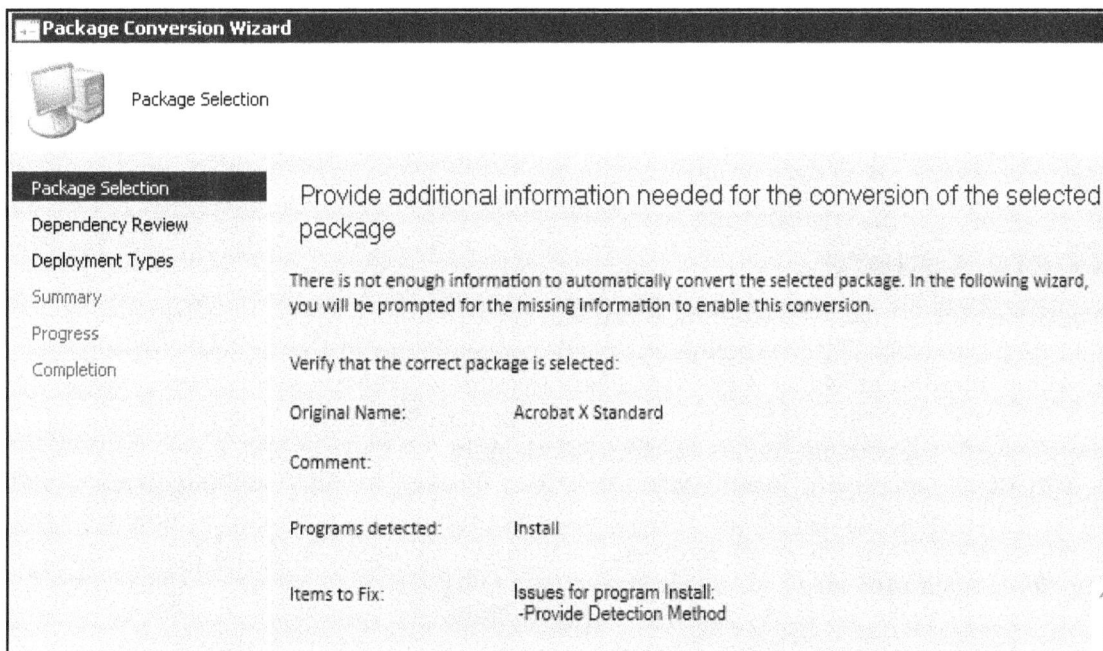

6. The first page of the **Package Conversion Wizard** describes the items required to fix. In our example, the classic program specified an executable (`.exe`) for installation. In order to convert to an application, we must specify the detection method for the product.

7. Under Deployment Types, select the first one in the list, and select Edit Detection Method. This action opens the familiar detection method dialogs to allow you to specify how to detect if the application is installed (filename and version, registry name and value, and so on). Repeat for additional deployment types and/or delete any unnecessary deployment types.

8. Continue to work through this process for all classic packages that can be migrated to a new application.

How it works...

PCM analyzes the classic package by analyzing the programs for a package. If we only have one program, and that program executes a Windows Installer file, the conversion process is very simple and automatic. If multiple programs are discovered, the PCM may not be able to programmatically determine the deployment types you desire to create for the application. PCM does a very good job of establishing a workflow to enable you to easily migrate packages to applications.

There's more...

After using the PCM a couple of times, you will get a good idea of how you may consider altering programs in CM07 to enable automatic conversion to an application. Generally speaking, Windows Installer is good, and easy to migrate, with a significant caveat related to repackaged applications. If you repackaged an application to an MSI, use care with detection rules. If you have detection rules based on the repackaged MSI, you may not be able to identify an existing install of the application that was installed without the wrapper. Also, with a repackaged application to MSI, ensure that the product GUID is unique for the application. Otherwise, we may detect an installation for product A, B, and C, instead of only the desired product A.

Creating and deploying Virtual Applications – App-V

Virtual Applications (APP-V) applications are by far the easiest applications to deploy. Also remember with applications, we can have multiple deployment types. For example, we may have an App-V deployment type for Microsoft Visio, as well as a Windows Installer deployment type. We can then create requirement rules.

Getting ready

Before we can create the application in CM, we need to have an App-V sequenced application. Also with CM, we can create a prerequisite on the application to install the App-V client, if it's not already installed.

How to do it...

Follow these steps to create and deploy an App-V application:

1. Navigate to **Software Library** | **Application Management** | **Applications**, then right-click and select **New Application**.
2. For **Application Type**, select **Microsoft Application Virtualization** and then browse to the manifest file (`.xml`) for the application.
3. Populate the **General Information** page of the wizard (**Application name**, **version**, and so on).
4. Complete the **Create Application Wizard**.
5. View properties of the new application, and edit the **Deployment Type**.
6. Select the **Dependencies** tab, and then click on **Add**.
7. Enter a friendly name, such as `App-v client prerequisite` and then click on the **Add** button.
8. Navigate to your Microsoft Application Virtualization client application, and enable both the x86 and x64 deployment types. (note that you need to create an App-V client install for x86 and x64 before completing this step).
9. On the **Add Dependency** dialog, ensure the **Auto Install** checkbox is enabled for each deployment type as shown in the following screenshot:

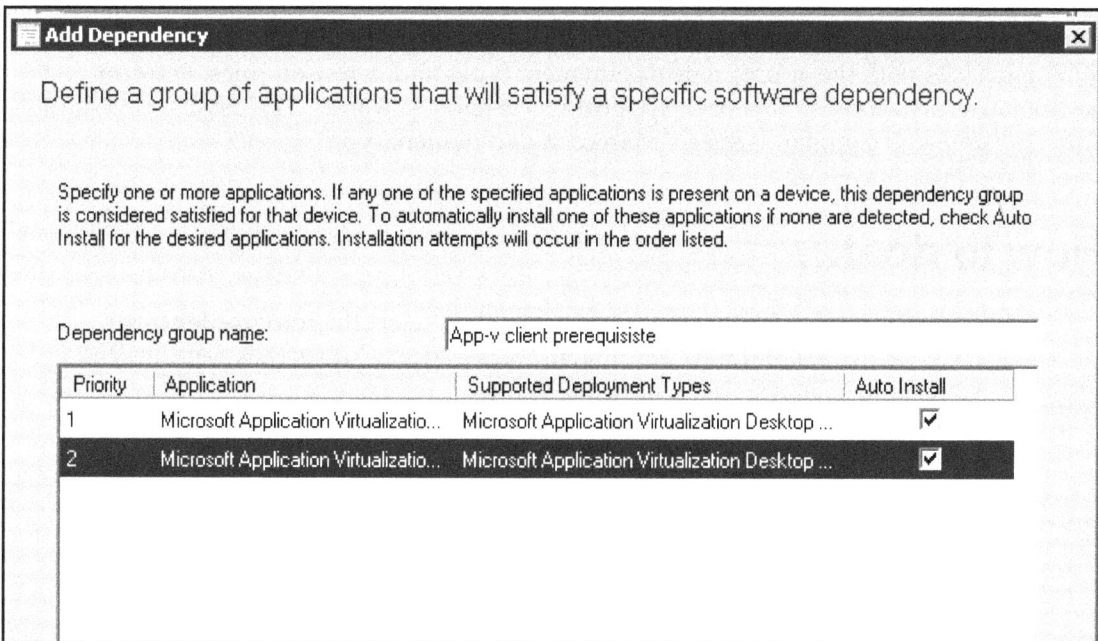

10. Click on **OK** to save the Deployment Type settings, and then click on **OK** again to save the Application Settings.
11. To deploy the application, right-click on the application and select **Deploy**.
12. Complete the **Deploy Software Wizard** to deploy the application.

How it works...

Clients will use the App-V 4.6 SP1 client (or later) to install these applications instead of the Windows Installer engine. They'll send status back on their success or failure to do so just like other applications.

Superseding applications

Use application supersedence to upgrade applications from a previous version.

Getting ready

Most of the work for supersedence requires precise applications configured for both the old and new application. For example, you are currently deploying an application named "7-Zip 9.20". A new version of 7-Zip (version 9.22) has been released. Create a new application for version 9.22 with the appropriate deployment types and detection rules. Perform additional tests to confirm that each application (version 9.20 and 9.22) installs successfully, and have uninstall commands specified in each deployment type.

How to do it...

1. View **Properties** for the application, and then select the **Supersedence** tab.
2. Click on the **Add** button, and then browse to the appropriate application that is being superseded by the new application.

3. In the **Specify Supersedence Relationship** dialog, map the existing deployment types to the deployment types for the new application version. Also, enable the **uninstall** checkbox to use the uninstall commands of the previous version of the product. If the uninstall checkbox is not enabled, CM will launch the installation process to supersede the previous version, assuming that the installation code will handle the upgrade/uninstall of the pre-existing product.

4. Deploy the new application. You have the deployment option to **Automatically upgrade any superseded version of this application**.

How it works...

Supersedence checks for the existence of previous application installations, based on detection rules and requirement rules. If a system is targeted with the new application, previous versions of the application may be upgraded (depending on how supersedence was configured), and if no previous version exists, the targeted application will simply install.

When you configure supersedence, you have the option to uninstall the previous version prior to installing the new version. This option will be selected differently for each application, as some vendors may support an upgrade (which may or may not require a previous version already installed), while other applications may require previous versions are uninstalled prior to installing the latest version. Work with the application vendor as well as test every possible scenario and simulate deployment before actual deployment. If you select the **Uninstall** option for the previous version, you must have uninstall information populated in the DT of the old application.

Also note that supersedence of an application does not make the previous version obsolete. You can deploy version 9.20 to one collection, and 9.22 (with supersedence) to a different collection.

Monitoring content and deployment status

With **Software Distribution**, content is king. If content is not available for an application installation, software updates, or operating system deployment, installations (obviously) fail, generating trouble tickets, and probably causing you to work extra hours.

Getting ready

To monitor content and deployment status, we must have proper visibility to this information in the CM console. Be advised that **Roles Based Administration** (**RBA**) may prevent you from seeing everything. Work with your CM admins to ensure you have access to the proper scope for supporting your end users (and computers).

How to do it...

1. Navigate to **Monitoring** | **Distribution Status** | **Content Status**.
2. Right-click on the title bar, and select **Group By** | **Type**. This will create groups based on the type to easily locate the desired content.
3. Select the name of the desired content, and observe the bottom detail pane to view distribution statistics.
4. If required, click on the **View Status** link to view additional issues related to CM.
5. If content is corrupt or missing, navigate back to the **Software Library** tab, and then view **Properties**, and finally the **Content Locations** tab.
6. From the **Content Locations** tab, select the appropriate action to validate content (hash check), redistribute content, or remove content from a DP.
7. Review the **Deployments** node to view the status of a deployment. Selecting the **View Status** action will show the current content status information.

How it works...

CM monitors the content of all packages and applications on the DPs, keeping track of versions and verifying integrity of the files. CM can also be scheduled to check the integrity repeatedly. Only when CM sees content on the DP as expected, will it offer the DP to clients. All of this monitoring is presented to users in the **Monitoring** node of the console.

Preparing for software updates

Painters will tell you that all the work goes into preparation; the painting itself is fast and easy. The same goes for CM software update management. It takes some work to get a proper setup in place before the easy work of day-to-day management can begin. We will now show you how to setup your **Software Update Point** (**SUP**) and sync it.

Getting ready

Installing WSUS and its dependencies has not changed since CM07. Make sure that you have WSUS 4.0 or later version installed on a server with IIS before proceeding. Note that, after the installation of WSUS, cancel out of the wizard. CM will do the configuration instead. You will want to make the machine account of your primary site server a local admin of the WSUS server.

How to do it...

1. Navigate to **Administration** | **Site Configuration** | **Servers and Site System Roles**.
2. Select the WSUS server in the right-hand pane (or right-click if the server is yet unknown and enter the FQDN and site code).
3. Select the **Software Update Point** and complete the wizard until you get to **Supersedence Rules**.

> This is new from CM12. If you never deploy superseded updates, you can now set them to automatically expire upon syncing. Expired updates can never be deployed. They won't cause errors, but they won't install either. Alternatively, if your company has issues with updates and has a need to keep some of the older updates around for a while, select a timeframe for when to expire them instead.

4. WSUS does not know which newer classifications and products are available until it syncs once. So choose as a classification and just one product you plan to send out. Complete the wizard and after a few minutes, watch the SUPSetup.log, and Security Updates as a classification and just one product you plan to send out. Complete the wizard and after a few minutes, watch the SUPSetup.log, and WSUSCtrl.log on the SUP, and the WCM.log on the primary site for errors.
5. To sync, navigate to **Software Library** | **Software Updates** | **All Software Updates**. In the ribbon, click on the **Synchronize Software Updates** button. Watch the wsyncmgr.log for errors.

6. After a complete sync, navigate to **Site Configuration** | **Sites**, select the primary site and select **Configure Site Components** | **Software Update Point**, and choose the classifications and products you plan to update.

How it works...

Admins do not log on to the WSUS console with CM. All configurations made inside the CM admin console are passed on to the WSUS server. Only after WSUS syncs will it know about all products Microsoft is making available for software updates.

There's more...

Once CM has been told where WSUS is, it can configure and operate it. But clients also need to be told to use it and where to find it.

The Active Software Update Point

Each primary site server and the CAS must have an **Active Software Update Point** designated.

To set the Active Software Update point, navigate to **Administration** | **Site Configuration** | **Sites** and in the right-hand pane choose the **Site server**, then in the ribbon, click on **Configure Site Components** and select **Software Update Point**.

Even if you make more than one SUP, only one can be selected as the active SUP. If you need more than one, you must cluster them using NLB and select the radio button for **Use Network Load Balancing cluster for active software update point**.

> Servers under a **Central Administrative Site** (**CAS**) will have **Sync Settings** grayed out as that is set only on the CAS.

Enable software updates on clients

With the server side of things ready, clients need to be told to use the SUPs instead of Microsoft updates.

Navigate to **Administration** | **Site Configuration** | **Client Settings**. You can either enable software updates for all machines (at this point, it just means scanning only) or you can create a custom client setting to apply to just a test collection.

Inside the settings window, select **Software Updates** and enable software updates on clients. At the next policy refresh of the client, it will have a local policy generated to use the SUP. If any GPO is set to designate an old WSUS server, it must be removed or the client will fail to scan.

Creating and monitoring software updates

Software updates management has changed dramatically in CM12 but not that much in CM. The change is a reflection of the entire task of managing updates being simplified.

Getting ready

Updates have to be downloaded to a source location before they can be pushed out to DPs. On a server of your choice (yes, the primary or CAS is OK for this too), create a share for the patches, for example, `FileServerPatches$`. The share permissions will need your ID to write the patches and the primary site server's machine account to read them.

How to do it...

Now it's time to actually create a package of software updates that can be used to target clients. This can be done by following the given steps:

1. Navigate to **Software Library** | **Software Updates** | **All Software Updates**. The right-hand side pane shows the first 1000 updates. It has a new search window which is what you will use to build saved searches of various types of updates.
2. To the right-hand of the search pane is a drop-down column **Add Criteria** – use it to select **Date Revised, Superseded, Title, Update Classification**, and **Vendor**. Click on **Add**.
3. Set **Date Revised** to **is less than or equal to** and **Last 1 month**.

4. Set **Superseded** to **No**.
5. Set **Title** to **does not contain** and then type `Itanium` in the text field to the right.
6. Set **Update Classification** to **Security Updates**.
7. Set **Vendor** to **Microsoft** and then click on the search button to the right of the search field.
8. In the ribbon, click on the **Save Current Search** button. From this point on, you can always get to this group of updates via the **Saved Searches** button in the ribbon instead of having to create it each time.
9. Assuming you wish to deploy these patches from the past month, you now highlight them all in the right-hand pane with a shift click and then right-click on **Create Software Update Group**. Give it a meaningful name when prompted, like **October Updates**.
10. In the admin console, right-click on your new software update group to **Show members**. This is where you can right-click on a patch and select **Edit Membership**. This allows you to remove a patch from this software update group or add it to others.
11. You can create another search and add it to this group as well.

Patches have yet to be downloaded. That can be done manually now as shown next, or chosen in the deployment wizard when you create a deployment targeting a collection:

1. Once you're happy with the patches showing in the group, it's time to download them. Navigate to the **Software Update Groups** node and in the right-hand pane, right-click on your newly created group and choose **Download**.
2. The wizard offers the option to download to an existing package or to create a new one. In this example, create a new one with the **Package Source** set to `FileServerPatches$October`. Although you could simply download all patches to the same folder, it might help in troubleshooting to break them out by the package.
3. Finally, the software update package has to be pushed to the DPs. To do that, simply click on the **Deployment Packages** node in the left-hand pane, and in the right-hand pane click on your new package. Click on **Distribute Content** in the ribbon to start the wizard, which will allow you to choose which DPs or DP groups you wish to send the updates to.
4. Allow the server some time to copy the package to the DP and click on **refresh** in the ribbon. The status of the content will be shown in the bottom right with a success message when ready.

How it works…

A software update deployment can use several software update packages at once. It's also possible to create multiple deployments targeting one collection. Using the **Windows Update Agent**, clients scan against the SUP, the content from the SUP and pull patches from the DP. Keep the latest Windows Update Agent available installed on clients for best scanning results.

There's more…

With everything in place to patch machines, the final step is to deploy the software updates to a collection.

Create a software update deployment

Navigate to **Software Library** | **Software Updates** | **Software Update Groups**. In the right-hand pane, select the group, then click on **Deploy** in the ribbon.

Name your deployment then browse to the collection you wish to target.

Complete the wizard using your personal preferences for showing or hiding updates, or suppressing or allowing reboots. If the updates were not previously downloaded, the wizard will allow you to do that now.

If you do not set a deadline in the wizard, clients will not install the updates in the deployment (unless there is another deployment targeting them). Deployed updates without a deadline will appear in Software Center on the client, allowing the user to optionally install the update.

Monitor the deployment

For a quick glance at how compliance of your update group stands throughout the company as a whole, the bottom pane of the software update group will show counts and percentages.

For a quick glance at the compliance of targeted machines from your deployment, navigate to **Monitoring** | **Deployments** and click on your deployment in the right-hand pane. The bottom pane will offer overall details, but you can click on **View Status** to drill down for more detail.

For detailed reports via SRS, navigate to **Monitoring** | **Reporting** | **Reports** and type `updates` in the search window to bring up a list of built-in reports related to software updates. **States 1 – Enforcement states for a deployment** is probably the first used to monitor a specific deployment.

See also

- For more information on the latest Windows Update Agent refer to `http://support.microsoft.com/kb/949104`

Leveraging Automatic Deployment Rules – ADRs

New to CM12 are **Automatic Deployment Rules** (**ADRs**). It's a way to bring to CM12 what WSUS had natively; the ability to automatically approve updates and deploy them. We'll show an example of how to create one to update **Endpoint Protection** definitions, but the concept can be used for all software updates.

Getting ready

Have a target collection created for a group of machines, which will serve as a pilot for new definitions before sending them to the rest of the company. Updates have to be downloaded to a source location before they can be pushed out to DPs. On a server of your choice (yes, the primary or CAS is OK for this too), create a share for the patches, for example, `FileServerPatches$`. The share permissions will need your ID to write the patches and the primary site server's machine account to read them.

How to do it…

1. From the CM admin console, navigate to **Software Library** ∣ **Software Updates** ∣ **Automatic Deployment Rules**.
2. In the ribbon, click on **Create Automatic Deployment Rule** and enter `EP Definitions` and then browse to your pilot collection.
3. Under **General**, check the radio button for **Add to an Existing Software Update Group** so that updates can be automatically downloaded. Leave the box checked for **Enable the deployment after this rule is run**.
4. Under **Software Updates**, select **Definition Updates** for **Update Classification**.
5. Under **Evaluation Schedule**, set the schedule for as often as you plan to pilot. If setting the schedule for production, set it to occur at least daily.
6. Under **Deployment Schedule**, set the installation deadline for **As soon as possible**.
7. Under **User Experience**, set user notifications to **Hide in Software Center and all notifications**.
8. Under **Download Settings**, set both radio buttons to **Download software updates from distribution point and install**.
9. Under **Deployment Package**, you are given the option to download to an existing package or to create a new one. In this example, create a new one with the **Package Source** set to `FileServerPatches$EPDefinitions`. Although you could simply download all patches to the same folder, it might help in troubleshooting to break them out by the package.
10. Complete the wizard then open the created ADR and go over every setting for possible mistakes.
11. Test the ADR by clicking on **Run Now** in the ribbon. After enough time has passed for the ADR to run and updates to download, click on **refresh** in the ribbon to see the **Last Error Description** in the right-hand pane. Review `ruleengine.log` for additional information.

How it works…

The ADR runs automatically on schedule, downloading the updates selected and creating new deployments.

There's more...

The ADR has also created a deployment. The status of that new deployment should be checked regularly by navigating to **Monitoring** | **Deployments**.

Deploying custom updates

Deploy custom updates using **Microsoft System Center Updates Publisher** (**SCUP**). Once configured, custom updates are synchronized, downloaded, and deployed just like all other Microsoft updates with CM. You will also find third-party catalogs from vendors like Adobe, HP, and Dell. You can leverage these catalogs with SCUP to easily detect and deploy hardware (firmware, BIOS, and so on) and software updates.

> So far, there is no official statement from Microsoft on the supportability of SCUP with CM current branch. But, there is a lot of feedback that SCUP works fine with CM.

Getting ready

To install custom updates, you must have a valid SoftwareUpdatePoint, as well as SCUP installed on either the server or your workstation. Search for the latest SCUP (current version is SCUP 2011) and download at: `http://www.microsoft.com/download`.

After installing SCUP, follow the integrated help for assistance in preparing the environment – a signing certificate is required to publish and deploy custom updates, as well as a group policy update to allow locally signed updates to be deployed through WSUS. You also need to deploy the certificate to clients so that they will trust the installation.

> Use SCUP to import catalogs from Adobe, Dell, and Hewlett-Packard. Work with your application vendor for SCUP support.

How to do it...

Follow these steps to create a SCUP install of 7-Zip:

1. Launch SCUP, and select **Create Software Update**.

2. On the **Package information** tab, browse to the filename to install (`7z920-x64.msi`). Also, specify the download URL. This can be a local UNC path, or an HTTP path. Note that the download URL is used at publish time. You will also see in the following screenshot that no command-line arguments have been added. SCUP automatically adds `/quiet /norestart` to all Windows Installer-based packages, so adding these commands to the command-line property will result in duplicate command-line arguments, causing a Windows Installer error.

Specify the package information for the software update

Package source: Package size: 1.38 MB

7z922-x64.msi   Browse...

☐ Use a local source to publish software update content
Download URL (or UNC):

\\CM2012TEST\source$\7-zip\7-zip_MSI\7z922-x64.msi

Example: http://www.woodgrovebank.com/mytool/mytool.msp

Binary language: Language Neutral   ▼

Success return codes:

                                    Example: 1, 2, 1029, 3023

Success pending reboot codes:

                                    Example: 1, 3, 127, 3023

Command line:

                                    Example (exe): /qn /norestart
                                    Example (msi/msp): name=value

          < Previous   Next >   Summary   Cancel

3. On the **Required Information** tab, populate all available information.
4. On the **Optional information** tab, populate all available information.
5. On the **Prerequisites** tab, add the prerequisite named **WSUS Detectoid – CPU Architecture: x64-based systems**, and select **Add Prerequisite**.
6. Skip the **Superseded Updates** tab.
7. Use **Installable Rules** to determine if the application should be installed. In our case, we already have a **WSUS Generated MSI Installable Rule (read only)**, as a result of browsing to the MSI in a previous step:

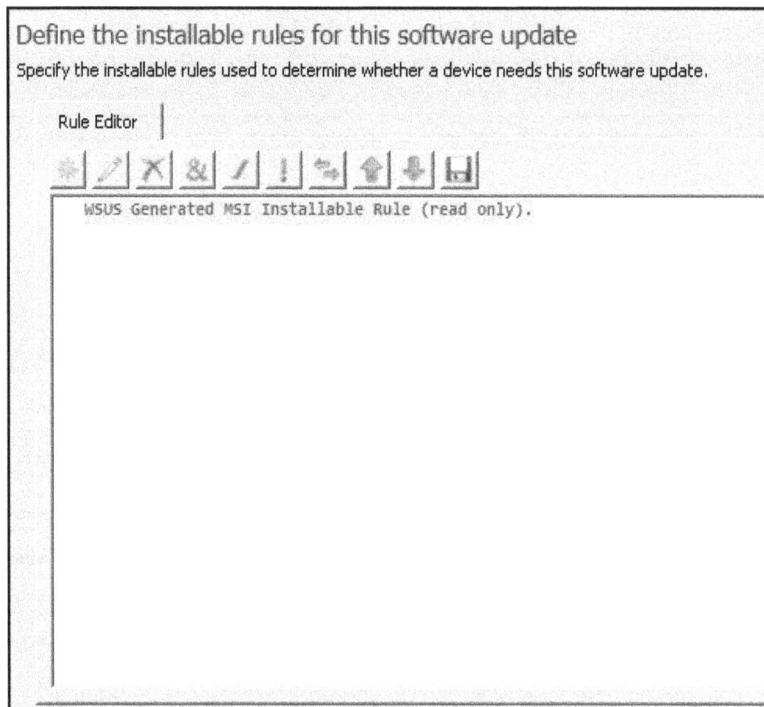

Define the installable rules for this software update
Specify the installable rules used to determine whether a device needs this software update.

Rule Editor

WSUS Generated MSI Installable Rule (read only).

8. On the **Installed Rules** tab, leave the default rule, and continue through the wizard.
9. Now use the SCUP console to browse to the custom update we just created, right-click on the update, and select **Publish**.
10. Select **Full Content** from the **Publish Software Updates Wizard**. Continue the wizard to complete the publishing process. View `%temp%SCUP.log` for more information.

11. Perform WSUS synchronization from CM, and then search Software Updates to locate new custom update.
12. Refresh the **All Software Updates** node. Search the node for the 7-Zip update, and follow your standard process for deploying software updates. The client experience will show all targeted software updates, including the custom update, as shown in the following screenshot:

Installation Status	Installed Software	Options			
SHOW	All ▼	☑ Show optional software			SEAR
					Find additional a
NAME		**TYPE**	**PUBLISHER**	**AVAILABLE AF...**	**S**
7-zip 9.22		Update	Custom Update	10/11/2011	A
Security Update for Microsoft .NET Framework 4 on Windows...		Update	Microsoft	10/11/2011	A
Security Update for Microsoft .NET Framework 4 on Windows...		Update	Microsoft	10/11/2011	A
Security Update for Microsoft .NET Framework 4 on Windows...		Update	Microsoft	10/11/2011	A
Security Update for Microsoft .NET Framework 4 on Windows...		Update	Microsoft	10/11/2011	A

7-zip 9.22

OVERVIEW		REQUIREMENTS		DESCRIPTION
Status:	Available	Restart required:	Might be required	7-zip 9.22
Help document:	Click here			
Bulletin ID:	None			
Article ID:	None			

How it works...

SCUP is a great way to deploy updates to applications, and can also be used to deploy core applications, if required.

> Microsoft System Update Packages (files that end with `.msu`) are not supported through SCUP. For more information on Microsoft System Update Packages refer
> to `http://support.microsoft.com/kb/934307http://technet.microsoft.com/en-us/systemcenter/bb741049`.

There's more…

As far as knowing when to use SCUP versus CM application deployment, as always, it depends. If you have baseline applications that you want to "set and forget", you could consider using SCUP. If you want to take advantage of the familiar patching process to deploy an application, patch, or setting, consider using SCUP. If you don't want to manage an additional certificate and GPO to configure SCUP, stay with Application Model.

See also

- Learn more about System Center Updates Publisher at `http://technet.microsoft.com/en-us/systemcenter/bb741049`

Leveraging Windows 10 Servicing to deploy features upgrades

In CM, you can create servicing plans to deploy the latest Windows 10 upgrades that Windows 10 computers are up to date. The new build upgrade will be deployed via SUP just like a traditional Windows update.

Getting ready

Make sure to check the following before deploy upgrades:

- WSUS 4.0 or later with the hotfix 3095113 and 3159706 must be installed on your SUP

- Specify the group policy setting, **Defer Upgrades and Updates**, to determine whether a computer is CB or CBB
- You must select the **Upgrades** classification and synchronize software updates

How to do it...

Follow these steps to create a Windows 10 servicing plan:

1. Navigate to **Software Library** | **Windows 10 Servicing** | **Servicing Plans**.
2. On the **Home** tab, in the **Create** group, click on **Create Servicing Plan**.
3. On the **General** page, specify the **Name** and **Description**. Click on **Next**.
4. On the **Servicing Plan** page, specify the **Target Collection**. Click on **Next**.
5. On the **Deployment Ring** page, specify the type of release (CB/CBB) and delay date. Click on **Next**.
6. On the **Deployment Schedule** page, configure the following settings:
    1. **Schedule evaluation**: Specify the time evaluation method by using UTC or the local time.
    2. **Software available time**: Specify when the software updates are available to clients.
    3. **Installation deadline**: Specify the installation deadline.
7. On the **User Experience** page, configure the following settings:
    1. **User notifications**: Specify whether to display the notification for the user.
    2. **Deadline behavior**: Specify the behavior that is to occur when the deadline is reached.
    3. **Device restart behavior**: Specify whether to suppress a system restart on servers and workstations.
8. On the **Deployment Package** page, select an existing package or create a new one. Click on **Next**.
9. On the **Distribution Points** page, specify the target DPs. Click on **Next**.
10. On the **Download Location** page, specify whether to download from the Internet or from your local network. Click on **Next**.
11. On the **Language Selection** page, select the languages. Click on **Next**.
12. On the **Summary** page, review the settings and click on **Next** twice.

After you have completed the wizard, the servicing plan will run. It will add the updates that meet the specified criteria to a software update group, download the updates to the content library on the site server, distribute the updates to the configured distribution points, and then deploy the software update group to clients in the target collection.

To deploy a specific update (CB) by following these steps:

1. Navigate to **Software Library | Windows 10 Servicing | All Windows 10 Updates.**
2. Select an upgrade, click on **Deploy** on the **Home** tab.
3. On the **Deploy Software Updates Wizard**, provide a **Deployment Name**, **description** and choose the **Collection.** Click on **Next**.
4. On **License Terms** Page, make sure the terms and accept it.
5. On the **Deployment Settings** page, set the **Type of deployment** as **Required** or **Available.** Click on **Next**.
6. On the **Scheduling** page, configure the following settings:
    1. **Schedule evaluation**: Specify the time evaluation method by using UTC or the local time.
    2. **Software available time**: Specify when the software updates are available to clients.
    3. **Installation deadline**: Specify the installation deadline.
7. On the **User Experience** page, configure the following settings:
    1. **User notifications**: Specify whether to display the notification for the user.
    2. **Deadline behavior**: Specify the behavior that is to occur when the deadline is reached.
    3. **Device restart behavior**: Specify whether to suppress a system restart on servers and workstations.
8. On the **Deployment Package** page, select an existing package or create a new one. Click on **Next**.
9. On the **Distribution Points** page, specify the target DPs. Click on **Next**.
10. On the **Download Location** page, specify whether to download from the Internet or from your local network. Click on **Next**.
11. On the **Language Selection** page, select the languages. Click on **Next**.
12. On the **Summary** page, review the settings and click on **Next** twice.

The process of deploying the upgrade for Windows 10 is basically same with the traditional update deployment.

How it works...

You can create multiple servicing plans to define the deployment rings that you want in your environment, and then monitor them in the Windows 10 servicing dashboard. Servicing plans use only the Upgrades classification, not cumulative updates for Windows 10.

You can use a TS to deploy an upgrade for each Windows 10 build, but it requires more manual work. However, a TS provides additional customized options, such as the pre-deployment and post-deployment actions. Refer to the details from `Chapter 2`, *Deploying Windows 10 with Operating System Deployment*.

There's more...

If you need to change the settings for an existing servicing plan, you can go to properties for the servicing plan.
To modify the properties of a servicing plan:

1. Navigate to **Software Library** | **Windows 10 Servicing** | **Servicing Plans.**
2. Select the servicing plan that you want to modify.
3. On the **Home** tab, click on **Properties** to open properties. Make the necessary changes.

You can enable the WSUS cleanup task from in SUP Component properties. It will run at the next software update synchronization. The expired software updates will be set to a status of declined on the WSUS server and the Windows Update Agent on computers will no longer scan these software updates. By default, the WSUS cleanup job runs every 30 days.

Follow these steps to enable WSUS cleanup task:

1. Navigate to **Administration** | **Overview** | **Site Configuration** | **Sites**.
2. Select top-tier (CAS or Stand-alone Primary) site.
3. Click on **Configure Site Components** in the **Settings** group, and then click on **Software Update Point.**
4. Click on the **Supersedence Rules** tab, select **Run WSUS cleanup wizard**, and then click on **OK**.

CM provides a new Windows as a Service dashboard. You can see the current organization's client deployment status from the dashboard:

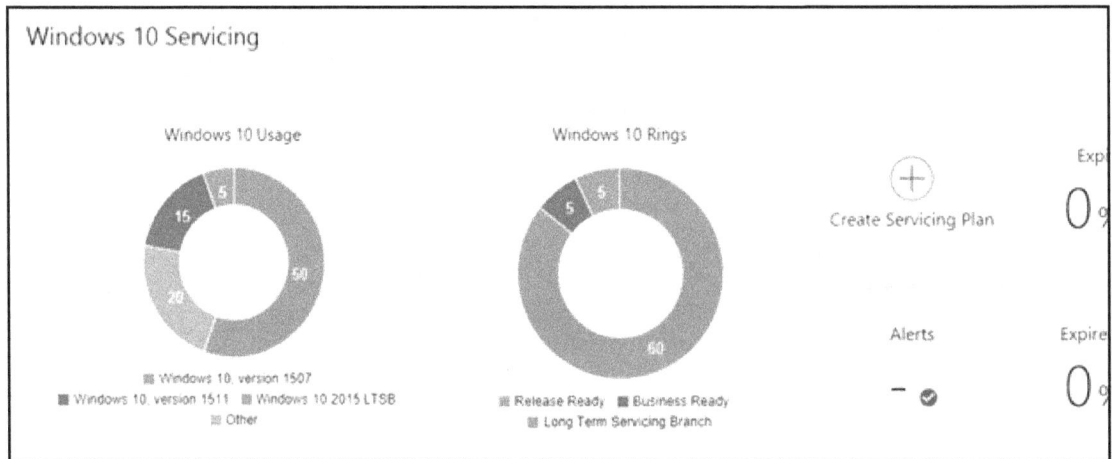

Also, quickly check the Windows 10 support lifecycle.

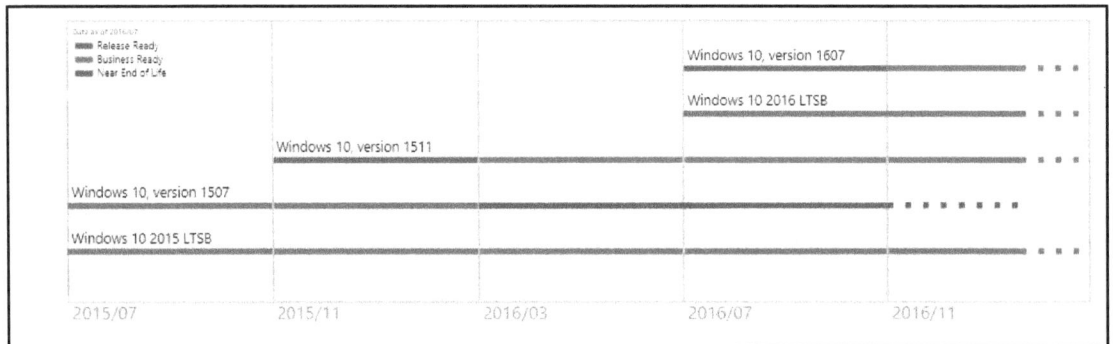

See also

- Learn more about WaaS management at `https://technet.microsoft.com/en-us/library/mt627931.aspx`

4
Managing Compliance Settings

In this chapter, we will cover the following recipes:

- Building Configuration Items the old way
- Building Configuration Items for Windows 10
- Creating and deploying a baseline
- Leveraging Security Compliance Manager
- Monitoring compliance with SSRS

Introduction

Compliance settings in CM (also known as **Desired Configuration Management (DCM)** in the past- CM07) have improved greatly since CM12. While CM12 introduced the **Remediation** feature which could enforce a list of settings, CM Current Branch brings **Compliance Settings** to a whole new level by leveraging that existing feature to manage **Mobile Devices** without CM agent installed (enrolled via Microsoft Intune).

In CM Current Branch, Compliance Settings is used for two purposes:

1. Enforce compliance settings to CM agent installed machines (such as Windows 10, Mac OS X, and Windows clients and servers).
2. Enforce security policies to agentless mobile devices (such as iOS, Android, or Windows 10 Mobile devices).

This chapter will cover the first scenario and the following chapter will cover the mobile device scenario case.

There are a variety of ways to use compliance settings. The one you are already aware of is **Software Updates**, which are nothing more than a bunch of **Configuration Items** (**CIs**) downloaded from Microsoft. When you bundle them in a deployment, you are basically creating a baseline with remediation.

Perhaps you are currently using software inventory to look for a program and you wish to keep your database footprint small by removing errors such as location, size, dates, and so on. If you just want to know whether the program is there or not, compliance settings can tell you that by looking for it via a registry, a WMI entry, or a file.

This chapter will cover the creation of CIs, grouping CIs into a baseline, and deploying the baseline to a collection of machines. We will also show you how to import configuration packs and how to monitor compliance with the baseline.

> CM Current Branch differentiates the type of CIs for **Windows 10** and **for other Windows versions**. When selecting **Windows Desktops and Servers**, every setting will have to be defined in a customized fashion (such as by defining a registry, a WMI entry, and a file to check). When selecting **Windows 10** as the targeted platform though, a list of comprehensive categories of policy is offered.

Keep in mind that any CI can be put into a baseline and targeted at a collection. The examples we show could be mixed and matched as you need. We offer them here mostly to show how to use the tool.

There are two types of CIs available in CM Current Branch. The first type, that we call **the old way**, is the legacy CI type available since CM12. The second type is the new type introduced in CM CB for **Windows 10**.

Building Configuration Items the old way

Assume your company requires all machines to adhere to the following four items:

- Users are required to use *Ctrl + Alt + Delete* to log in
- The local guest account must be disabled
- The Internet Connection Sharing service must be disabled
- A recent antivirus definition file

Each of these settings can be verified with a single CI returning a single compliant or noncompliant state, or each setting can get its own CI and return a state for each setting. The latter generates more state messages, but it can provide more detail in reporting. In this scenario, we'll just put all these settings into a single CI.

Getting ready

Create a text file called `virus.def` in the `Windows\Temp` folder of the computer running the CM admin console. You can replace this file and location with the correct file of your company's antivirus definition file as needed in the following *How to do it...* section.

How to do it...

1. In the admin console, navigate to **Assets and Compliance** | **Compliance Settings** | **Configuration Items** and click on **Create Configuration Item** in the ribbon to launch **Create Configuration Item Wizard**.

2. Under **General**, enter `Company Security Policy` for **Name**. Since we are going to create a custom CI, select **Windows Desktops and Servers (custom)** as the type of the CI. Check **Client** and **Server** as a category to easily find or search for this CI again.

3. Under **General** | **Supported Platforms**, leave all the operating systems checked as this CI will be checked against all of them (for a server CI, you might just check the server operating system).

4. Under **General** | **Settings**, click on **New** to create a new setting.

At this point, you have two options: manually enter the information or browse to a machine where the setting exists. We'll show the option to manually enter the information first:

1. Under **General**, enter `disablecad` for **name**, select **Integer** for **Data type**, enter `SOFTWARE\Microsoft\Windows\CurrentVersion\Policies\System` for the **Key**, and **disablecad** for **value**. Click on **Apply**.

2. Under **Compliance Rules**, click on **New** and then enter `disablecad Equals 0` for **name**. Enter `0` for **value**, check the remediation box and select **Information** for the severity level. Click on **OK:**

For the situation where you have a computer you can browse to obtain the registry information, use the following **Browse** option:

1. Under **General**, click on **Browse** and enter the name of a computer where the setting is already made and click on **Connect**, or if the machine you are currently on has the setting, navigate the registry tree in the left-hand pane to `HKEY_LOCAL_MACHINE\SOFTWARE\Microsoft\Windows\CurrentVersion\Po` `licies\System` and then in the right-hand pane click on **disablecad**. Uncheck the box that states that the rule defines compliance (because it is the setting of zero that matters here, not that the key exists). Check the second box to show **Equals** and **0** so that machines with a value of 0 for this key will be deemed compliant. Click on **OK:**

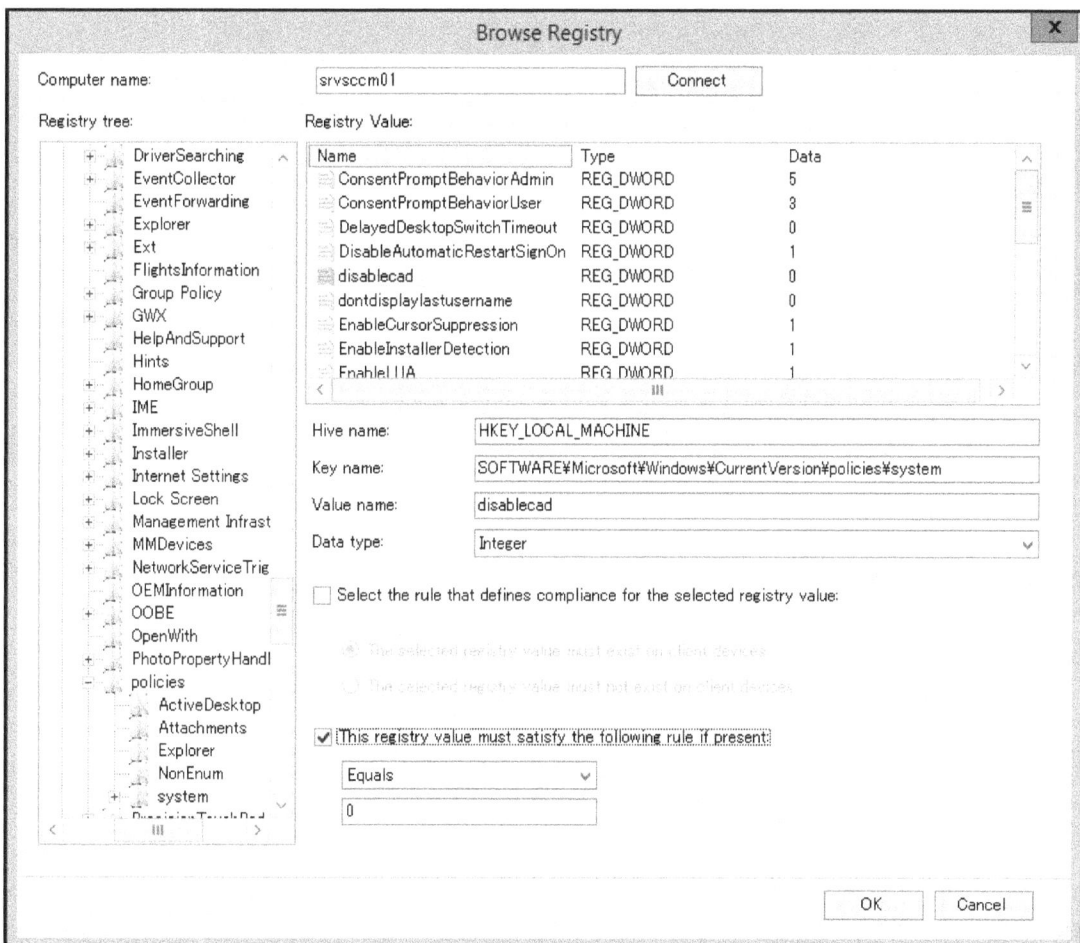

2. To enforce this new setting, click on the **Compliance Rules** tab, click on **disablecad Equals 0**, then click on **Edit...** and check the box to remediate the noncompliant rules. Click on **OK** twice to return to the **General | Settings** area of the wizard. Skip ahead to the *How it works...* recipe.

You now have one of the four compliance settings visible in **Create Configuration Item Wizard** with three more to add.

How it works...

After adding the remaining rules for this one CI, it can be added to an existing or new baseline and targeted to a collection for both monitoring and enforcement. Clients will pick it up as policy just like they pick up policies for software updates or applications. If found to be noncompliant, clients will be instructed to change bad settings to comply with the company policy wherever you have set a CI to remediate.

> The client's compliance evaluation results are cached locally, for **15 minutes**. For this reason, the client will not re-evaluate its compliance within this **15 minute** window, even if you specify a shorter evaluation compliance schedule.

There's more...

Now let's add the three remaining rules to this CI so that it can be placed into a baseline.

Disabling the local guest account

To do this, perform the following steps:

1. While still in **Create Configuration Item Wizard**, under **General | Settings**, click on **New...** to create a new setting.
2. Under **General**, enter `Disabled Guest Acct` for **name**. Choose **WQL query** for **Setting type** and **Boolean** for **Data type**.
3. Enter `Win32_UserAccount` for **Class** and `Disabled` for **property**. Type `SID like '%501' and LocalAccount = 1` for the **WQL query WHERE clause**. Click on **Apply**.

4. Now, under **ComplianceRules**, click on **New** and enter `Disabled Guest Acct` for **Name**, click on the remediation box and choose **Information** for **Noncompliance severity for reports**.

5. Click on **OK** twice to return to **Create Configuration Item Wizard**.

Disabling Internet Connection Sharing

To do this, perform the following steps:

1. While still in **Create Configuration Item Wizard**, under **General | Settings**, click on **New** to create a new setting.

2. Under **General**, either browse to a machine with the correct settings or enter the following manually. If browsing, be sure to return to the compliance rules to check the remediation box.

3. Enter `Disable ICS` for **Name**, **Registry value** for **Setting type**, **Integer** for **Data type**, `SYSTEM\CurrentControlSet\services\SharedAccess` for the **Key**, and `Start` for **Value**.

4. Under **Compliance Rules**, click on **New** and enter `Start Equals 4` for **Name**, and `4` for **value**. Check the remediation box and select **Information** for**Noncompliance severity for reports**.

5. Click on **OK** twice to return to **Create Configuration Item Wizard**.

Verifying recent antivirus definition

This can be done by performing the following steps:

1. While still in **Create Configuration Item Wizard**, under**General | Settings**, click on **New** to create a new setting.

2. Under **General**, enter `virus.def` for **name** and **File system** for **Setting type**. Click on **Browse** and navigate to **Windows | Temp folder** in the left-hand pane and click on **virus.def** in the right-hand pane. (If you did not create the file earlier, you can create it now to select it.)

3. Check the box for **The selected file must be compliant with the following rules**. Click on **Add** and select **Greater than** for **Operator**. Change the date on **Value** to 3 days ago and then click on **OK**.

> Notice that there are now two rules listed under Compliance Rules; one that the file exists and one that looks for it to be recent. A failure of either would return noncompliance for a client.

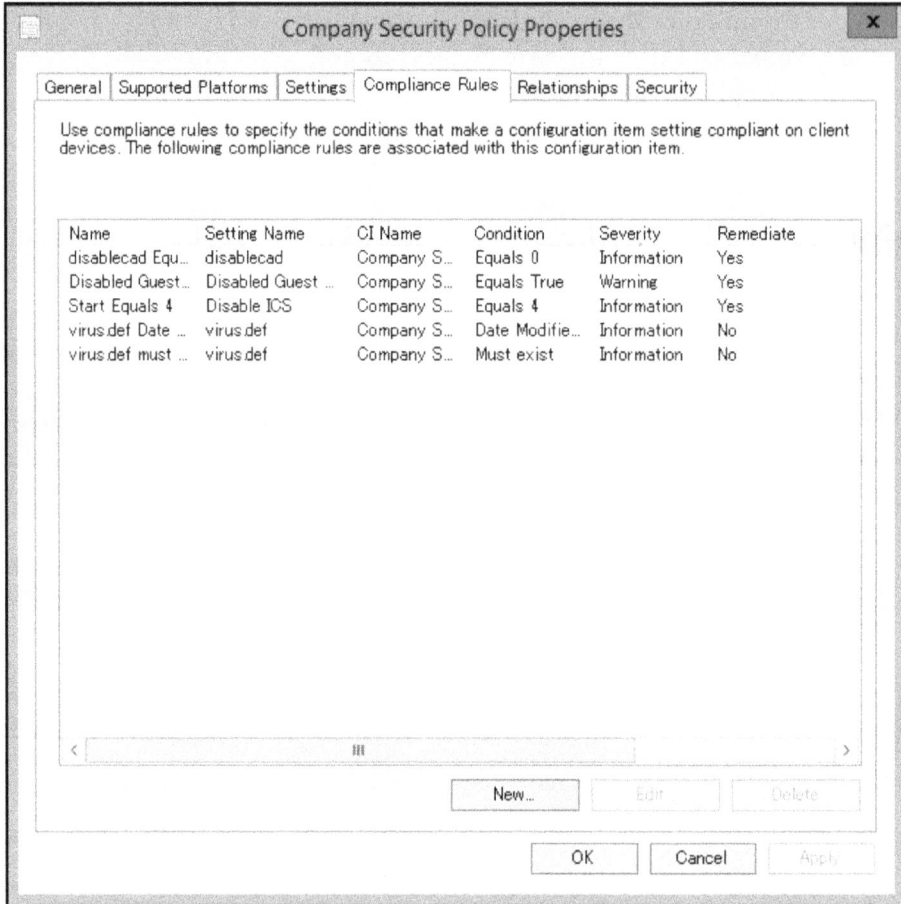

4. You should now see four settings in the **Create Configuration Item Wizard**. Click on **Next** to verify that you see five compliance rules listed where three are set to remediate.

5. Click on **Next** for the summary and close the wizard to reveal your new policy **Company Server Policy** in the right-hand pane of Configuration Items.

See also

- Many great tips for creating CIs can be found at `http://mofmaster.com`
- **CP Studio** is a commercial add-on tool to help build rules, found at `http://www.silect.com/products/cp-studio`

Building Configuration Items for Windows 10

CM Current Branch has added many handy features to manage Windows 10. Compliance Settings also include improvement when it comes to Windows 10. The CI that we called "the old way" lets you verify and remediate any custom settings/registry/WMI/files and so on. The CI type for Windows 10, though, will offer something which is more like a GPO. Indeed, this CI proposes predefined settings such as password policy, device policy, and so on.

Let's assume that your company wants to **disable bluetooth** on all Windows 10 computers. You will see next that a CI for Windows 10 offers a very simple way to do that.

Getting ready

Nothing to prepare this time before we create a CI for Windows 10. You can directly jump into the *How to do it...* section!

How to do...

1. In the CM admin console, navigate to **Assets and Compliance | Compliance Settings | Configuration Items** and click on **Create Configuration Item** in the ribbon to launch **Create Configuration Item Wizard**.
2. Under **General**, enter `Company Security Policy for Windows 10` for **Name**. Since we are going to create a custom CI, select **Windows 10** as the type of the CI. Check **Client** as a category to easily find or search for this CI again.
3. Under **General | Supported Platforms**, you will only find **Windows 10** as this CI will only apply to Windows 10 operating systems. Be sure that **Windows 10** is checked.

4. Under **General | Device Settings**, in the list of available settings groups, select **Device** and click on **Next**.

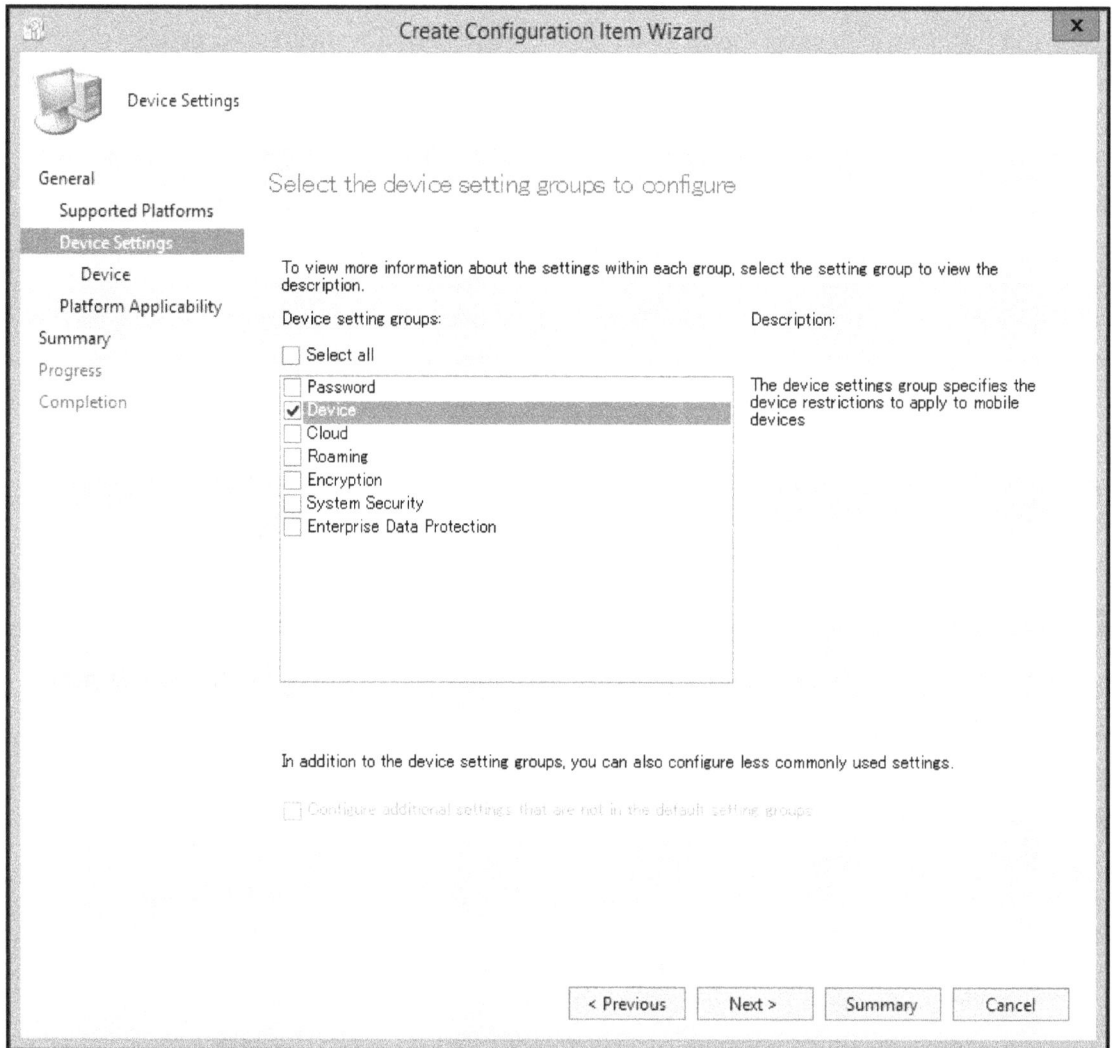

5. In the available settings list, select **Prohibited** as a value for **Bluetooth**. Be sure that the option **Remediate noncompliant settings** is checked and select the severity report accordingly.
6. Click on **Next** twice to finish the **Create Configuration Item Wizard**.

You now have a CI targeting specifically Windows 10 computers and which will remediate automatically if the computer is not compliant.

How it works...

The CI created for Windows 10 can be added to an existing or new baseline and targeted to a collection containing Windows 10 computers. When deployed as part of a baseline, this CI works exactly the same way as the legacy CI. The only difference is that in a legacy CI, you have to create a **setting** to monitor, as well as the **compliance rule** which will be used to remediate noncompliant settings:

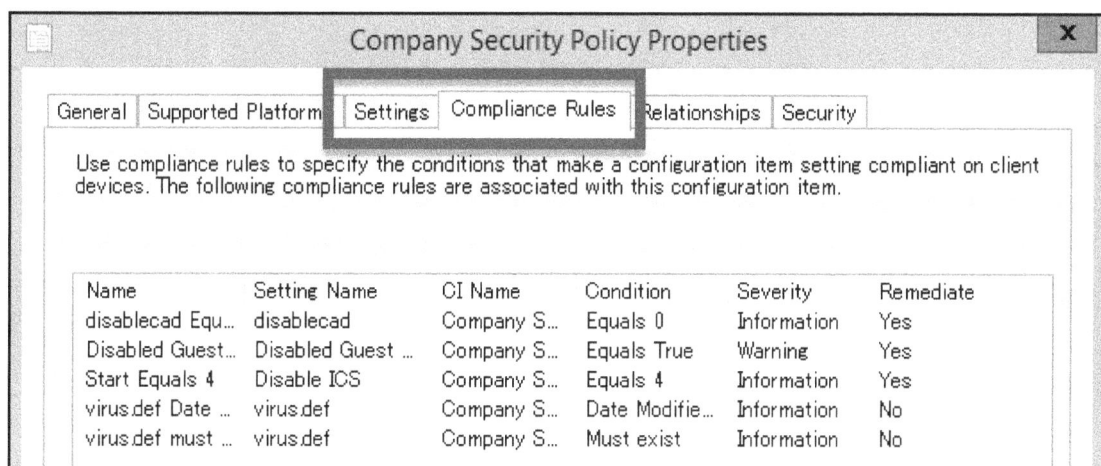

Whereas in the new CI for Windows 10, only **built-in compliance rules** are available:

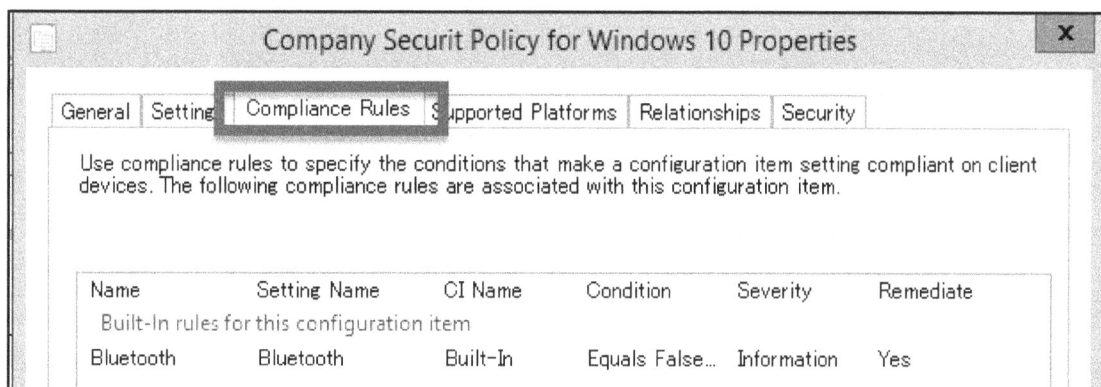

There's more...

Even though you created a CI for Windows 10, once it has been created, you can edit that CI and add some custom settings and compliance rules as explained in the *Building Configuration Items the old way* recipe.

Creating and deploying a baseline

Baselines are rules you target to collections of machines to test for compliance. A software update deployment is a form of a baseline. It contains a group of patches and rules to test for clients. In CM, baselines can also remediate the settings you want to change.

Getting ready

You should now see a CI called **Company Security Policy** in the right-hand pane of **Configuration Items** under **Assets and Compliance** | **Compliance Settings** | **Configuration Items**. If not, complete the previous task to create it. If you don't already have a collection created to pilot baselines to, create one before proceeding.

How to do it...

1. Enter Company Security Baseline for **Name**. Click on **Add** and choose **Configuration Items** to open a list of possible CIs to add. Click on **Company Security Policy** and then click on **Add. Do the same for Company Security Policy for Windows 10** and then click on **OK**.

2. In the CM admin console, navigate to **Assets and Compliance** | **Compliance Settings** | **Configuration Baselines** and click on **Create Configuration Baseline** in the ribbon to launch **Create Configuration Baseline Wizard**.

> Notice that this baseline could have multiple CIs, software updates, or other baselines added to it. It's best just to build baselines up a little bit at a time rather than to add everything at once.

3. Check **Client** and **Server** as categories to easily see or search for it in the console later on. Click on **OK** to commit the CI to the new baseline. This baseline should now show in the right-hand pane as **Company Security Baseline**.

How it works...

Once deployed, clients will evaluate their state for each CI in a baseline and report that back with a state message as either compliant or noncompliant. These state messages will show up in built-in reports. When remediation is selected on a CI, the rule will be enforced so the machine becomes compliant.

There's more...

Once a baseline has been created, it's ready to deploy to a collection. Piloting the baseline before sending it to all machines is always recommended and is especially important when selected CIs are set to remediate.

Piloting the baseline

1. From the CM admin console under **Assets and Compliance** | **Compliance Settings** | **Configuration Baselines**, click on **Company Security Baseline** then click on **Deploy** in the ribbon. **Company Server Baseline** should show in the right-hand box.
2. Check the box to **Remediate noncompliant rules when supported**. Optionally, check the box to **Allow remediation outside the maintenance window**. Leaving the box unchecked means a noncompliant machine will remain in its current state until the next window opens. Generally, for security-based baselines, this box is checked.
3. Click on **Browse** and choose your pilot collection. Click on **OK**.

Testing the baseline

The CI selected for the baseline will look for a text file called `virus.def` in `%widir%\temp`. On a machine in the pilot collection, delete that file if it exists and initiate a machine policy refresh from the CM client control panel applet.

Wait for a minute, and then click on the **Configurations** tab of the control panel applet and click on **Refresh**. The new baseline should appear. Click on **Evaluate**. When **Evaluation State** switches from **In Progress** to **Idle**, **Compliance State** should change to **Non-Compliant**. Click on **View Report** to verify the details. Note that viewing reports requires admin rights and if UAC is set to high, a password will be required to view the results:

Non-Compliant Rules:

Setting Name	Setting Type	Setting Description	Rule Name	Rule Description	Severity	Instance Data			
						Expression	Current Value	Instance Source	Rule Type
virus.def	File		virus.def must exist		Information	NotEquals 0	0		Existential

A similar test would be required to rename an old file in the `Windows\Temp` folder to `virus.def`. Run the evaluation again. This time it should fail based on the old date.

Finally, create a new file called `virus.def` and run the evaluation to see **Compliance State** change to **Compliant**.

Once you are happy with the baseline, you can change the target to any production collection you wish.

Managing revisions

Each time you change a CI, its revision level is incremented by one. Baselines also have revision levels. Revisions are helpful in two ways. One is in reports where clients showing old revision numbers are yet to evaluate your changes. The other is in managing new releases of baselines.

Right-click on **Company Server Baseline** and choose **Properties**. Click on the **Evaluation Conditions** tab. Select **Company Server Policy** for **Configuration data**. Click on **Change Revision** and select **Always Use Latest**.

This has set the baseline to report back (and enforce if remediation was selected) the latest version of **Company Server Policy** created.

See also

- Microsoft TechNet `https://technet.microsoft.com/en-us/library/mt 595713.aspx`

Leveraging Security Compliance Manager

In July 2016, Microsoft updated a well known tool called **Microsoft Security Compliance Manager 4.0** (**SCM**) to manage baselines. With SCM, you can download prebuilt baselines, clone and edit for your own use, compare to Microsoft defaults, and, most importantly, export a cab file to be imported into CM to make new baselines.

SCM itself hasn't been changed much since the previous version (SCM 3.0) but the content has always been updated and baselines for the latest version of Windows 10 (build 1511 at the time of writing) are available for download within the tool:

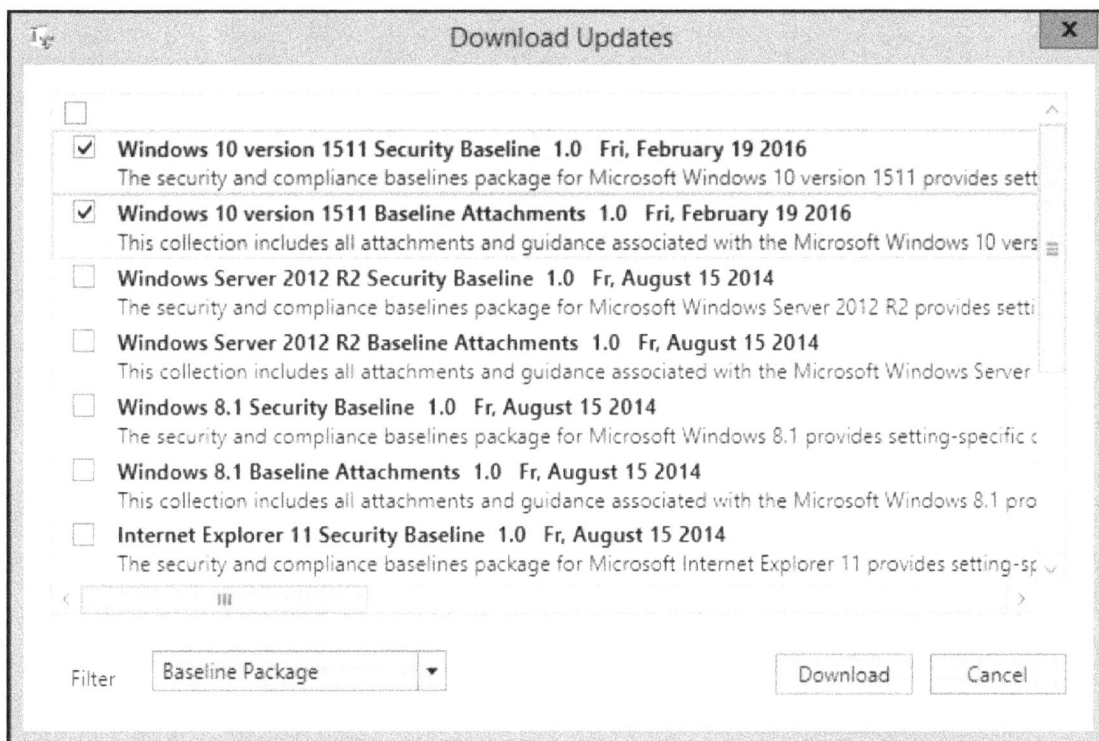

CM gives you the ability to do revisions of baselines so that as you change them over time, you can phase out old ones and enforce or report on new ones. But we advise you to maintain the same revisions in SCM so that you can fully leverage its full capabilities.

> On top of SCM baselines, Microsoft provides another type of baselines in **System Center Configuration Manager Vulnerability Assessment Configuration Pack (VACP)**. This contains vulnerability assessment baselines which allows you to scan managed systems for common missing security updates and misconfigurations which might make client computers more vulnerable to attack. For more information about VACP, refer to the blog post `https://blogs.technet.microsoft.com/enterpri semobility/2016/04/28/release-announcement-vulnerability-asses sment-configuration-pack/`. Note also that VACP reports are not available in CM Current Branch yet but will be released along with **version 1606** of **Configuration Manager Current Branch**.

Getting ready

Download and install **SCM 3.0**. Get well acquainted with SCM before proceeding. What we are going to do is clone the enterprise class Windows 10 1511 security baseline in SCM and export a cab file for use in CM as a new baseline.

How to do it...

1. From the SCM console, clone the **Win10-1511 Computer Security Compliance 1.0** baseline by selecting it in the left-hand pane, then navigate to **Baseline | Duplicate** in the right-hand pane. Enter `My-Company Win10-Computer` for **Baseline Name** and then click on **Save**.

2. This new baseline can now be edited from the defaults. You might already be aware of some changes you need to make or match your company's policy. You may make them at this time, but for the purposes of this exercise, we will just make two changes.

3. Find the setting called **Interactive logon: Message title for users attempting to log on** and click on it. Uncheck the box for **Not Defined**. Enter `Warning` in the textbox for **Customize setting value**, then click on **Collapse**.

4. Find the setting called **Interactive logon: Message text for users attempting to log on** and click on it. Uncheck the box for **Not Defined**. Enter `Unauthorized users will be prosecuted` in the textbox for **Customize setting value**, then click on **Collapse**.

> **TIP**
>
> Note that SCM makes the alterations to the default stand out in bold so that your company's changes are easily identified. Note also that settings available in the Windows 10 baseline are all grouped by category. When importing this baseline in CM, you will get one CI per group.

At this point, you can modify other settings as needed to match your company's policies. But it's important to understand that not every setting shown in SCM can be exported correctly.

In the right-hand pane of SCM, navigate to **Export** | **SCCM DCM 2007 (.cab)** to export the My-Company Win10-Computer baseline.

> **i**
>
> You might get an error message when you try to export a baseline. Usually, it means that your baseline contains settings that are not supported by the DCM Export. The error message points you to a log file which clearly specifies which settings were ignored during the export.

> **TIP**
>
> Guest account status is one of those settings that cannot be exported. A workaround is to create a custom CI to verify this setting in another way (like we did using WMI query).

How it works...

SCM is a great tool to manage your security baselines. It gets updates from Microsoft regularly. It can export baselines into GPOs for active directory and as cab files for CM. You deploy these baselines to monitor for drift from company standards.

There's more...

Now it's time to import the baseline back into CM. To do this, perform the following steps:

1. From the CM12 admin console, navigate to **Assets and Compliance** | **Compliance Settings** | **Configuration Baselines** and click on **Import Configuration Data** in the ribbon.

2. Click on **Add…** and browse to the cab file you exported from SCM. Click on **Yes** for the publisher warning. Click on **Next** twice to exit **Import Configuration Data Wizard**.

You should now see many new CIs with a name starting with **My-Company-Win10-Computer** in the right-hand pane. Each of them could be deployed to a pilot collection of your choice at this point.

Recall that this baseline could not properly export the guest account status from SCM. Since you already created a CI that does that, we can add that to this baseline.

Adding an additional CI to the baseline

1. In the admin console, navigate to **Assets and Compliance | Compliance Settings | Configuration Baselines**. Click on **My-Company-Win10-Computer**, then click on **Properties** in the ribbon.
2. Click on **Categories** and assign **Client** to this baseline.
3. From the **Evaluate Conditions** tab, click on **Add** and select **Configuration Items**. Select **Company Security Policy** and click on **Add**, then click on **OK**.
4. Should an error pop up about the description length, shorten the verbiage for **Description** in the **General** tab. Click on **OK**.

> Note that this imported CI checks for more than just guest account state, so you could optionally create a new CI to check for only that state.

This baseline is now ready to be piloted. When pilot machines show either a compliant or noncompliant state (not error), the baseline can be deployed to any collection of Windows 10 machines.

See also

- Microsoft Security Guidance official blog `https://blogs.technet.microsoft.com/secguide/`
- Microsoft Security Compliance Manager `http://www.microsoft.com/scm`

Monitoring compliance with SSRS

We previously showed how to use the CM control panel applet to look at compliance, but that is useful for just one machine at a time. There are several ways to monitor the compliance of a baseline in CM for all users or computers.

One way to view compliance is just to view the **Monitoring** node of the CM console. Another way is to view **SQL Server Reporting Services** (**SSRS**) reports. Slicker yet, is to leverage subscriptions via text file to a share, or an e-mail from SSRS. We will show you how to set up an e-mail subscription on behalf of your boss. Then we will show how to drop a file daily, which lists noncompliant assets for your security team.

Getting ready

The **My-Company-Win10-Computer** baseline created earlier should have been piloted by now and should be deployed to a collection of Windows 10 machines. Refer to Chapter 9, *Managing Reports and Queries* to set up SSRS if you have not already done so.

How to do it...

1. Install the **SMTP feature** using Server Manager onto any server of your choice.
2. Configure the SMTP properties to allow access from your SSRS server's IP (if remote).
3. On your SSRS server, open **Reporting Services Configuration Manager**. From the **E-mail Settings** tab, enter the FQDN of your SMTP server for **SMTP Server**, and enter your team's group e-mail address (or your own) for **Sender Address**. Click on **Apply**.
4. From the **Execution Account** tab, enter a domain account and password, if one is not already listed. Click on **Apply**. This account must be mapped to the CM database with both the **Public** and **smsschm_users** roles for proper access. This account is needed so that reports can be generated for subscriptions on behalf of subscribers.

How it works...

SSRS e-mails the Compliance drift report according to a recurring schedule that you set. It uses SMTP to send an attachment or embedded report to the e-mail you specify. The automated process should help free your time and remove the manual process for your boss to go find a website.

There's more...

Creating an e-mail based subscription

Now it's time to make the subscription. To do this perform the following steps:

1. From the CM admin console, navigate to **Monitoring** I **Reporting** I **Reports** and search for the report named **Summary compliance by configuration items for a configuration baseline** in the right-hand pane. Right-click on the report and select **Create Subscription**.

2. Under **Subscription Delivery**, select **E-mail** for **Report delivered** by. Enter your e-mail address for **To** (after testing, change this to your boss' e-mail). Type `@ReportName was executed at @ExecutionTime` for **Subject**. Check the boxes to include **link** and **report**. Select **MHTML (web archive)** for **Render Format**. Click on **Next**.

3. Under **Subscription Schedule**, select a time 2 minutes from now (after testing, change this time to something appropriate, for example, daily at 7:00 am, or Mondays at 8:00 am). Click on **Next**. Under **Subscription Parameters**, select **My-Company-Win10-Computer** for **Configuration Baseline Name**. Select **<All Values>** for **Category**. Select **<All Values>** for **Minimum Security**. Select the Windows 10 collection you targeted the baseline to for collection. Click on **Next** twice and then click on **Close**.

After testing, return to replace your e-mail address with that of your boss'. Also select an appropriate schedule for the report to be e-mailed.

Creating a file-based subscription

Often security prohibits the use of SMTP or you just might not have access. An alternative is available by way of a file-based subscription. A new detailed drift report can be regenerated each day and dropped into a share where your admins can look anytime without degrading the performance of SSRS. To do this, perform the following steps:

1. From the CM admin console, navigate to **Monitoring** | **Reporting** | **Reports** and search for the report named **Summary compliance by configuration baseline** in the right-hand pane. Right-click on the report and select **Create Subscription**.

2. Under **Subscription Delivery**, select **Windows File Share** for the Report that is delivered. Enter `Win10 Drift Report` for **File Name**. Enter the UNC path to a share where you make this report available, for example, `\\Server\SRSReports$` for **Path**. Select **HTML 4.0** for **Render Format**. Enter the SSRS execution account and password for **User Name** and **Password**. Type `Windows 10 Drift Report` for **Description**. Click on **Next**.

3. Under **Subscription Schedule**, select a time 2 minutes from now (after testing, change this time to something appropriate, for example, daily at 7:00 am, or Mondays at 8:00 am.). Click on **Next**.

4. Under **Subscription Parameters**, select **My-Company-Win10-Computer** for **Configuration Baseline Name**. Select **<All Values>** for **Category**. Select **<All Values>** for **Minimum Security**. Click on **Next** twice, and then click on **Close**.

After testing, return to select a schedule that is appropriate for the report to be regenerated and viewed.

> Note that the specified share created will need the appropriate share and NTFS permissions added for the security team's Active Directory group. The SSRS execution account will need write permissions to that share.

See also

- Microsoft MSDN e-mail setup for SSRS: `https://msdn.microsoft.com/en-us/library/ms159155(v=sql.120).aspx`
- E-mail Delivery in Reporting Services for SQL Server 2016: `https://msdn.microsoft.com/en-us/library/ms160334.aspx`

5

Managing Mobile Devices using Configuration Manager with Microsoft Intune

In this chapter, we will cover the following recipes:

- Creating a Microsoft Intune subscription
- Connecting Microsoft Intune to CM
- Creating and deploying MDM policies
- Using Conditional Access to control devices' access to Office 365 services
- Managing mobile devices enrolled in Microsoft Intune via the CM console

Introduction

Even though **Mobile Device Management** (**MDM**) has existed from CM07 days, it has been greatly improved thanks to the release of a new way to manage mobile devices using Microsoft Intune. When I talk about mobile devices, I am not only talking about iOS, Android, or Windows Mobile but also about Windows 10, which is managed in the same way. MDM products such as Microsoft Intune implements the **Open Management Alliance Device Management** (**OMA-DM**) specification for remote mobile device management. OMA-DM is a standardized way to manage mobile devices using different operating systems. MDM management differs from the CM management, which requires a CM client on the managed device.

The trending **Bring Your Own Device (BYOD)** or **Choose Your Own Device (CYOD)** scenarios leverage MDM to manage mobile devices. Users (BYOD) or administrators (CYOD) are able to enroll a device into an MDM solution in order to get access to corporate data. On the other side, MDM is able to deploy policies, applications, and push remote actions (such as remote lock or remote wipe).

Creating a Microsoft Intune subscription

Among many MDM solutions available on the market, Microsoft offers its own solution called **Microsoft Intune**. Microsoft Intune is a management solution which allows managing mobile devices from the cloud. There is nothing to install on premises, everything runs in the cloud and administrators will execute all the administrative tasks from a web portal.

> Microsoft Intune is part of a security solution suite provided by Microsoft called **Enterprise Mobility Suite (EMS)**. This suite contains **Microsoft Intune** as well as **Azure AD Premium (AADP)** and **Azure AD Rights Management Services (AADRMS)**. If you know that your company has licenses for EMS, then you will be able to use Microsoft Intune as part of this license agreement.

One of the biggest benefits of using Microsoft Intune over other MDM solutions is its capacity to integrate with CM, giving a hybrid management solution: Intune to manage mobile devices, CM to manage desktop devices. Once Intune has been integrated with CM (Hybrid mode), CM will offer a one-stop solution to manage both mobile and desktop devices.

Microsoft Intune is a paid service but a free 30-day trial is available to try this solution. This trial can be transformed into a paid subscription later on. Access `https://www.microsoft.com/en-us/cloud-platform/microsoft-intune`and click on the **Try now** button to signup for a free 30-day trial.

Getting ready

Before being able to integrate Microsoft Intune with CM, we first need to create an Intune subscription. If your organization has already created an Intune subscription, you can skip the following section and jump directly to the *Connecting Microsoft Intune to CM* section.

How to do it...

To sign up for a Microsoft Intune subscription, perform the following steps:

1. Access the Microsoft Intune official site at `https://www.microsoft.com/en-us/cloud-platform/microsoft-intune-features` and click on the **Try now** button on the top right of the page.
2. In Step 1, fill your company's information
3. Step 2 is crucial. You have to define the **cloud domain name** (that is `domainname.onmicrosoft.com`). Be very careful when deciding this domain name because you won't be able to change it later. The cloud domain name you decide here will become the Azure AD domain name used as a directory by Microsoft Intune. For the username, use per example *admin* since it will be the first administrator account of Microsoft Intune tenant.
4. In the last step, Step 3, just make the robot verification and you're ready to go!

How it works...

The previous steps will create a new Microsoft Intune tenant. This tenant, similar to other Microsoft cloud services, leverages Azure AD for identity.

If you create a new Azure AD domain, you will manage Azure AD from the Office 365 portal: `https://portal.office.com`.

If you attach the new Intune tenant to an existing Azure AD, then you have the choice between managing it from the Office 365 portal or the Azure portal `https://manage.windowsazure.com`.

There's more...

Once you have signed up for a Microsoft Intune subscription, you can access to the Intune Administration web portal from the following URL: `https://manage.microsoft.com`.

To log into the web portal, you need to specify the admin account (that is, `admin@sccmcookbook.onmicrosoft.com`) and the password you specified during the sign up process.

You can only open Microsoft Intune administration web portal from Internet Explorer or Firefox browsers because this web portal is based on Silverlight. This means you won't be able to administer Microsoft Intune from a browser like Chrome or Safari, which don't support Silverlight. However, the direction Microsoft Intune engineering is taking is to move the whole Silverlight-based web portal to the new Azure portal, which is HTML5 based. By the time you read this, it's possible the transition has already been made. In fact, because Intune is updated so often, you should expect some deviations from what you see in the rest of the chapter.

Since we are going to integrate Microsoft Intune to CM, it is crucial not to configure anything from the web portal. All the Intune configuration and administration will be done from the CM console. If you configure anything from the web portal, you might get in trouble when trying to integrate Microsoft Intune to CM.

See also

- Intune quick start guide: `https://docs.microsoft.com/en-us/intune/get-started/start-with-a-paid-subscription-to-microsoft-intune`

Connecting Microsoft Intune to CM

The main goal of connecting Microsoft Intune to CM is to offer the administrator a one-stop solution to administer mobile devices as well as desktop devices. But that is not the only benefit coming from that integration. Here's a non-complete list of improvements when integrating with CM:

- Management using PowerShell (Intune doesn't provide any PowerShell interface)
- **Role Based Access Control (RBAC)**
- Advanced User and Device grouping
- Scalibility (Standalone Intune tenant supports up to 50,000 devices. CM integrated with Intune can manage up to 300,000 devices)

Microsoft provides a detailed list of pros and cons of standalone versus hybrid mode, which will help you decide whether to use Microsoft Intune in a standalone or hybrid way `https://technet.microsoft.com/en-us/library/mt706478.aspx`.

Getting ready

To make that integration, you need to prepare the following:

1. An active Microsoft Intune subscription and the admin account credentials.
2. A synchronized **Active Directory** (**AD**) to Azure AD. The synchronization of your on-premises AD to Azure AD is not covered in this book. Refer to the online documentation to install the synchronization tool (Azure AD Connect) and sync your AD to Azure AD: `https://azure.microsoft.com/en-us/documentation/articles/active-directory-aadconnect/`.

> **TIP**
>
> If your organization is already using online services such as Microsoft Office 365, there is a strong chance that the synchronization between your on-premises AD and Azure AD is already implemented.

3. An **AD group** containing users who are authorized to enroll a device and a **User Collection** in CM which is based on that AD group.

Let's first create the AD group on a **domain controller** (**DC**). Connect to a DC and follow these steps:

1. Open the **Active Directory Users and Computers** console.
2. Create a new security group called `Microsoft Intune Users`.
3. Go to the **Members** tab and add some users who you want to authorize to enroll their devices; then click on **Apply**.

Now access your CM console and follow these steps:

1. In the admin console, navigate to **Assets and Compliance** | **User Collections** and **select Create User Collection** from the **Home** tab in the ribbon.
2. Enter the name of the collection (*Intune Users*, for instance) and select **All Users and User Groups** as a limiting collection.

3. On the **Membership** Rules page, select **Add Rule** then **Query Rule**. Name the query `Intune Users in AD` then click on **Edit Query Statement**. By clicking on **Show Query Language**, you can manually edit the collection query. Copy and paste the following query:

```
select
SMS_R_USER.ResourceID,SMS_R_USER.ResourceType,
SMS_R_USER.Name,SMS_R_USE
R.UniqueUserName,SMS_R_USER.WindowsNTDomain
from SMS_R_User where SMS_R_User.UserGroupName =
"<Enter your domain name here>\\Microsoft Intune Users"
```

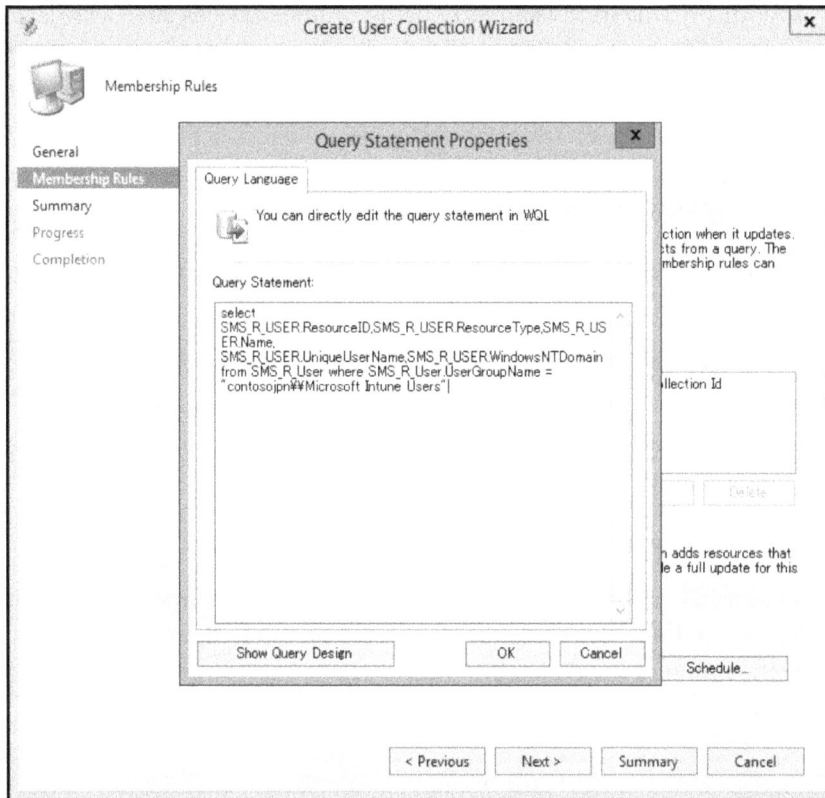

4. Continue the wizard to completion.

After having refreshed that new user collection, you should see members appearing:

Icon	Name	Limiting Collection	Member Count	Members Visible on Site
	All User Groups	All Users and User...	3	3
	All Users	All Users and User...	10	10
	All Users and User Groups		13	13
	Intune Users	All Users and User...	2	2

User Collections 4 items

Now you are ready to connect Microsoft Intune to CM.

How to do it...

Access the top site of the CM hierarchy and follow these steps:

1. In the admin console, navigate to **Administration** | **Cloud Services** | **Microsoft Intune Subscriptions** and select **Add Microsoft Intune Subscription** from the **Home** tab in the ribbon to start the **Create Microsoft Intune Subscription Wizard** window.

2. The **Introduction** page can be skipped.

3. On the **Subscription** page of the wizard, select the **Sign In** button and enter the Microsoft Intune admin credentials in the login page.

> When starting to use Microsoft cloud solutions like Microsoft Intune, Azure or Office 365, admin credentials management becomes a big deal. Let's say you have three people who will manage Intune. A good practice is not to share the first admin account (*admin@sccmcookbook.onmicrosoft.com*) you created during the tenant creation amongst those three administrators. But instead, it is recommended to create a specific admin account for each of them and only grant them the needed rights. That way, if a person leaves the company, you will only need to disable his account instead of having to change the password of a shared admin account.

4. On the **General** page, specify the **user collection** called *Intune Users* that we defined earlier in this chapter. Then enter **Company name**, select a **Color scheme** and select the **Configuration Manager Site code** to assign to mobile devices. Before going to the next wizard page, select the **maximum number of devices** a user can enroll.

5. On the **Company Contact Information** page, enter any contact information that will be displayed in the company portal.

6. On the **Company Logo** page, you can customize the company portal. Specify whether you want to show a company logo and whether you want to display the company name next to that logo.

7. On the **Device Enrollment Manager** page, you can add a device enrollment manager. The device enrollment manager account is a special Intune account with permission to enroll more than five devices.

8. Continue the wizard to completion.

> Any settings you defined in the previous wizard can be modified later by going into the **Properties** of the *Microsoft Intune Subscription* that has been added:

> If, when attempting to add a Microsoft Intune subscription to CM, you get the message **This operation can not be completed at this time**, then it means that the Intune tenant you are trying to associate with CM already has the authority set to Intune standalone. This may happen if you were using Intune as a standalone implementation for a while and then decided to integrate it with CM. In order to fix this issue, there is no alternative but to call the *Microsoft Premier support* to reset the Intune tenant's authority.

After having connected Microsoft Intune to CM, you need to configure which platform will be supported. For Android, Windows 10, and Windows 10 Mobile you only have to tick on the checkbox, but for iOS, you will have to get an **Apple Push Notification services** (**APNs**) certificate from Apple.

Android management setup

1. In the admin console, navigate to **Administration** | **Cloud Services** | **Microsoft Intune** Subscriptions and select **Configure Platforms** from the **Home** tab in the ribbon and select **Android**.
2. In **Microsoft Intune Subscription Properties**, just check the **Enable Android enrollment** option.

Windows 10 management setup

1. In the admin console, navigate to **Administration** | **Cloud Services** | **Microsoft Intune Subscriptions** and select**Configure Platforms** from the **Home** tab in the ribbon and select **Windows**.
2. In **Microsoft Intune Subscription Properties**, just check the **Enable Windows enrollment** option and skip the **code-signing certificate** which is only used for Windows 8.1.

Windows 10 Mobile management setup

1. In the admin console, navigate to **Administration** | **Cloud Services** | **Microsoft Intune Subscriptions** and select the **Configure** Platforms from the **Home** tab in the ribbon and select **Windows Phone**.

2. In the **Microsoft Intune Subscription Properties**, just check the **Windows Phone 8.1** and **Windows 10** Mobile option and select **None** for the certificate option.

iOS management setup

1. In the admin console, navigate to **Administration** ❘ **Cloud Services** ❘ **Microsoft Intune Subscriptions** and select the **Create APNs certificate** request from the **Home** tab in the ribbon to create a **certificate request** that we will submit to Apple.

2. In the **Request Apple Push Notification Service Certificate Signing Request** window, enter the filename of the request and click on **Download**. Once the request is successfully completed, click on the **Apple Push Certificate Portal** link to submit that certificate request to Apple:

Request Apple Push Notification Service Certificate Signing Request ☒

Specify the file where you want to save the downloaded Certificate Signing Request. This is required to request the Apple Push Notification Service (APNs) certificate. You will be prompted for your Microsoft Intune organizational account to complete the download.

File Name: `C:¥Users¥a-shd¥Desktop¥ios.csr` [Browse...]

After you download the Certificate Signing Request, you must perform the following steps to complete APNs setup:

Step 1: Submit the request to the Apple Push Certificate Portal and download the APNs certificate.

Step 2: Upload the APNs certificate to Microsoft Intune through the Configuration Manager console.

Status: Complete

[Download] [Close]

---

3. The browser will open the **Apple Push Certificate Portal** and you will be required to sign in with an Apple ID. If you don't already have one, just create a new one, it is completely free. (I recommend creating a generic one for your company.) Once signed in, click on the **Create a Certificate** button located on the top right-hand side of that page, accept the terms of use, then select the CSR file generated by CM in the previous step and click on the **Upload** button.

If you are using Internet Explorer to generate the APN certificate, after uploading the CSR file, you will get a notification to save a `.JSON` file. This file is not the APN certificate so just ignore it. Instead, go back to the first page of **Apple Push Certificates Portal** and click on the **Download** button on the right side of your recently created certificate. You should now get a notification to download a file named `MDM_MicrosoftCorporation_Certificate.pem`. This is the APN certificate file.

4. Come back to the CM admin console and this time select the **Configure Platforms** from the Home tab in the ribbon and select **iOS**.
5. In **Microsoft Intune Subscription Properties**, just check the **Enable iOS** and **Mac OS X** (MDM) enrollment option.
6. In the **APNs certificate** section, select the **APN certificate** that you previously downloaded from the Apple website. It is also strongly recommended to enable **Show an alert before the APNs certificate expires**:

It is extremely vital to renew the APNs certificate before it expires. If the APNs certificate expires, iOS devices will no longer be managed and must all be enrolled again. By default, Apple will notify you by e-mail 1 month before the APNs certificate expires. We also strongly recommend using the alert option in CM.

How it works...

Once the integration between Microsoft Intune and Configuration Manager has been done, every configuration related to Intune you make from the CM console will be replicated to the cloud. That replication interval is set to 5 minutes and is managed by the new CM site system role called **Service Connection Point** (**SCP**), which replaced Windows Intune Connector from CM12.

The replication interval is fixed and cannot be changed. Thus, whenever you enroll a device or send a remote wipe action, it might take up to 5 minutes to get reflected.

The SCP is the only point of contact between CM and Microsoft Intune. Each hierarchy supports a single instance of this role. For those with a CAS, the top level SUP is a common choice for the SCP role.

There's more...

To verify that the integration between Microsoft Intune and CM is a success, try to enroll a mobile device and verify that it appears in the CM console. The following steps have been performed using an Android device but are similar for iOS or Windows Mobile:

1. Using an **Android mobile** device, access the **Google Play application** store and search for **Microsoft Intune Company Portal**:

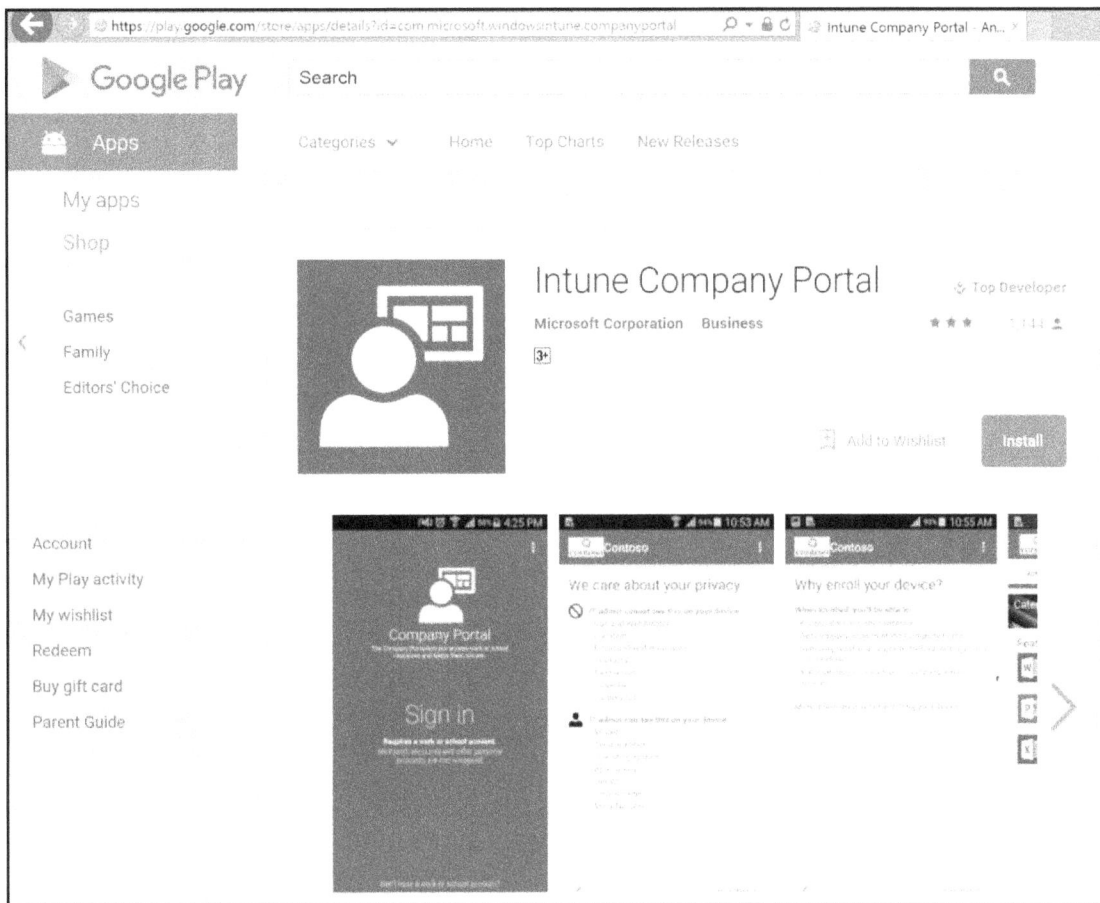

2. Install the **Microsoft Intune Company Portal** app and launch it.
3. Go through the enrollment wizard on the Android device to register it to Microsoft Intune. The user account used to register that device should be part of the user collection specified during the Microsoft Intune integration to CM.
4. Wait at least 5 minutes and verify that the enrolled device appears in the CM console.

Mobile devices enrolled in Microsoft Intune will appear in the pre-existing **All Mobile Devices** collection. When deploying MDM policy, you can either deploy it to that collection or create a dedicated one (for piloting, for instance).

CM offers different logs to help troubleshooting the SCP replication between CM and Microsoft Intune. These logs can be found in the **Logs** folder of the **CM installation directory** (commonly `C:\Program Files\Microsoft Configuration Manager\Logs`). The following are the log files found:

- `Cloudusersync.log`: This records license enablement for users
- `Dmpdownloader.log`: This records details on messages downloaded from Microsoft Intune
- `Dmpuploader.log`: This records details for uploading policies to Microsoft Intune
- `outgoingcontentmanager.log`: This records the content uploaded to Microsoft Intune

See also

- For information about the service connection point in System Center Configuration Manager, go to `https://technet.microsoft.com/en-us/library/mt627781.aspx`

Creating and deploying MDM policies

Once a device has been enrolled in Microsoft Intune, the next step is to create and deploy an MDM policy to that device. As explained previously, in an Intune and CM integrated configuration, all the settings are done using the CM console. An MDM policy is very similar to what we have seen in Chapter 4, *Managing Compliance Settings* about Compliance Settings. It basically sets all the settings that will be applied to a mobile device. By default, it autoremediates any settings that are not compliant.

Let's assume that your company's security policy requires to disable the camera on every Android mobile device that is managed by Microsoft Intune.

Getting ready

There is nothing specific that needs to be deployed. Watch the mobile device to verify the effect of the MDM policy once applied to the device.

If you don't have a physical Android device to do the MDM testing, there's an open source project which proposes **Android x86** version (`http://www. android-x86.org/`). This means you can run Android in a VM running on Hyper-V (or any other virtualization platform). Just keep in mind the limitation of such an x86 platform. For instance, since Office for Android is only published for the **ARM** platform, you won't be able to install Office for Android on your x86 Android platform. However, you can install **Microsoft Intune Company Portal** to enroll that VM and test that the policies apply correctly.

How to do it...

1. In the admin console, navigate to **Assets and Compliance** | **Compliance Settings** | **Configuration Items** and click on **Create Configuration Item** in the ribbon to launch **Create Configuration Item Wizard**.
2. Under **General**, enter `Company Security Policy for Android` for **Name**. Select **Android** and **Samsung KNOX** as **Configuration Item** type. Check client as a category to easily find or search for this CI again.
3. Under **General** | **Supported Platforms**, leave all Android versions checked as this
CI will be checked against all of them.
4. Under **General** | **Device Settings**, select **Security** under **Device setting** groups.
5. Under **General** | **Device Settings** | **Security**, select **Prohibited** as a value for **Camera** and select **Critical** for the severity level.
6. Continue the wizard to completion.

You should now see a CI called **Company Server Policy for Android** in the right-hand pane of **Configuration Items**, under **Assets and Compliance** | **Compliance Settings** | **Configuration Items**. Also, note that the Device Type of that CI is Mobile and not Windows.

To deploy that freshly created CI, we just need to add it to a MDM policy (baseline) and deploy it to a device collection containing Android devices.

1. In the CM admin console, navigate to **Assets and Compliance** | **Compliance Settings** | **Configuration Baselines** and click on **Create Configuration Baseline** in the ribbon to launch **Create Configuration Baseline Wizard**.

2. Enter `Company MDM Policy for Android` for **Name**. Click on **Add** and choose **Configuration Items** to open a list of possible CIs to add. Click on **Company Security Policy for Android**, then click on **Add** and then on **OK**.

3. Check **Client** as categories to easily see or search for it in the console later on. Click on **OK** to commit the CI to the new baseline. This baseline should now show in the right-hand pane as **Company MDM Policy for Android**.

How it works…

The settings offered in each **Device settings** group depends on the platform you selected in the first place for that CI. We saw in the previous paragraph that when selecting **Android** as a platform, the Security device settings group only offers three available settings: **Camera**, **YouTube**, and **Power off**.

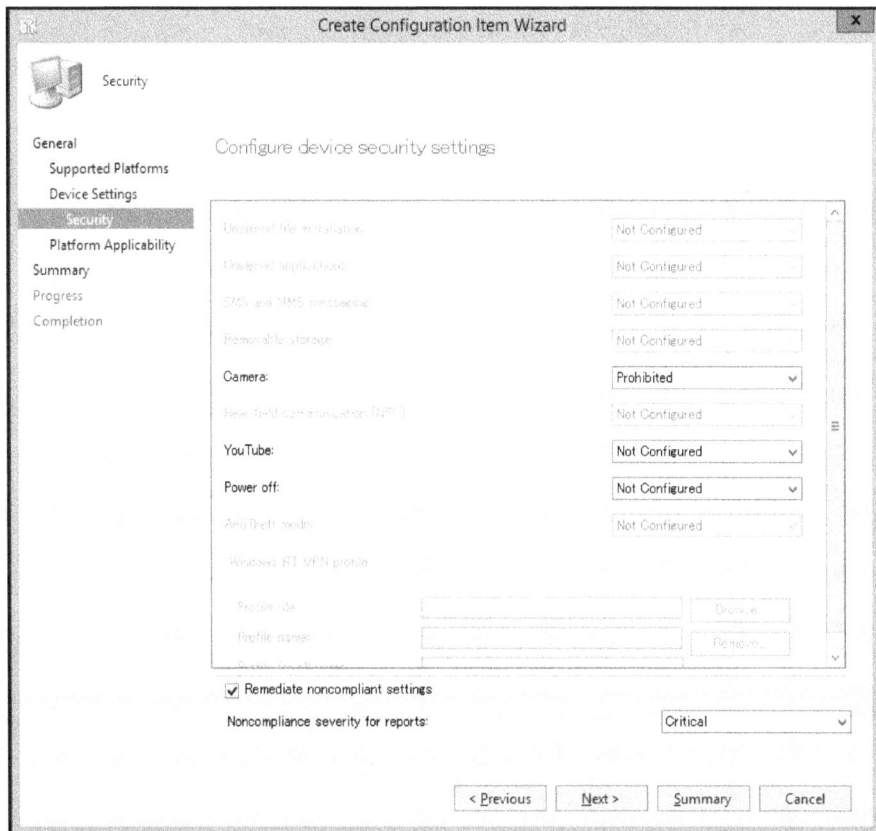

The available **device settings** group and **settings** in each group are automatically filtered based on the targeted platform for that CI. You can find all the available settings for each platform in the following TechNet documentation: `https://technet.microsoft.com /en-us/library/mt629318.aspx`.

There's more...

Once a baseline has been created, it's ready to be deployed to a collection. Piloting the base line before sending it to all machines is always recommended and is especially important when selected CIs are set to remediate.

Deploying the MDM policy

1. From the CM admin console under **Assets and Compliance** | **Compliance Settings** | **Configuration Baselines**, click on **Company MDM Policy for Android**, then click on **Deploy** in the ribbon. **Company MDM Policy for Android** should show in the right-hand box.
2. Check the box to **Remediate noncompliant rules when supported**. Optionally, check the box to **Allow remediation outside the maintenance window**. Leaving the box unchecked means a noncompliant machine will remain in its current state until the next window opens. Generally, for security-based baselines, this box is checked.
3. Click on **Browse** and choose your pilot collection. Click on **OK**.

Verifying the application of the MDM policy

The MDM policy for Android has been deployed and it will take a few minutes to synchronize to Microsoft Intune services in the cloud.

Remember that the sync between CM and Microsoft Intune occurs every **5 minutes** and can be monitored using the `dmpuploader.log` log file. When the sync occurs, you should see in the log file something similar to the following screenshot:

```
Retrieve cloud service version ...
Retrieve cloud service version ...
Retrieve cloud service version ...
Found sync start for replication group CloudDmp
StartUpload for replication group CloudDmp last sync version 7508 ...
Startload succeeded with transmission ID 36ac676d-ee5a-47f2-a900-a562c1153f3f
Expecting sync data or sync end message, however message type is DRS_SyncPing
EndUpload transmission 36ac676d-ee5a-47f2-a900-a562c1153f3f final data version 7509 succeeded
Retrieve cloud service version ...
```

Once the policy is applied to the Android device, try to open the `camera` app. You should get the following message:

In case the MDM policy hasn't been applied yet, you can open **Microsoft Intune Company Portal** to manually trigger a policy refresh. Navigate to the **Settings** menu and click on **SYNC** under **Security Policy**. Wait for a few minutes and try again to open the `camera` app:

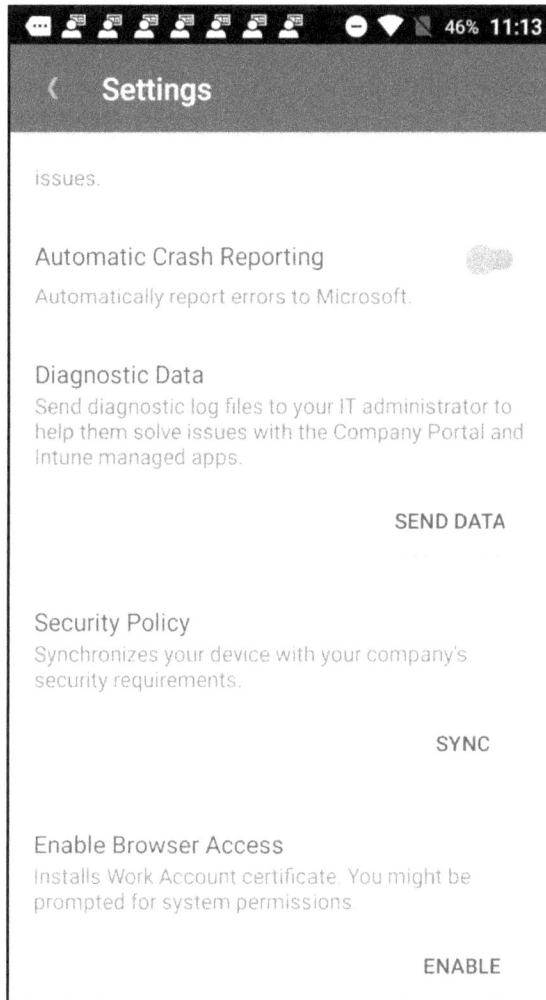

When a policy or an app is deployed, Intune immediately begins attempting to notify the device that it should check in with the Intune service. This typically takes less than 5 minutes. If a device doesn't check in to get the policy after the first notification is sent, Intune makes three more attempts. If the device is offline (for example, it is turned off or not connected to a network), it might not receive the notifications. In this case, the device will get the policy on its next scheduled check-in with the Intune service as follows:

- iOS and Mac OS X: Every 6 hours
- Android: Every 8 hours
- Windows Phone/Mobile: Every 8 hours
- Enrolled Windows RT devices: Every 24 hours
- Windows 8.1 and Windows 10 PCs enrolled as devices: Every 8 hours

Once you are happy with the MDM policy, you can change the target to any production collection you wish.

See also

- How to create CI for Android: https://technet.microsoft.com/en-us/library/mt629346.aspx
- How to create CI for iOS and Mac OS: https://technet.microsoft.com/en-us/library/mt629339.aspx
- How to create CI for Windows 10: https://technet.microsoft.com/en-us/library/mt629341.aspx
- How to create CI for Windows Mobile: https://technet.microsoft.com/en-us/library/mt629325.aspx

Using Conditional Access to control devices' access to Office 365 services

One of the biggest concerns we hear constantly from administrators is how to implement a BYOD scenario while securing access to the corporate apps and data accessed from a mobile device. Using an MDM solution like Microsoft Intune coupled with CM, a mobile device can be secured by applying MDM policies. But how to make sure that any mobile device which has access to corporate apps and data is secured by Microsoft Intune and is compliant with the company's rules? Microsoft came up with a simple solution called **Conditional Access** (**CA**), which leverages a new type of policy called **compliance policy**.

To protect company data, you need to make sure that the devices used to access corporate apps and data, comply with certain rules like using a PIN to access the device, and encryption of data stored on the device. A set of such rules is referred to as a **compliance policy.**

By defining a compliance policy, we can define whether a device complies to the corporate security policy. And based on that resultant **compliance status**, access to services like on premises Exchange or Office 365 services can be blocked. That connectivity to corporate services based on rules is called **Conditional Access**.

Getting ready

Before enabling conditional access in Microsoft Intune, we first need to define a **compliance policy** containing the conditions to allow access Office 365 services.

To continue with the Android example, let's create a compliance policy for Android.

1. In the admin console, navigate to **Assets and Compliance** | **Compliance Settings** | **Compliance Policies** and click on **Create Compliance Policy** in the ribbon to launch **Create Compliance Policy Wizard**.
2. Under **General**, enter *Company Compliance Policy for Android for Name*. Select **Compliance rule for devices managed without Configuration Manager Clients** and **Android and Samsung KNOX**.

3. On the **Supported** Platforms page, select all **versions of Android**.

4. Under **Rules**, you will get different conditions that are available for Android. Modify any existing condition based on your corporate security policy.

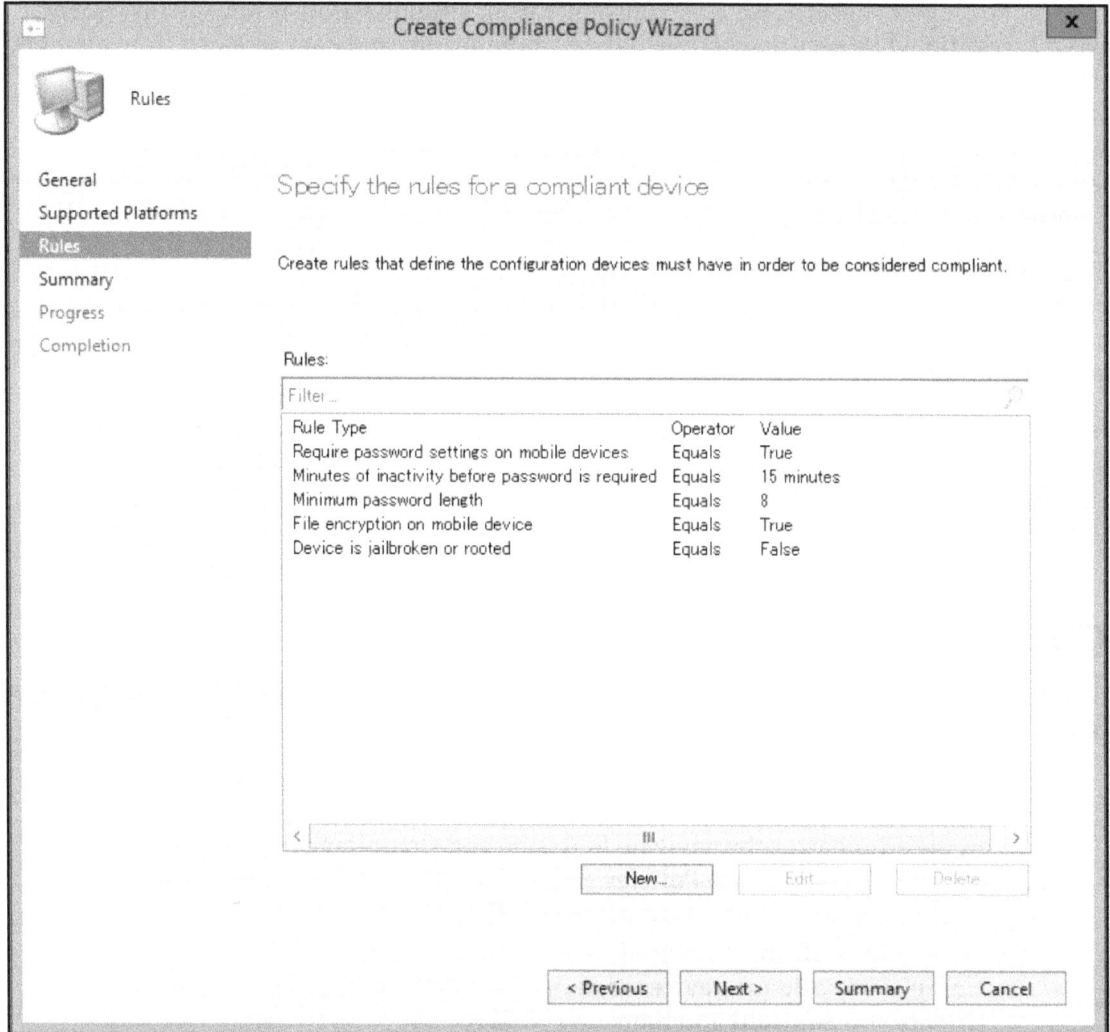

5. Continue the wizard to completion.

By default, that compliance policy will monitor that the mobile device is configured as follows:

- A password is defined
- The minimum password length is 6
- The inactivity time before a password is required is 15 min
- The device filesystem is encrypted
- The device is not rooted or jailbroken

If one of these conditions is not true, then the device will be reported as **non compliant**. And that compliance status will be used for **conditional access**. Before enabling conditional access, one last step is to **deploy** that compliance policy to Intune users.

1. From the CM admin console under **Assets and Compliance | Compliance Settings | Compliance Policies**, click on **Company Compliance Policy for Android**, then click on **Deploy** in the ribbon.
2. Click on **Browse** and choose the **Intune users user collection**. Click on **OK**.
3. Change the **evaluation schedule** of that policy accordingly. Remember that this represents the time before a noncompliant device loses access to corporate data.

How to do it...

Now that we have defined a compliance policy for Android, let's enable conditional access for **Exchange Online**. The same can be done for on-premises **Exchange**, **Dynamics CRM Online**, and **Skype for Business**.

1. In the admin console, navigate to **Assets and Compliance | Compliance Settings | Conditional Access | Exchange Online** and click on **Configure conditional access policy** for in the Intune console in the right pane. This is one of the very few settings we have to configure from the Intune web portal.
2. The Internet Explorer will open and log into the **Microsoft Intune portal** using the administrator credentials (that is, `admin@xxx.onmicrosoft.com`).

3. In the Intune web console, navigate to **Policy** | **Conditional Access** | **Exchange Online** and select **Enable conditional access policy** in the right pane:

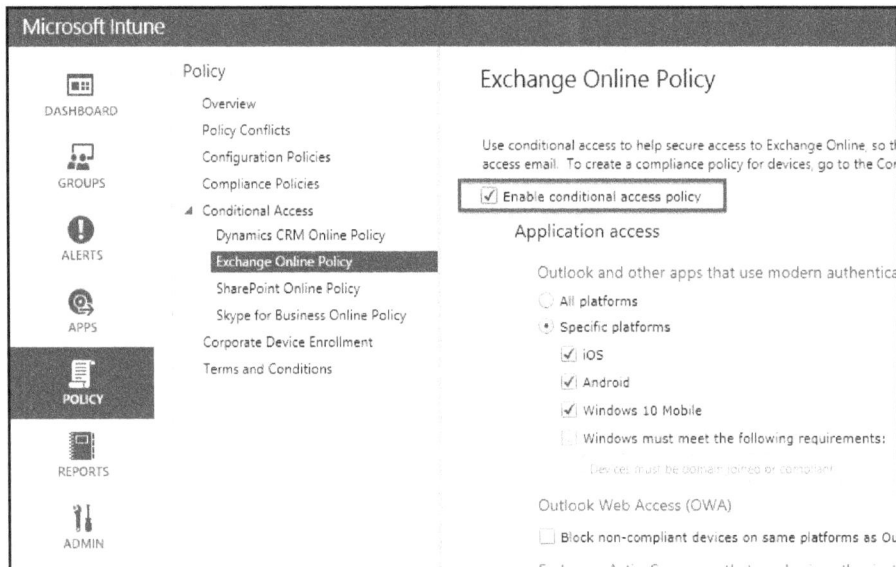

4. Under **Application access**, specify the platforms which are targeted by that **conditional access**. It is recommended to enable each mobile platform (iOS, Android, and Windows 10 Mobile).

5. Under **Policy deployment**, select the targeted group. In our case, it will be the **Microsoft Intune Users** group. Select **Selected security** groups, click on **Modify** then select the **Microsoft Intune Users** group.

6. Save the policy.

Conditional access for Exchange Online is now enabled and mobile devices which are not enrolled in Intune and that do not comply with the compliance policy defined previously, won't be able to access Exchange Online.

> When a non compliant device or a device not managed by Intune tries to access Exchange Online, it will receive an e-mail explaining the reason for being denied. Once that device is enrolled in Intune and is compliant, e-mails will start to flow automatically.

How it works...

You might think that **Conditional Access** for Exchange Online is a feature of Microsoft Intune. Actually it's a combined feature of **Azure AD**, **Office 365** and **Microsoft Intune**. Whenever a device is managed by Intune and is in a compliant/non compliant state, their information is stored as attributes of the device object in Azure AD. Office 365 services, which are based on Azure AD, will verify those *managed* and *compliance* state, then *allow/deny* access to those devices.

When you enable **CA** in the Intune web portal, it actually enables this feature in Office 365 which leverages Azure AD.

Here is a typical flow of CA taken from the Microsoft site:

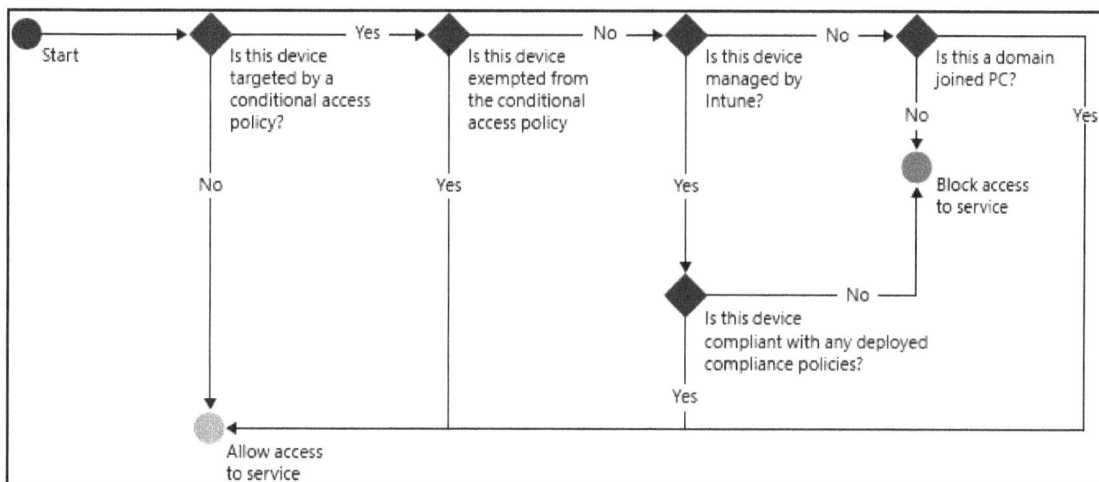

There's more...

Be very careful before enabling **Conditional Access** for everyone in your company because some might lose access to their e-mails until they enroll their device. First enable some pilot users and verify that everything works as expected. Then enable CA for every Intune user. (You can use that **Microsoft Intune Users** security group we created previously.)

Conditional Access won't work with device enrolled using **Device Enrollment Manager** (**DEM**). This is because when a device is registered in Intune using a DEM account, it won't be linked to a user. And CA, as seen before, only targets users. If you enable CA for a user using a device enrolled using a DEM account, the user won't be able to access his/her e-mails because Office 365 won't find that device linked to the user object in Azure AD. It will consider that device not managed and not compliant. If you have such users, exempt them from the CA configuration.

See also

- Limitations of devices enrolled with a device enrollment manager account: `https://docs.microsoft.com/en-us/intune/deploy-use/enroll-corporate-owned-devices-with-the-device-enrollment-manager-in-microsoft-intune`

Managing mobile devices enrolled in Microsoft Intune via the CM console

CM integrated with Microsoft Intune offers a single-point solution to manage both desktop devices and mobile devices (through Intune). Once a mobile device is enrolled in Intune, it will appear in the CM console and you will be able to get the **software inventory** of that device as well as executing remote tasks on it like **remote lock** or **remote wipe**.

There are four remote tasks we can run from the CM console:

1. A full wipe to restore the device to its factory settings.
2. A selective wipe to remove only company data.
3. A remote lock to help secure a device that might be lost.
4. Reset the device `passcode`.

Getting ready

The content of **software inventory** collected from mobile devices depends on one important parameter: the **device ownership**. You can change the ownership of devices to **Company** or **Personal** if a device is managed through Microsoft Intune.

1. In the admin console, navigate to **Assets and Compliance** | **Devices** and select **Change Ownership** by right-clicking on a mobile device:

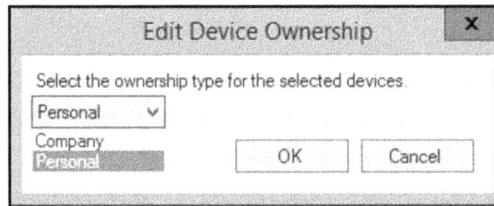

This parameter is used to control how much inventory is collected from users devices, here are the possible values:

- If a device is set as **Personal**, then only the apps deployed and installed by Intune will appear in the software inventory
- If a device is set as **Company**, then all apps installed on the user's device will appear in the software inventory.

Mobile device **software inventory** can be seen by running **Resource Explorer.**

1. In the admin console, navigate to **Assets and Compliance** | **Devices** and right-click on a mobile device in the right pane.
2. Right-click on **Mobile Device** | **Start** | **Resource Explorer**.
3. Under **Hardware** | **Mobile Device Installed Applications**, you will find in the right pane a list of all installed applications on that mobile device:

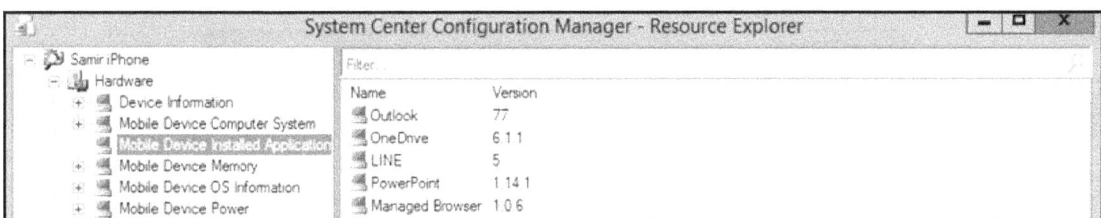

How to do it...

Each of the remote tasks can be done from the CM console where each mobile device registered in Intune is listed.

Full wipe action

Executing this action resets the mobile device back to factory defaults, thus permanently removes all the users and corporate data of the device.

1. In the admin console, navigate to **Assets and Compliance** | **Devices** and right-click a mobile device in the right pane.
2. Click on **Remote Device Actions** in **Device Group**, and then select **Retire/Wipe**.
3. Select **Wipe the mobile device and retire it from Configuration Manager** and click on **OK**.

Selective wipe action

Executing this action only removes company data:

1. In the admin console, navigate to **Assets and Compliance** | **Devices** and right-click on a mobile device in the right pane.
2. Click on **Remote Device Actions** in **Device Group**, and then select **Retire/Wipe**.
3. Select **Wipe company content and retire the mobile device from Configuration Manager** and click on **OK**:

> There is an exhaustive list of what is deleted during a selective wipe depending on the mobile platform on the following TechNet site `https ://technet.microsoft.com/en-us/library/mt634519.aspx`.

Remote lock

This action will lock the mobile device remotely:

1. In the admin console, navigate to **Assets and Compliance** | **Devices** and right-click on a mobile device in the right pane.
2. Click on **Remote Device Actions** in **Device Group**, and then select **Remote Lock**.

Passcode reset

This action will lock the mobile device remotely.

1. In the admin console, navigate to **Assets and Compliance** | **Devices** and right-click on a mobile device in the right pane.
2. Click on **Remote Device Actions** in **Device Group**, and then select **Passcode Reset**.

How it works...

Remote tasks are directly pushed to mobile devices. The push notification leverages a specific network made available by each mobile platform vendor:

- APNs (Apple Push Notification services) for iOS
- GCM (Google Cloud Messaging) for Android
- WNS (Windows Notification Services) for Windows

Whenever a remote task is run from the CM console, that task is sent to Microsoft Intune, which will then contact the appropriate push notification service depending on the mobile platform. By using this notification network, the mobile device will get the remote task immediately wherever it is located.

There's more...

For the remote lock and passcode reset actions, you can verify the task state from the CM console.

1. In the admin console, navigate to **Assets and Compliance** | **Devices** and right-click on a mobile device in the right pane.
2. To verify the `passcode` and reset the status, click on **Remote Device Actions** in **Device Group**, and then select **Show Passcode State**.
3. To verify the remote lock status and reset the status, click on **Remote Device Actions** in **Device Group**, and then select **Show Remote Lock State**.

6
Managing Sites

In this chapter, we will cover the following recipes:

- Managing collections
- Configuring site maintenance
- Managing site communications
- Configuring Discovery
- Managing Boundary Groups
- Managing role-based security
- Configuring the Application Catalog
- Managing and validating content for DPs and DP groups

Introduction

Managing sites in CM will be a different experience than with CM07, unless you have a single primary site (in which case the experience will be similar). This chapter will cover some of those differences, as well as information for configuring some of the site roles for your environment. You will also learn how to create collections, leverage **Role-based Administration** (**RBA**), and support clients over the Internet without a VPN connection.

Managing collections

A key component of CM is a **collection**. Collections contain one or more devices or users, and are used for targeting software deployments, operating-system deployments, client settings, and compliance settings. The members of a collection can be statically configured or set to be dynamically updated on a defined schedule. Collections in CM12 offer extended functionality compared to CM07. Here are some of the highlights:

- Client Settings (polling interval, remote control configuration, and so on) can be configured and deployed to one or more collections
- Right-click on a collection and select **Add Resources** to quickly add direct membership rules to a collection (hint→you can add multiple systems at one time if you use a comma-separated list)
- A collection can only contain devices or users, but never both
- Every collection requires a limiting collection
- Include and exclude rules simplify WQL queries
- Sub-collections no longer exist. Create folders for organization purposes, if required

This recipe will walk you through how to use some of the new collection features.

Getting ready

We will step through the process of creating a collection of "All Workstations that do not have Office 2010 Installed." To perform this task we should have healthy systems in our environment, and the ability to create collections.

How to do it...

First, we will create a collection of All Office 2010 Clients, and then we will create a collection of Systems without Office 2010.

1. Navigate to **Assets and Compliance** | **Device Collections**, select **Create** | **Create Device Collection** from the ribbon.

2. Enter a collection name `All Office 2010 Clients`. Click on **Browse** to select the limiting collection named **All Desktop and Server Clients**. Click on **Next**.

3. On the **Membership Rules** page click on **Add Rule** and select **Query Rule**.

4. Enter the name of the query as `All Office 2010 Clients` and click on **Edit Query Statement**.

5. On the **Query Statement Properties** dialog select the **Criteria** tab, and then click on the starburst to create query criteria.

6. Leave the default **Criterion Type** of **Simple Value**. Click on the **Select** button.

7. On the **Select Attribute** dialog, select **Add/Remove Programs** for the **Attribute class**, and **Display Name** for the **Attribute**, as shown in the following screenshot. Click on **OK**, as shown in the following screenshot:

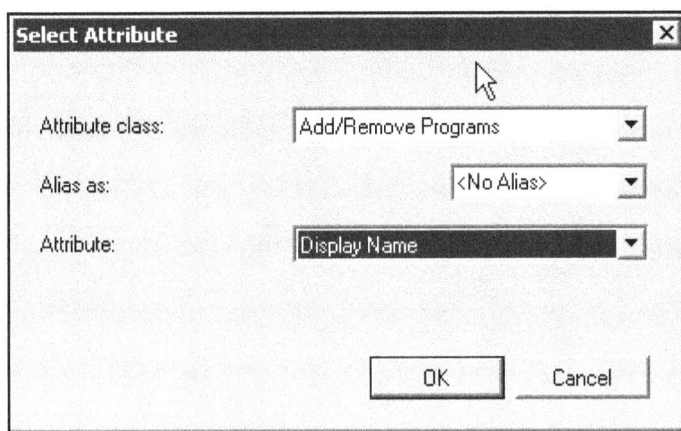

8. On the **Criterion Properties** dialog change the **Operator** to **is like**, and enter `Microsoft Office%2010` for **Value**. As shown in the following screenshot, select **OK**. To close the **Criterion Properties** dialog.

9. The percent symbol passes through various names of the product, but the product must start with **Microsoft Office** and end with **2010**. If you look at the possible Office 2010 names offered by Microsoft, this simple trick will capture them all:

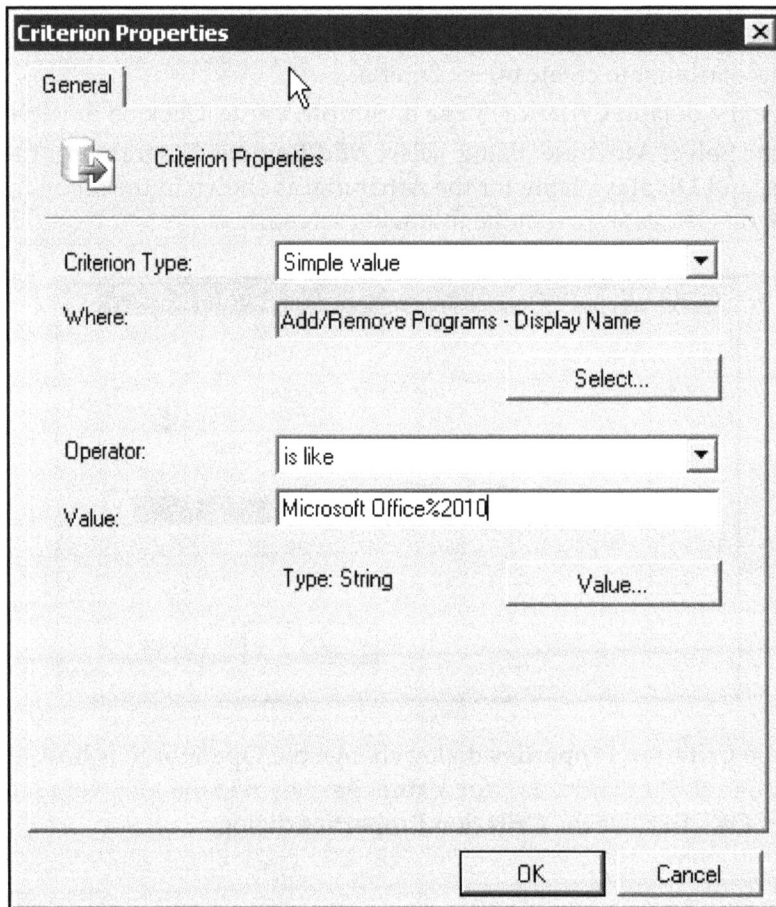

Criterion Properties

General |

Criterion Properties

Criterion Type: Simple value

Where: Add/Remove Programs - Display Name

                    Select...

Operator: is like

Value: Microsoft Office%2010

                    Type: String   Value...

OK   Cancel

10. Repeat steps 5 to 8, but use the **Attribute Class** named **Add/Remove Programs (64)** to include systems with office 2010 x64 installed.

11. On the **Criteria** tab, toggle the **and** statement to a **or** statement by clicking on the **&|** button, as shown in the following screenshot. Click on **OK:**

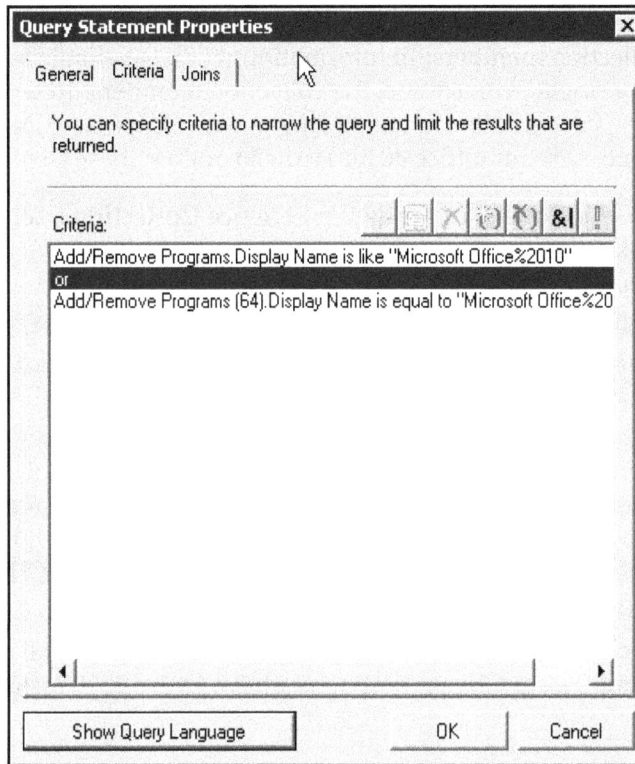

12. You can verify the query statement by selecting the **Show Query Language** button in the preceding figure. The WQL statement should appear as follows:

```
select *  from  SMS_R_System  inner join
SMS_G_System_ADD_REMOVE_PROGRAMS on
SMS_G_System_ADD_REMOVE_PROGRAMS.ResourceId =
SMS_R_System.ResourceId inner join
SMS_G_System_ADD_REMOVE_PROGRAMS_64 on
SMS_G_System_ADD_REMOVE_PROGRAMS_64.ResourceId =
SMS_R_System.ResourceId where
SMS_G_System_ADD_REMOVE_PROGRAMS.DisplayName like "Microsoft
Office%2010" or SMS_G_System_ADD_REMOVE_PROGRAMS_64.DisplayName
like "Microsoft Office%2010"
```

13. Click on **Next** to view the summary for **Create Device Collection Wizard**, and click on **Next** then on **Close** to complete the wizard.

Depending on whether you have a **Central Administration Site** (**CAS**), and the number of primary sites, the collection membership information will be available in approximately 10 minutes. If you have a single primary site, the collection membership will update within a few minutes. You now have a collection of all clients with Office 2010. Now you will create a collection of all clients without Office 2010. To do so, follow these steps:

1. Navigate to **Assets and Compliance** | **Device Collections**, select **Create** | **Create Device Collection** from the ribbon.

2. Enter a collection name `All Clients without Office 2010` and select the limiting collection named **All Desktop and Server Clients**. Click on **Next**.

3. On the **Membership Rules** page click on **Add Rule** and select **Exclude Collections**. Select the **All Office 2010 Clients** collection.

4. Add one additional query rule of named **All Systems** and click on **OK**. This is an empty query using the default query rule **Select * from SMS_R_System**. You will be given a warning prompt that this is returning all systems. Even though this WQL appears to display all systems, it will only show those systems that appear in the limited collection of **All Desktop and Server Clients**.

5. Complete the wizard to create the new collection.

6. After the collection evaluates, you will have a collection of all clients in **All Desktop and Server Clients** that do not have Office 2010 installed.

How it works...

The exclude collection rule allows us to easily exclude collections. To accomplish the same task in CM07, we would have to create a WQL Sub Select query to obtain the same results. Review `Colleval.log` on each primary site server to monitor collection evaluation. You could add additional exclusion rules. For example, if you have a collection named **All Servers**, you could exclude that collection to ensure that none of your servers will ever appear in the **All Clients without Office 2010** collection.

There's more...

The steps in this recipe walked through the process of easily excluding a collection of systems. Now let's step through more functionality in CM12 collections.

Creating maintenance windows

Use maintenance windows to ensure that the following features only execute during specified times:

- Software and software update deployments
- Compliance settings deployment
- Operating system and task sequence deployments

Each of these deployments allows the admin to configure the deployment to ignore maintenance windows so that windows can be overridden when absolutely necessary.

> Some admins create a non-recurring maintenance window in the past on their server collection, so that software is never installed, unless a new maintenance window is configured for a future date.

Review `ServiceWindowManager.log` in the client logs to view service window information.

Here are a few additional notes about maintenance windows:

- Only the action of installing (or compliance settings remediation) adheres to maintenance windows. If a deployment is configured to download and execute, the download is not restricted to the maintenance window.
- A program will only run if the maximum allowed run time is less than the size of the window.
- If a system has more than one maintenance window, and doesn't overlap, then each window will be treated individually.
- If a system has overlapping maintenance windows, then the union of the windows will apply can create one larger window for deployments.
- Maintenance windows are ignored when a user initiates an action. For example, installing software from the Software Center or launching software updates from a balloon notification in the system tray, will override any maintenance windows.

Configuring power management

Power management is a very important topic in today's greener, more efficient world. CM allows you to control power management on a collection level (for device collections only). We can also create a custom client setting and deploy to a collection, which will allow an end user to opt out of power management, if needed.

If you're familiar with power management in CM07 R3, the significant change in CM current branch is that we can create a custom client settings policy to allow users to opt out of power management.

Before we deploy power management enforcement, we should spend some time monitoring current power usage. The default hardware inventory in client settings will automatically inventory power management information from each client. Review the power management reports to understand your power usage.

If you use a third-party power management application, consider disabling the hardware inventory classes that begin with "Power," as much of the data would be duplicative (and unnecessary) due to the third-party power management information.

There are three main settings on collection properties for power management:

- **Do not specify power management settings**: This is a default setting, which basically does not apply any power management settings for this collection.
- **Never apply power management settings to computers in this collection**: This setting takes precedence over any other power management setting, and prevents any power management for systems in the collection. For critical systems (such as kiosk systems, or systems running a manufacturing process), we may actually want to enforce power management, and specify peak and non-peak plans of **always on** to ensure systems remain powered on at all times.
- **Specify power management settings for this collection**: This setting allows us to configure the granular settings for the peak and non-peak power policy. Configure these settings as required. Select a default setting, or select the **Customized** setting to configure settings such as **turn off display after (minutes)**, **Lid Close action**, and so on.
- The **Wakeup time** setting applies only to desktop OS of Windows 7 and later and does not rely on magic packets, or anything remote from the system to power it on. Wake timers are used on the system to wake it up at the specified time. Once the system is awake, it will follow the power plan being enforced at that time. If CM12 has some work to do such as software distribution, and patching, CM will keep the client awake with activity.

If we apply power settings to an XP or Server 2003 system, and then later decide to remove the power policy, the settings we applied are "tattooed" on to the system – users can then modify them once we have removed the policy. For newer operating systems, power policy is reverted to their original values when we stop managing power from CM12.

If a system resides in multiple collections that are being power managed, the client will use the least-restrictive (or conservative) power management settings. Also note that server operating systems are not supported for power management in CM. Review `pwrmgmt.log` and `PwrProvider.log` on the client for troubleshooting power management issues.

Configuring alerts

The **Alerts** tab on collection properties allow us to configure in-console alerts related to client status (health check, remediation, and activity) and endpoint protection alerts (malware detection, and so on).

Import/export and copying collections

A right-click on any collection will allow us to export or copy the selected collection, and a right-click on the **Device Collections** node allows us to import a collection to our site. We need to mention a couple caveats related to the functions with collections.

- If we export a collection that contains direct membership rules, the **resourceID** will probably be associated with a different system when imported into a different CM12 environment. Use caution when importing collections – verify that the membership includes only that what was intended.
- When we copy a collection, the limiting collection of the copy is actually the collection we copied from. For example, let's say we have a collection named `All Systems in Austin`, and it has a collection limit to `All Workstations`. When we copy that collection, the copy will be named `All Systems in Austin[1]`, and be collection limited to `All systems in Austin`, instead of the `All Workstations` collection.

See also

Review the following Microsoft TechNet Documentations:

- Collections: `http://technet.microsoft.com/en-us/library/gg682169.aspx`
- Maintenance Windows: `https://technet.microsoft.com/en-us/library/mt629354.aspx`
- Power Management : `https://technet.microsoft.com/en-us/library/mt629349.aspx`

Configuring site maintenance

Right after you get your site up and running, you will want to start things off on the right foot. Tell the CM how to manage itself right at the start and it will save you headaches down the road. You won't want to rely on default settings for long, for example, backups are disabled by default.

Getting ready

Have a completed installation of a primary site with roles and configurations set up, as needed, before proceeding.

How to do it...

To configure site maintenance, follow these steps:

1. Navigate to **Administration | Site Configuration**. In the right-hand pane, each site in your hierarchy is listed. The console will offer varying configuration options based on the type of site you choose in the right-hand pane. For example, the **Client Installation Settings** offerings are grayed out on a CAS as clients never assign to it.

2. For each primary or CAS in the right-hand pane, select the site in the right-hand pane then click on **Site Maintenance** in the ribbon. The **Site Maintenance** window opens showing a list of tasks. We're going to set some important ones right now. Note that not everything listed here can be set on the CAS, as it has only 10 built-in tasks.

3. Select **Rebuild Indexes** and click on **Edit**. Select **Enable this task** and choose a day of the week where the server is least busy (the default of midnight Sunday is good as many clients are powered down and not much is going on). This is a rather resource intensive task, but necessary to help SQL find data in the database. Click on **OK**.

4. Select **Backup Site Server** and click on **Edit**. Select **Enable this task** and choose a time of day that most of the client processing for the day has been completed. Click on **Set Paths** to set a location for backup files to be stored. All inboxes and the database will be backed up, so be sure to have enough space when making this choice. Click on **OK**. Check the **Enable alerts for backup task failures** checkbox, as this backup method is currently the only supported method to restore a site; you will want to know if it fails. Click on **OK**.

5. For each task you are not using, click on it and then click on **Disable**. For example, if you are not using file collection (a very rarely used feature), click on **Delete Aged Collected Files** and then click on **Disable**.

6. Click on **Name** in the title bar to sort by name. For each of the **Delete Aged** tasks, edit them to prune data to a shorter lifespan than the defaults if possible. For example, if you don't need to know about how much RAM was on machines 3 months ago (you need only the past 3 weeks), select **Delete Aged Inventory History**, click on **Edit**, and set **Delete date older than (days)** to **21**. Click on **OK**.

How it works...

CM is a smart tool that can be told how to take care of itself if you just tell it what you want it to do. There are side benefits to modifying the defaults. For example, by deleting data you don't need more often, you keep the database size smaller. This helps SQL find things faster and makes for faster backups and less chance of running out of disk space.

There's more...

Be sure to go through all the site maintenance tasks and adjust to your needs. Before going on to the next site, there are some other beneficial settings you can make while in the **Sites** node of the console.

Setting up a Network Access Account

For primary servers only: select the primary server in the right-hand pane and click on **Configure Site Components** in the ribbon.

Select **Software Distribution** and click on the **Network Access Account** tab. Click **Set** and **New Account** and then **Browse** to select an AD account. Enter its password and click on **Verify**. Click on **OK**.

> This account should be a member of Domain Users only. There is no reason for any higher security. It is used only when a machine account fails to grab data from a DP, during an OS Deployment prior to the domain join or for workgroup machines which have no machine accounts.

Disabling unused Status Filter Rules

For all primary sites and the CAS, select the server in the right-hand pane and click on **Status Filter Rules**.

> CM monitors itself and writes issues to the event log. If you're not monitoring the event log, you can disable these messages. Alternatively, you can choose to run a program to take action.

A good example here is the rule, **Detect when the status of the transaction log for the site database changes to Critical because it could not be accessed**. Click on **Edit** and then click on the **Actions** tab. Generally, you could check the **Write to the Configuration Manager database** checkbox and then monitor this in an SRS report. But in this case, CM can't write anything because the transaction log isn't working; all CM to SQL activity is stuck. Instead, you could check **Run a program** and call out something such as Blat.exe, the command-line mail client to e-mail you about it.

Designating a fallback site

In the right-hand pane, select the CAS (if you don't have one, choose your primary). Click on **Hierarchy Settings** in the ribbon and check the **Use a fallback site** checkbox and select a site that clients will assign to should their boundaries not be in a group.

This simple act gets clients assigned and manageable when boundary information is sketchy or unknown. As that information is learned over time and entered into proper Boundary Groups, the fallback site should be used less and less.

The fallback site assists in getting a client assigned initially; it does nothing for you in case of a site failure. It does not reassign clients in case of a site failure!

See also

Review the following Microsoft TechNet documentation:

- Configure Maintenance Tasks for Configuration Manager Sites: https://technet.microsoft.com/en-us/library/mt605186.aspx
- Configuring Site Components in Configuration Manager: http://technet.microsoft.com/en-us/library/hh427329.aspx
- Blat: http://www.blat.net/

Managing site communications

For site-to-site data communications CM12 will use as much bandwidth as possible to transfer files. In most environments, this default setting may be acceptable. In environments with site systems in remote locations over slow WAN links, we may want to throttle bandwidth utilization.

Getting ready

In order to configure bandwidth throttling, we must have at least two different site systems. This could be Primary Site to Secondary Site, Primary Site to Distribution Point, CAS to Primary Site, and so on.

How to do it...

To configure bandwidth throttling between site servers, follow these steps:

1. Navigate to **Administration** | **Overview** | **Hierarchy Configuration** | **Addresses**, select the desired source and destination site, and choose **Properties**.
2. Use the **Schedule** tab to specify when data can be sent to the destination, based on priority. Each type of content (such as package, application, and image) has a configurable priority.
3. Use the **Rate Limits** tab to control how the data is actually sent. We can choose **Pulse mode** or select **Limited to specified maximum transfer rates by hour**. By choosing the second option, we can set the percentage of available bandwidth to be used during specific hours of the day.

> Review Sender.log to monitor bandwidth restriction configurations.

There's more...

A new feature to CM12 is a standalone **Distribution Point** (**DP**) that leverages the sender technology. Previous to CM12 we had to use a Branch Distribution Point or a Secondary Site (with DP) to control bandwidth utilization. CM12 makes a standalone DP feasible now that we can control sending to it.

For site-to-site content transfer, review `sender.log`. For site-to-standalone DP content transfer, review `PkgXfermgr.log`.

Configuring bandwidth restrictions on standalone DPs

To configure bandwidth restrictions on standalone DPs, follow these steps:

1. Navigate to **Administration** | **Overview** | **Distribution Points**, select the desired standalone DP, and choose **Properties**.
2. A standalone DP will have two additional tabs, **Schedule** and **Rate Limits**.
3. Use the **Schedule** tab to specify when data can be sent to the destination, based on priority. Each type of content (package, application, image, and so on) has a configurable priority.
4. Use the **Rate Limits** tab to control how the data is actually sent. We can choose **Pulse mode** or select **Limited to specified maximum transfer rates by hour**. By choosing the second option, we can set the percentage of available bandwidth to use during specific hours of the day.

Configuring Discovery

We use discovery to import computer, user, and group resources into CM12. Discovery can also be used to discover network infrastructure, as well as IP Subnets and Active Directory Sites in Active Directory Forests.

Getting ready

Enabling discovery is one of the first items we configure in CM. **Heartbeat discovery** is automatically enabled when we install a primary site. **Forest Discovery** is the only discovery method that can be enabled on a CAS. Enabling discovery is very similar for each method (other than heartbeat), so we will only step through the process one time.

How to do it...

To enable **Active Directory (AD) Forest Discovery**, follow these steps:

1. Enable the **Enable Active Directory Forest Discovery** checkbox.
2. Select **Properties** from the ribbon.
3. Navigate to **Administration | Hierarchy Configuration | Discovery Methods**, and select **Active Directory Forest Discovery** from the Details pane.
4. Choose any additional options for Forest Discovery:
   - Automatically create Active Directory site boundaries when they are discovered
   - Automatically create IP Range boundaries when they are discovered
5. Configure the run schedule.
6. Click on **OK** to save settings.

How it works...

By default, AD Forest Discovery will query the forest where the site server resides and depending on the configured options, it will automatically create boundaries in CM12 for AD sites and IP subnet boundaries. Review `ADForestDisc.log` for more information.

> Although the thought of automatically creating boundaries sounds a little scary to the CM07 admin, you will sleep better at night knowing that boundaries must be added to a boundary group before they're actually used by CM12.

After AD Forest Discovery has run successfully (and if you enabled the auto creation of boundaries), view the **Boundaries** node to review the created boundaries.

If you want to manually initiate a discovery action, simply highlight the desired discovery method, and select **Run Full Discovery Now**.

There's more...

If you need to enable Forest Discovery for additional forests, perform the following steps:

1. Navigate to **Administration | Hierarchy Configuration | Active Directory** node, and select **Add Forest** from the ribbon.
2. From the **Add Forest** dialog, enter the domain suffix to discover.

3. If the computer account for the site server has read permissions to the forest, we are finished with the **General** tab. If the computer account does not have read rights, as when connecting to an untrusted forest, we can specify an account that does have proper rights. This account is considered a "global account", and will also be used for publishing to active directory.

4. In the **Publishing** tab, select the desired sites to be published to Active Directory in the specified Forest.

Enabling Active Directory System Discovery

Use AD System Discovery to allow CM to discover computers from AD. While still in the **Discovery Methods** node of the admin console, perform the following steps:

1. Select **Active Directory System Discovery**, and then click on **Properties** in the ribbon.

2. Check the **Enable Active Directory System Discovery** checkbox, and then click on the orange starburst to select the AD container to discover.

3. Enter an LDAP path, or click on **Browse** to search and select a path.

4. Select whether to recursively search child containers, and/or discover objects within AD Groups.

5. If the Local System account of the site server does not have access, specify an account that can query Active Directory.

6. On the **Polling Schedule** tab, adjust the frequency for full discovery if required.

7. Check the **Enable Delta Discovery** checkbox to find objects in between full discovery. Delta discovery finds objects based on a higher number **Update Sequence Number** (**USN**) than the last delta discovery.

8. Use the **Active Directory Attributes** tab to include any additional attributes in discovery – this could be helpful for additional information that's stored in active directory, so that it can be queried and associated to CM12 data.

9. Use the **Option** tab to filter inactive or old computers from discovery.

10. Click on **OK** to complete the AD System Discovery configuration.

11. Monitor `ADSysDis.log` for more information.

Enabling Active Directory User Discovery

This process is very similar to Active Directory System Discovery. Take a close look at User Attributes in Active Directory. Some companies extend AD Schema to include additional user attributes (or use existing ones) to capture data such as employee ID, employee manager, location, e-mail address, and phone number. By discovering this data with CM, you may be able to create some helpful reports with additional business information than just CM12 out of the box. Monitor `ADUsrDis.log` for more information.

Enabling Active Directory Group Discovery

CM12's **Active Directory Group Discovery** replaces **AD Security Group** and **AD System Group** discoveries from CM07. AD group discovery in CM12 is much more "surgical" in that we can specify the individual groups to discover. Our goal is to discover a smaller number of groups than all groups in a domain – generally, a much smaller number is used in CM than what is in Active Directory, and discovering a smaller number decreases the time and effort required by your site server for group discovery.

The settings for this discovery method are very similar to the previous methods. Simply specify the desired group(s) or location(s), and specify an account if required. Configure the polling schedule, and then the **Option** tab to filter out inactive or old systems from discovery.

See also

- Review the Microsoft Documentation for information about Heartbeat and Network discovery:
  `https://technet.microsoft.com/en-us/library/mt621991.aspx`

Managing Boundary Groups

Boundary Groups is a new concept in CM12, and take the old site boundaries of CM07 to a new level of flexibility. Boundary Groups are used to determine client site assignment and content location for both **Distribution Points** (**DPs**) and **State Migration Points** (**SMPs**).

Clients that are connected through the Internet do not use Boundary Groups for site assignment or content location requests.

Just configuring a boundary in CM12 will not help with site assignment or content location. A boundary must be added to a Boundary Group before it is actually used by CM12.

Getting ready

In order to manage Boundary Groups, we must first create one or more boundaries.

In the admin console, navigate to **Administration** | **Hierarchy Configuration** | **Boundaries**. Click on **Create Boundary** from the ribbon. From this dialog, we can enter an **Active Directory Site**, **IP Subnet**, **IPv6 Prefix**, or **IP Address Range**. As an alternative to entering each boundary manually, you can follow the steps in the previous recipe to run Forest Discovery and automatically create AD Site and/or IP range boundaries.

Why are IP address ranges always a better bet than Subnets?
An incorrect mask on a subnet may cause site assignments to fail. Ranges always work.

How to do it...

Follow these steps to create a Boundary Group:

1. Navigate to **Administration** | **Hierarchy Configuration** | **Boundary Groups**, and then click **Create BoundaryGroup** from the ribbon.
2. Enter a descriptive name and description, and then click on **Add**. The **Add Boundaries** dialog appears.
3. Select one or more boundaries from the dialog and click on **OK**.
4. Click on the **General** tab to configure additional options.
5. If this group will be used for site assignment, enable the checkbox, as well as specify the assigned site. (The defined site will also perform all client push operations for the Boundary Group.)
6. Under **Content Location**, click on the **Add** button and specify all site systems to associate to this Boundary Group, and then click on **OK**.
7. Finally, click on **OK** to create the new Boundary Group.

How it works...

As you can see, Boundary Groups are used for both client site assignment and content location for both DPs and SMPs. These Boundary Groups are published to Active Directory (if AD Publishing is enabled) by CM (watch `hman.log` to confirm.)

> Regarding site assignment, the **Server Location Point** role in CM07 has been integrated into the **Management Point** (**MP**) role in CM12. So for clients that can't query AD (or if AD publishing isn't enabled), you can configure clients to contact the MP for content location and site assignment information.

There's more...

A boundary can be added to more than one boundary group. We can also classify each boundary as a fast or slow connection to the site system(s). Overlapping Boundaries for content is nondeterministic-a client will randomly choose between available site systems, giving priority to any site system identified as a fast connection.

> Ensure there are no overlapping boundaries configured for site assignment. If a client is in the boundaries of multiple site systems with different site assignments, the result is non-deterministic and not supported.

Adding or editing Boundary Groups from the Boundaries node

Simply right-click on one or more boundaries in the **Boundaries** node, and select **Add Selected Items | Add Selected Items to Existing Boundary Groups** (or choose **Add Selected Items to New Boundary Group**). Complete the wizard in the same way we did in the previous steps.

See also

- Microsoft documentation for additional information about boundary configuration: http://technet.microsoft.com/en-us/library/hh427326.aspx .

- The MVPs have had some lengthy discussion of the value of entering subnets, versus IP ranges. Review Jason Sandy's post on **Why IP Subnet Boundaries are Evil** at `http://blog.configmgrftw.com/?p=343`.

Managing role-based security

Role-based Access Security (**RBAC**) is new to CM12. It offers the ability to segregate administrators with ease. In CM07 admins either used extra primary sites or scripts kicked off by status filters to separate admins from each other. Now it can be done in just a few minutes, right from the console.

We are going to use RBAC to divvy up roles for workstation and server admins so that neither sees the other's assets.

Getting ready

Create two AD user groups-**CM Wkstn Admins** and **CM Server Admins**. Populate each with a unique test account or real user accounts.

How to do it...

We start by creating one collection for workstations and one for servers:

1. In the admin console, navigate to **Assets and Compliance | Device Collections** and click on **Create Device Collection** in the ribbon.
2. For **Name**, enter `All Managed Workstations`. Click on **Browse** and select **All Desktop and Server Clients**. Click on **Next**.
3. Click on **Add Rule** and select **Query Rule**. Enter `Wkstn Only` for **Name**. Click on **Edit Query Statement**.
4. Choose the **Criteria** tab and click on the yellow starburst.
5. Under **Criterion Properties**, click **Select**. For **Attribute class**, select **System Resource**.

> **TIP**
>
> Click on the drop-down pane and enter the system resource's name to get there faster than scrolling.

6. For **Attribute**, select **Operating System Name and Version**. Click on **OK**.

7. Under **Criterion Properties**, enter `Microsoft Windows NT Workstation%` for **Value**. For **Operator**, select **is like**. Click on **OK** thrice to return to **Create Device Collection Wizard**.

> Entering `%workstation%` would work too, but entering as much text before the percent at the end gives SQL a head start and is easier on the server.

8. The default refresh cycle occurs every seven days. Click on **Schedule** to set it to recur every day or something more appropriate for your needs. Click on **Next** twice and then on **Close** to exit the wizard.

Repeat the steps 1 to 8 to create a server collection called **All Managed Servers**. For step 7, enter `Microsoft Windows NT %Server%` for **Value**. (The long name trick won't work here because there is an NT Server and an NT Advanced Server).

How it works...

You now have two collections which update at least daily and will serve as the foundation for each of the admin roles to be defined. These collections will be the basis for each admin group. Once an admin (or AD group) has been limited to a collection, all collections created will be ultimately be limited by the defined limited collection for the admin.

There's more...

Now it's time for the easy work; wrap security around these new collections and tell CM who will have what access to them.

Creating scopes to manage security boundaries

We start by creating a scope for each group we plan to manage:

1. In the admin console, navigate to **Administration | Security | Security Scopes** and click on **Create Security Scope** in the ribbon.

2. For **Security scope name**, enter `Wkstn Admins`. Enter any meaningful description under **Description**. Click on **OK**.

3. Repeat the previous steps, but enter `Server Admins` for **Security scope name** to create a security scope to bind the server admins.

Defining administrator groups

CM now needs to be told about your AD user groups and how you wish to restrict them. To define administrator groups

1. Navigate to **Administration** | **Security** | **Administrative Users** and click on **Add User or Group** in the ribbon.
2. Click on **Browse** and choose the **CM Wkstn Admin** group.
3. Click on **Add** and select **Application Administrator** and **Software Update Manager**. Click on **OK**.

> Clicking on one of the roles fills the description pane to help guide you when making choices.

4. Under **Security scopes and collection**, highlight all collections and scopes and click on **Remove** to remove them.
5. Click on **Add** and select **Security Scope**. Check the checkbox next to **Wkstn Admins** and click on **OK**.
6. Click on **Add** and select **Collection**. In the left pane of **Select Collections**, choose **Device Collections**, and then click **All Managed Workstations** in the right-hand pane. Click **OK** twice to exit the wizard.

Repeat the preceding steps for the CM Server Admin group (choosing to lock Server Admins down to the **All Managed Servers** collection.

Setting security scopes on DPs

One last item is to let these new application admins have access to park software on DPs. Navigate to **Administration** | **Security** | **Distribution Points** and highlight your DPs in the right-hand pane. Click on **Set Security Scopes** in the ribbon and check the **Server Admins** and **Wkstn Admins** checkboxes.

What you have just done is grant two groups the ability to manage their own assets with no chance of one group touching the other. Each group can send software and patches. Additional roles could be granted to them as needed.

You can also copy roles, rename them and edit them to meet any need you might have other than the 14 defaults offered.

See also

* Microsoft Team Blog regarding RBAC: `http://blogs.technet.com/b/configmg rteam/archive/2011/09/23/introducing-role-based-administration-in-sy stem-center-2012-configuration-manager.aspx`

Configuring the Application Catalog

The **Application Catalog** is used for User and User Group targeted applications. If you only plan to use machine-targeted distributions, you will not need to configure the Application Catalog. See `Chapter 3`, *Applications and Software Updates*, for what has changed in the new software center.

Getting ready

The Application Catalog requires two different roles; the **Application Catalog Web Service Point**, and the **Application Catalog Website Point**. The Application Catalog Web Service Point must reside in the same forest as the site database. The application website can exist in a different forest, if required. There are several prerequisites for installing the Application Catalog- review `http://technet.microsoft.com/en-us/library/gg682145.aspx` for a complete list. For our test environment, we use the following steps to fully configure Windows Server 2008 R2 for all site server roles:

1. Download the latest installer for .NET Framework 4.0 (full version). Run the following command from an administrative command prompt:

   dotNetFx40_Full_x86_x64.exe" /passive /norestart

2. Open an administrative command prompt, and run the following command:

```
powershell -command "& {import-module servermanager;add-
windowsfeature FS-FileServer,Web-Static-Content,Web-Default-
Doc,Web-Dir-Browsing,Web-Http-Errors,Web-Http-Redirect,Web-Asp-
Net,Web-Net-Ext,Web-ISAPI-Ext,Web-ISAPI-Filter,Web-Http-
Logging,Web-Log-Libraries,Web-Request-Monitor,Web-Http-
Tracing,Web-Windows-Auth,Web-Filtering,Web-Stat-Compression,Web-
Dyn-Compression,Web-Mgmt-Console,Web-Metabase,Web-WMI,BITS-
Compact-Server,BITS-IIS-Ext,RDC,RSAT-Web-Server,RSAT-Bits-
Server}"
```

Now that all required features are installed, proceed to the next section to install the roles.

In some scenarios, such as when IIS is installed or reconfigured after the .NET Framework version 4.0 is installed, you must explicitly enable ASP.NET version 4.0. For example, on a 64-bit computer that runs the .NET Framework version 4.0.30319, run the following command: `%windir%\Microsoft.NET\Framework64\v4.0.30319\aspnet_regi is.exe -i -enable`

How to do it...

1. Navigate to **Administration | Site Configuration | Servers and Site System Roles**, right-click on the desired site server, and select **Add Site System Roles**.
2. Verify the settings on the **General** page, and select **Next**.
3. On the **System Role Selection**, enable the checkbox for **Application Catalog Web Service Point** and **Application Catalog Website Point**, and then select **Next**.
4. Follow **Add Site System Roles Wizard** to completion, specifying any custom configuration required (HTTPS instead of HTTP, port configuration, URL, and so on). Note that we can also specify a custom organizational name, as well as a custom theme color for the website.

How it works...

Review `SMSAWEBSVCSetup.log` and `awebsvcMSI.log` for the web service setup configuration, and `portlwebMSI.log` and `SMSPORTALWEBSetup.log` for the website installation. After installation, monitor `awebsctl.log` for the web service state, and `portlctl.log` for the Application Catalog website.

There's more…

Once the Application Catalog is active, client systems will have an active link in Software Center named **Find additional applications from the Application Catalog**. We can also control which catalog is launched from this link by using custom client settings.

See also

For more information about installing the Application Catalog, refer to the Microsoft documentation at `http://technet.microsoft.com/en-us/library/hh489603.aspx`.

Managing and validating content for DPs and DP groups

It's very important to take a good look at DP Groups in CM12. Here are some highlights of DP Groups in CM12:

- DP Groups are global-they can be configured from any primary site or CAS, and are replicated throughout the hierarchy.
- DP can be a member of many groups.
- DP group can be limited to a Role-based Scope, so only certain admins have access to certain DP Groups.
- Content can be monitored at a DP group level.
- DP Groups can be associated to one or more collections, so that when we distribute software we can choose to *Automatically deploy content to associated DP Groups*.
- When we add a DP to an existing DP group, all content that has already been targeted to the DP group will automatically be distributed to the new member DP in the group. However, when you remove a DP from a DP group, the DP group-targeted content does not automatically remove from the DP.

Getting ready

In order to add DPs to one or more DP groups, we must have DPs configured in our environment. After that, we're ready to roll.

How to do it...

Use the following steps to add DPs to a new or existing DP group:

1. Navigate to **Administration | Overview | Distribution Points**.
2. In the **Distribution Points** details pane, select one or more DPs.
3. From the **Home** tab on the ribbon, click on **Add Selected Items**, and then choose whether to add to an existing or new DP group.
4. For a new DP group, enter a valid name for the DP group.
5. Click on the **Add** button under the **Collections** tab to associate one or more collections to the DP group.
6. Click on the **Add** button under the **Members** tab to add/remove members from the DP group.
7. Click on the **OK** button to save changes.

How it works...

CM treats groups of DPs as a single unit. Add a DP to a group and you won't have to go manually send all packages to it like you did in CM07.

There's more...

Once we have DP groups configured, we can leverage them for content distribution and collection association.

- For content distribution, we can select one or more objects with content (packages, applications, images, and so on), and target them to a DP group.
- Here's a brief explanation for how collection association works with a DP group:
  - Admin creates a new deployment
  - In the **New Deployment** wizard, admin selects a target collection that has an associated DP group.
  - A new checkbox is enabled in the wizard – **Use default distribution point groups associated to this collection**. If the admin enables this checkbox, the associated DP group is automatically selected in the wizard, and content will be distributed to all target groups.

Monitoring the content status

1. Navigate to **Monitoring** | **Overview** | **Distribution Status** | **Content Status**.
2. If you have a lot of content, you may want to organize what you see in this view. Right-click on the title bar, and select **Group ByType**. You can then right-click on a type, and select **Collapse All At This Level**. You can then easily navigate to view content status.

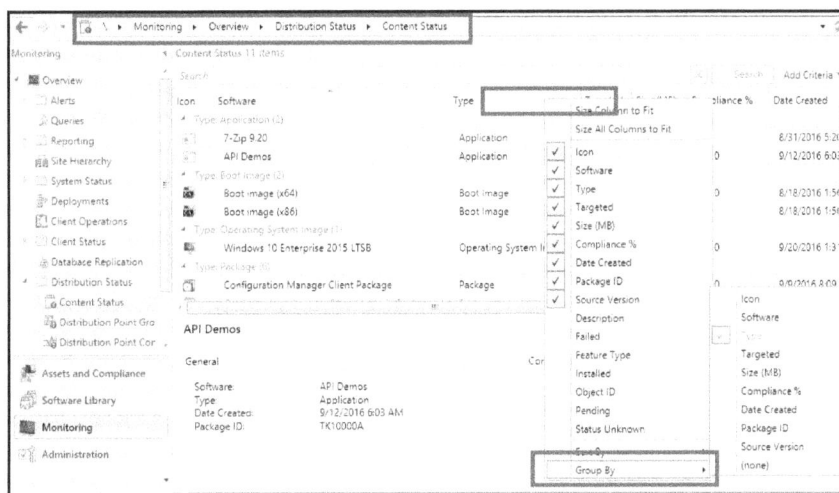

3. Locate and highlight the desired content to view **Completion Statistics**.
4. Click **View Status** to view detailed content status.

If the content status shows content in an unexpected state (in progress, error, and so on), first run the **Validate Content** action (discussed later in this recipe) to verify current status.

Monitoring DP group status

The DP group status is a great way to check status. For example, in our environment, we leverage some Workstation DPs in remote sites for OS Deployment only. We have a DP group of All OSD DPs, and have given our OSD Admins the ability to distribute to these DPs. So now, the OSD admin can simply select a task sequence, send content to the DP group for OSD, and then monitor status of only OSD-required packages from the **DP Group Status** node.

Monitoring the DP configuration status

To verify current status of a single DP, use the **Distribution Point Configuration Status** node, and select the desired DP – this will show status for all content targeted to the selected DP. Click on the **Details** tab to view status messages for the DP.

Validating the content

Content validation that can be used to confirm that content on a DP, including packages, applications, and OSD image, are still there and that none of the files have been corrupted. Some admins may be all-too-familiar with "Hash mismatch" errors when downloading and installing content in CM07. Use content validation to detect mismatch errors before your users encounter them and generate trouble tickets.

What causes hash mismatch errors anyway?
A hash mismatch issue is reported when the client downloads files for install, calculates a hash, and that hash doesn't match with the expected hash from CM. CM generates a failure to protect the integrity of the installation.

Basically, downloaded files don't match the files CM expected the system to download. This can occur if a file is added to package source on purpose, or even unknowingly just by browsing a DP share (`thumbs.db` generated by the operating system is often the culprit). CM12 helps this experience in two ways:

- The content library should effectively prevent human intent or error to add/replace files to a file source for `ConfigMgr`.
- The content validation process will detect any hash issues and display results in DP Monitoring.

We can configure content validation to run on a regular interval by modifying the **Distribution Point** properties. We can also perform content validation from the **Content Location** tab of any content source such as Package, Application Deployment Type, and Image.

Content Validation only validates the content store. If you have added the option to **Copy the content in the package to a package share on distribution points**, the DP share content will not be validated. Only use DP shares when absolutely necessary, such as when using the option to not download content, and run from DP instead.

Review `SMSDPMon.log` on the DP for validation details. We can also run `smsdpmon.exe LAB00025` (where the package ID is `LAB00025`) from the `\bin\` directory of the DP to check content on a specific package.

See also

Review Microsoft Documentation for more information about Content Validation:
`https://technet.microsoft.com/en-us/library/mt620087.aspx`.

7
Managing Clients

In this chapter, we will cover the following recipes:

- Deploying clients
- Upgrading client agents
- Managing client health
- Managing client settings
- Enabling Device Health Attestation in Windows 10
- Monitoring client installation and activity
- Making use of user-centric improvements
- Configuring power management

Introduction

This chapter is all about the CM client. You will learn multiple methods to deploy the client, as well as how to be proactive in monitoring the health of the client agent. Client health in CM is a giant leap forward in detecting, automatically repairing, and reporting on its health and activity (officially called as **client status**).

Another fantastic feature in CM is **client settings**. You can configure and deploy specific settings (inventory classes, software metering, software inventory, and all other client settings) to one or more collections. This allows you (for example) to reduce the classes for hardware inventory on servers, while continuing to inventory workstation systems. Also items such as end user notifications can be controlled at a collection level.

Power management is also an important feature of CM. As an admin, you can allow users to opt out of corporate power management configurations, or you can enforce specific power settings, based on collections.

Deploying clients

CM offers several ways to deploy the client on computers. We'll show our favorite method first, **Software Update Point** (**SUP**) based installation, and then show the popular `client push` method. This is our favorite because it allows you to leverage GPO on the client to pull the client installation from the SUP, instead of the traditional client push installation, where the server must connect, copy, and remotely start an installation.

Getting ready

You should have a fully functional primary and management point (one or more) before attempting to install and assign clients. For SUP-based installation, a functioning, active SUP at the primary, to which you intend to assign clients, must be in place.

How to do it...

1. From any computer with **Group Policy Management Console** (**GPMC**) installed, open GPMC and navigate to **Group Policy Objects**. Right-click on **Group Policy Objects** and select **New**. Enter `CM Client Install via SUP` for the name and click on **OK**.

2. Navigate to **CM Client Install via SUP** in the left-hand pane, right-click on it and select **Edit**.

3. In the left-hand pane of **Group Policy Management Editor**, navigate to **Computer Configuration | Policies | Administrative Templates | Windows Components | Windows Update**.

4. In the right-hand pane, right-click on **Specify intranet Microsoft update service location** and select **Edit**. Click on the **Enabled** radio button:

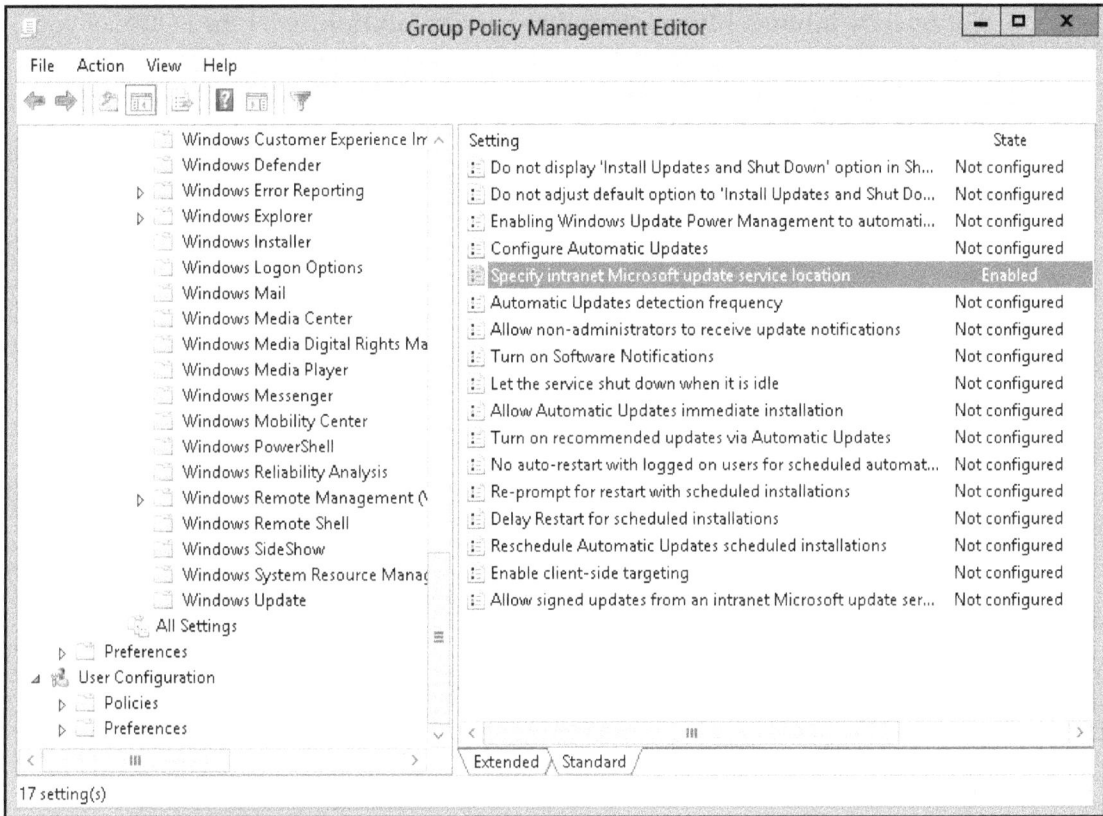

5. For **Comment**, enter `Install clients for ABC`, where ABC is the site code of the primary site.

6. For **Specify intranet Microsoft update service location**, enter the FQDN of your active SUP and port, for example, `http://myactivesup.mycompany.com:8530`. Enter this information for the intranet statistics server as well, as shown in the following screenshot:

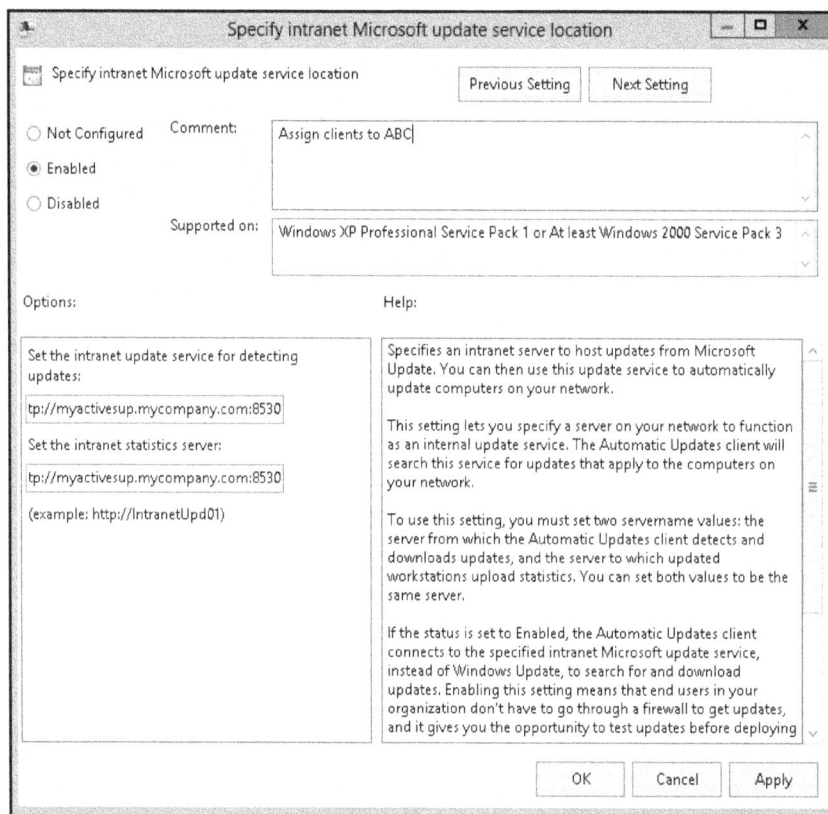

7. Navigate to **Administrative Templates** in the left-hand pane, right-click on it and select **Add/Remove Templates**. Click on **Add** and browse to the CM setup files (`SMSSETUP\TOOLS\ConfigMgrADMTemplates`) and select `ConfigMgrInstallation.adm`. Click on **Open** and then on **Close**.

8. In the right-hand pane, double-click to navigate to **Classic Administrative Templates (ADM)** | **Configuration Manager 2012** | **Configuration Manager 2012 Client** | **Configure Configuration Manager Client 2012 Client Deployment Settings**. Even though this policy is called "Configuration Manager 2012", it does still apply to **Configuration Manager Current Branch**.

9. Click on the **Enabled** radio button and enter SMSSITECODE=ABC for **CCMSetup**, where ABC is the site code of your primary site. Click on **OK** to exit the editor.

> The active SUP you enter must not be assigned to the CAS. Only an active SUP from a primary is entered here (because clients only communicate with primary and secondary sites, and never directly to the CAS). When there are multiple primary sites, you may have multiple GPOs, with custom site codes for each GPO. You could target each GPO to an AD Site to prevent conflicting GPOs. It's possible to have certain sites where this method might not work best in all locations.

10. Click on **CM Client Install via SUP** in the left-hand pane of the GPMC then click on the **Details** tab in the right-hand pane and select **User configuration settings disabled**. Click on **OK**.

11. This GPO can now be linked to a pilot OU of computers simply by navigating to that OU, right-clicking on it, and selecting **Link an Existing GPO**. After proper testing, it can be linked instead to an OU of all machines that the primary manages. You can also link to an AD site.

12. In the CM admin console, navigate to **Administration | Site Configuration | Sites** and select the primary site in the right-hand pane. Click on **Client Installation Settings** in the ribbon and select **Software Update-Based Client Installation**. Check the checkbox and click on **OK**.

How it works...

The GPO assigns the active SUP to clients linked to it. The next time they attempt to check for updates, they'll talk to the active SUP and not Microsoft. Step 12 publishes the current client files to the SUP for computers to use for installation. If the client is uninstalled by the user, this policy will force the client to be reinstalled just as if it were a missing patch.

There's more...

The most common method used in the past has been the client push installation. While this method might be easier for domain admins, it has some serious drawbacks. First, CM has to employ some method of discovery to find computers and put them into its database. Then the admin must have access to an account which has local admin access to all computers getting the client. Finally, there are potential security, networking, and name resolution issues to overcome as this installation method is the one time ever the CM server reaches out to the client, rather than pulled from the computer.

Discovering computers

We've already described how to get computers into CM by way of AD discovery in the *Configuring discovery* recipe in `Chapter 6`, *Managing Sites*. After discovery has been run, create a collection of computers you wish to install the client on. Because there is no inventory on such systems, the collection must be based on what little CM knows from discovery such as name, operating system, or subnet. It's advised to pilot to a small collection first because clean-up efforts from mistakes can be costly.

Configuring security

Obtain an account that has local admin rights on all the machines in the collection. Alternatively, you can grant the machine account of the primary site server to a local admin. You can use **Group Policy Preferences** in the GPMC to add this account to a GPO linked to an OU with the targeted computers.

1. If the firewall has been enabled on clients, it will have to be opened for File and Printer Sharing for domain locations. This can be done via GPO if using Windows native firewall or using the appropriate third-party tools for their product.
2. Admin shares must also be enabled on computers, so if that has been disabled in the past, it will have to be re-enabled.
3. Navigate to **Administration** | **Site Configuration** | **Sites** in the left-hand pane and select the primary site in the right-hand pane (this will have to be done for each primary where you want client push to work).
4. Click on **Client Installation Settings** in the ribbon and select **Client Push Installation**. Click on the **Accounts** tab then click on the yellow star burst to enter a **New Account**. Click on **Browse** to locate the account you previously created that is a local administrator on computers the client will be pushed to. Click on **Verify** and enter a name of a share where you have the CM client files staged. If clicking on **Test connection** fails, you will have to grant your client push account read permissions. Click on **OK**.
5. Click on the **Installation Properties** tab and enter `SMSSITECODE=ABC`, where `ABC` is the site code of the primary site. You may also enter other properties here such as `SMSMP` or `SMSCACHESIZE`. Click on **OK**.

Pushing the client to a collection

Navigate to the collection you prepared under `Discovering Computers`, right-click on the collection and select **Install Client**. Click on **Next**.

Under **Installation Options**, select any of the three boxes that make sense. Note that the second box forces a reinstallation of the client. Click on **Next** twice and then on **Close** to complete the wizard.

You can monitor the process live by viewing the log on the server (`logs\ccm.log`). Failed push records can be found in `inboxes\ccrretry.box`. (They can be opened with `Notepad`.)

Pushing the client to all computers automatically

After you've pushed successfully to collections and verified that all is well, you may optionally push to any computers CM ever discovers.

1. Navigate to **Administration** | **Site Configuration** | **Sites** in the left-hand pane and select the primary site in the right-hand pane (this will have to be done for each primary where you want client push to always push to newly discovered clients).
2. Click on **Client Installation Settings** in the ribbon and select **Client Push Installation**. From the **General** tab, check the checkbox to **Enable automatic site-wide client push installation**.
3. For **System types**, check any or all of the three checkboxes as desired. Only check the radio button for domain controllers if you intend to always push to them as well (this is rare).

See also

- How to Install Clients to Windows Computers in Configuration Manager: `https://msdn.microsoft.com/en-us/library/mt627891.aspx`
- Client Installation Properties which can be set in the installation properties tab: `https://technet.microsoft.com/en-us/library/mt489016.aspx`

Upgrading client agents

Similar to the latest Windows 10, Configuration Manager also gets frequent updates. These updates (or build) usually include a **CM client update**. This was the same back in CM12 when a new **Cumulative Update** (**CU**) was released, a new CM client version was also included. CM12 introduced a new feature called **Automatic Client Upgrade** to automatically upgrade all the CM clients to the latest version. Even though it was a great feature, many people considered that feature risky because it would deploy to all CM clients a new agent version without being really tested and where deploying the new agent manually like an application deployment.

To fill this gap, CM Current Branch introduced an improvement to the **Automatic Client Upgrade** by being able to deploy the new client version to a **pre-production collection**. Then if that pre-production deployment was successful, the administrator can decide to **promote** the client upgrade deployment to all the remaining production clients.

This two-step client upgrade deployment reduces the risk of deploying a new client version to a whole CM Site without being tested.

Getting ready

Create a new collection for pre-production client upgrade deployment and add some test computers to that collection. Then if you don't already have a new CM version available in the CM console, wait for a new build to be available under **Updates and Servicing**.

How to do it...

1. In the CM console, under **Administration** | **Cloud Services** | **Updates and Servicing**, select an available new CM version (for instance, **Configuration Manager 1602** if your site is running CM 1511) and client **Install Update Pack** in the ribbon menu.

2. In the **Configuration Manager Updates Wizard**, under **Client Update Options**, select **Validate in pre-production collection** and browse/select the pre-production collection we created previously:

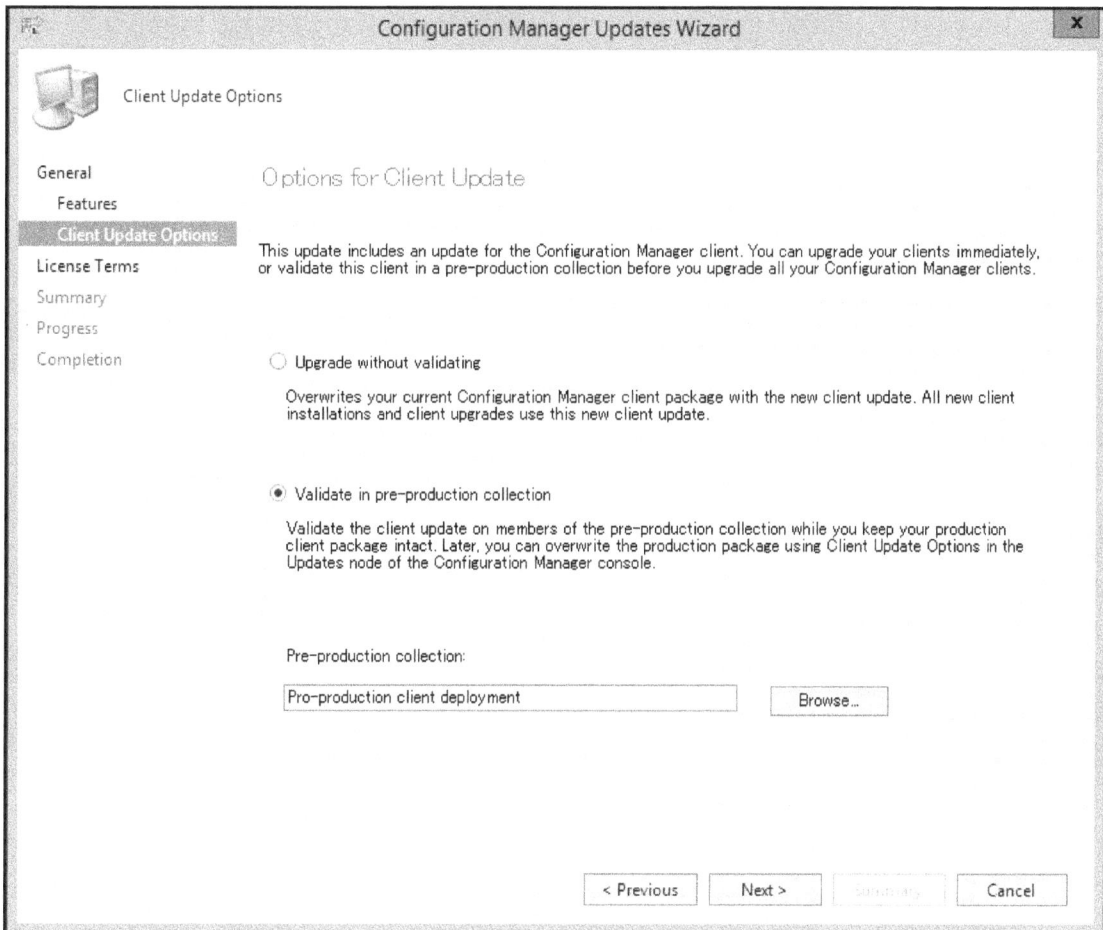

3. Complete the wizard and the installation of the CM version will begin.

> **TIP**
>
> When you deploy a client upgrade to a pre-production collection, computers in that collection will start installing the new client as soon as clients receive the policy.

How it works...

Once the CM update installation has finished, you should notice that the computers in the pre-production collection got upgraded too to the latest CM client agent version.

You can verify the CM client version by adding the **Client Version** column from the device list view (version 5.00.8355.1307 in the following screenshot).

Icon	Name	Client Type	Client	Site Code	Client Activity	Client Version
	SURFACEPRO4	Computer	Yes	P01	Active	5.00.8355.1307

Pro-production client deployment 1 items
Search

You can also verify the CM client version for production and pre-production under **Administration** | **Site Configuration** | **Sites** | **Hierarchy Settings** | **Client Upgrade**:

Hierarchy Settings Properties

General | Client Approval and Conflicting Records | Client Upgrade

Configure settings that control how clients automatically upgrade.

Production client version: 5.00.8355.1307
Last modified: 8/16/2016 12:49:26 PM

☑ Upgrade all clients in the hierarchy using production client

☐ Do not upgrade servers

Automatically upgrade clients within days: 7

Pre-production client version: 5.00.8355.1307
Last modified: 8/16/2016 12:49:15 PM

☐ Upgrade all clients in the pre-production collection automatically using pre-production client

Pre-production collection :

[   ] [Browse...]

> **TIP**
>
> When you have Automatic Client Upgrade enabled, each client adds a scheduled task called "**Configuration Manager Client Upgrade Task**". Computers will upgrade to the new client based on that scheduled task. Depending on the number of days (let's say 30 days) you mentioned in the autmatic client upgrade option, the "Next run time" of the task will be anywhere from 1 to 30 days out from the current date.

There's more…

Once you're satisfied with the pre-production deployment, you can decide to promote the new CM agent version to production. In that case, if you have enabled the **Upgrade all clients in the hierarchy using production client** option, all the clients in your CM site will automatically be upgraded to the latest CM agent that you already validated on the pre-production collection.

To promote the CM agent, follow these steps:

1. In the CM console, navigate to **Administration** | **Cloud Services** | **Updates and Servicing**, right-click the new CM version you just installed and select **Client Update Options.**

2. Select **I am ready to make pre-production client version available to production** and select **OK**.

If you go back to **Hierarchy Settings**, you can verify that the **Production client version** is the same as the **Pre-production client version**.

See also

- How to test client upgrades in pre-production collection in CM: `https://techne t.microsoft.com/en-us/library/mt612863.aspx`

Managing client health

Good news! CM manages client health for you by invoking `CcmEval.exe` via a scheduled task. By using a scheduled task, `CcmEval` has no dependency on a healthy CM client. Actually, there is one small dependency – `CcmEval` is configured automatically by the CM client, so the client installation has to be healthy at one point to configure the ccmeval cycle. Both `CcmEval` and SMS Agent Host (the service for CM client agent) perform checks against each other regularly, to ensure that both are configured properly. The client is routinely checked for issues which are reported back to CM, but the problems found are fixed on the fly as well!

If a client component or service fail to repair, that too gets reported back to CM so you can investigate as needed. We'll show how to make sure clients are healthy.

Getting ready

Have a running CM site with at least one assigned client.

How to do it...

Assume all clients are healthy because CM is more self-healing than ever! Seriously.

Trust but verify. OK, so we know you'll want to see for yourself that clients are healthy. Beyond just sending a test distribution (even simulated), the console is the first place to start looking.

1. In the CM admin console, navigate to **Monitoring | Client Status**. The right-hand pane shows a great overview of client health.
2. Under **Statistics**, you can **Browse** to any **Collection** to pinpoint results.
3. Under **Overall Client Status**, each group of states can be clicked to drill down and see each machine's state.

To familiarize you with the steps involved, we're going to break a client and watch `CcmEval.exe` fix it:

1. If you have not associated log files with the **Configuration Manager Trace Log Tool (Trace)**, do so now by finding it in the CM setup files (`SMSSETUP\TOOLS\CMTrace.exe`) and double-click on it. Click on **OK** to make the association.

> Optionally, to make things more readable in `Trace`, navigate to `File\Preferences` and remove `Thread` and `Component`.

2. From any working CM client, disable the **SMS Agent Host** service.
3. From Windows, navigate to the client's log folder (`%windir%\CCM\Logs`) and double-click on `CcmEval.log`.
4. When Trace opens `CcmEval.log`, leave it open, and navigate in Windows up one folder and find `CcmEval.exe`.
5. Grant `INTERACTIVE` full permissions to `CcmEval.exe`. Ignore the warning about changing permissions on system files.
6. Right-click on it and choose **Run as administrator**. Go back to watch the `CcmEval.log` window in Trace.

7. The evaluation kicks off and you can watch it testing various items (each test can be seen directly in `%windir%\ccm\CcmEval.xml`), as shown in this screenshot:

```
==========[ ccmeval started in process 2972 ]==========
Loading manifest file: C:\Windows\CCM\CcmEval.xml
Successfully loaded ccmeval manifest file.
Begin evaluating client health rules.
Successfully retrieved all client health checks.
Evaluating health check rule {4AB7D77D-3BB0-4EAB-BEFD-7C0F7DA10296} : Verify WMI service exists.
Evaluating health check rule {518C0699-03F8-4F38-85C4-4D319EAEFC05} : Verify/Remediate WMI service startup type.
Evaluating health check rule {7F4B6E15-2221-455B-9615-93C379E470D5} : Verify/Remediate WMI service status.
Evaluating health check rule {A81778B5-9A1E-4A52-9C6E-6939CEFAA118} : WMI Repository Integrity Test.
Evaluating health check rule {14E6774A-1795-4E09-B17D-B6F36A124205} : WMI Repository Read/Write Test.
Evaluating health check rule {5CC6C949-5001-4765-84B4-DD4FDC1E6940} : Verify BITS exists.
Evaluating health check rule {C6E29CF5-F9B2-450B-AE61-C4B256A75023} : Verify/Remediate BITS startup type.
Evaluating health check rule {CF4EFD8F-9A1E-4A89-BB35-7021D51767DB} : Verify/Remediate client and client prerequisites installation.
Evaluating health check rule {8883C683-04C8-4228-BB76-2EDD666BA781} : Verify SMS Agent Host service exists.
Evaluating health check rule {13F46523-5B82-417d-A363-A644E80CAD76} : Verify/Remediate SMS Agent Host service startup type.
Attempting to change service startup type for service 'CcmExec' to 'Automatic'.
Successfully changed service startup type for service 'CcmExec' to 'Automatic'.
Result: Remediation Succeeded, ResultCode: 0, ResultType: 0, ResultDetail:
Evaluating health check rule {70BECB51-44A1-4b46-8A23-6EA3D345B677} : Verify/Remediate SMS Agent Host service status.
Evaluating health check rule {C35E790D-4C05-40A8-BB46-A68578966D19} : WMI Event Sink Test.
```

8. Verify that the SMS Agent Host service has now been reset to **Automatic (Delayed Start)**. This was a manual test, but shows what the scheduled task does every day.

How it works...

By default a scheduled task runs on every CM client to check for health once a day. That task simply calls out `CcmEval.exe` from the client's installation folder to run various checks. Every step repaired or that has failed to repair is reported back to CM.

There's more...

The data sent back to CM can be viewed right in the console or via SRS reports. A great benefit of SRS is that any health report can be subscribed to, which can alert you to problems.

Viewing health in the console

You need to follow these steps for viewing health in the console:

1. From the CM admin console, navigate to **Monitoring | Client Status | Client Check** and in the right-hand pane click on **X client check passed** (where X is the count of systems passing a health check).

2. The console opens to **Assets and Compliance | Devices | Clients** that passed client check. If the list is too long to find the machine where you disabled the SMS Agent Host, enter the name of the system in the search pane and hit Enter.

3. Click on the computer in the right-hand pane and notice that under **Client Check Information**, **Remediation** is listed as **Successful**.

4. Click on the **Client Check Detail** tab at the bottom of the right pane to view the result of remediation steps taken.

Viewing health in SRS reports

For viewing health in SRS reports, you need to follow these steps:

1. In the CM console, navigate to **Monitoring | Reporting | Reports** and enter `client status` in the search pane, and then hit Enter.

2. Right-click on the **Client Remediation Summary** report and select **Run**.
    * For **Values**, select a collection containing the remediated computer.
    * For **Remediation Result**, select **Remediation Succeeded**.

3. Click on **OK**. Then click on **View Report**.

Viewing alerts in the console

Before you can view an alert, you have to set one up. Here is how to set one that will alert you when remediation is failing, which means CM can't fix something and you have to do so yourself:

1. In the CM console, navigate to **Assets and Compliance | Device Collections** and choose a collection for which you would like alerts to be set up on.

2. Right-click on that collection and click on the **Alerts** tab. Click on **Add**.

3. Check the checkbox for **Client remediation success falls before the threshold (%)**. Click on **OK**.

4. For **Raise alert if client remediation success rate is below**, enter 95. Click on **OK**.

5. The new alert will be shown under **Monitoring | Alerts** as **Low client remediation rate alert for collection (your collection)**. Hopefully, you will never see it change from **Never Triggered**.

Disabling client remediation

Occasionally, there are times when remediation won't be wanted. Perhaps a server team demands that you allow them to fix a client instead of `CcmEval.exe`. In such cases, you can disable the remediation feature (but still report on faulty clients).

To do so, use `regedit` to change the string value from **FALSE** to **TRUE** on the **NotifyOnly** key, as

`HKEY_LOCAL_MACHINE\SOFTWARE\Microsoft\CCM\CcmEval\NotifyOnly = True`.
Refer to the following screenshot:

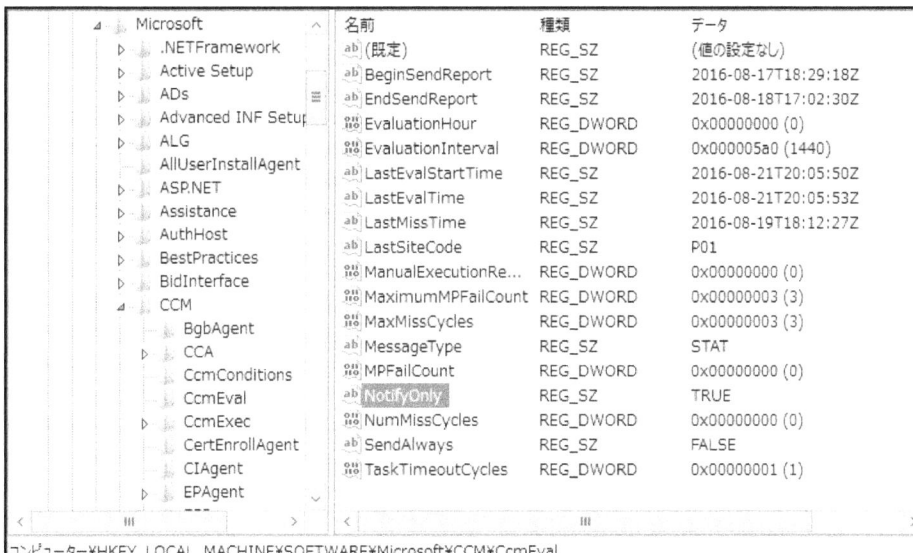

See also

- How to Configure Client Status in ConfigMgr: `https://technet.microsoft.com/en-us/library/mt627874.aspx`

Managing client settings

Client Settings in CM is a very flexible way to manage CM client settings. Indeed, CM offers **Default Client Settings** that are applied to all machines in a site but also provides **Custom Client Devices Settings** and **Custom Client User Settings** that can be targeted to specific collections for more granularity.

Deploying custom client settings to just one collection keeps network traffic down and the database size smaller. For example, if the sales department needs software inventory data on their `C:\Sales` folder, only their machines will look for it and send that data back, instead of the entire company.

We're going to show a couple examples of how custom settings can be used.

Getting ready

In the CM admin console, navigate to **Administration | Client Settings** and double-click on **Default Client Settings** in the right-hand pane.

Go over each of the 20 policies one by one, adjusting schedules, dates, Company Name, and so on, as needed that will be applied to all machines in the company. Click on **OK** to exit. From this point on, it will be far more common to create custom settings. As an example, let's create one now that disables Remote Tools for all servers.

How to do it...

1. From the CM admin console, navigate to **Administration | Client Settings** and click on **Create Custom Client Device Settings** in the ribbon.
2. For **Name** enter `Disable Remote Tools`.
3. For **Description** enter `This policy disables remote tools wherever it is deployed`.
4. For **Select the custom settings to be enforced on client devices**, click on **Remote Tools**. This causes a new option called **Remote Tools** to appear in the left-hand pane of the **Create Custom Client Device Settings** window; click on it.

5. Click on **Configure** in the right-hand pane and uncheck the **Enable Remote Control on client computers** checkbox (it should be disabled by default). Click on **OK** twice.

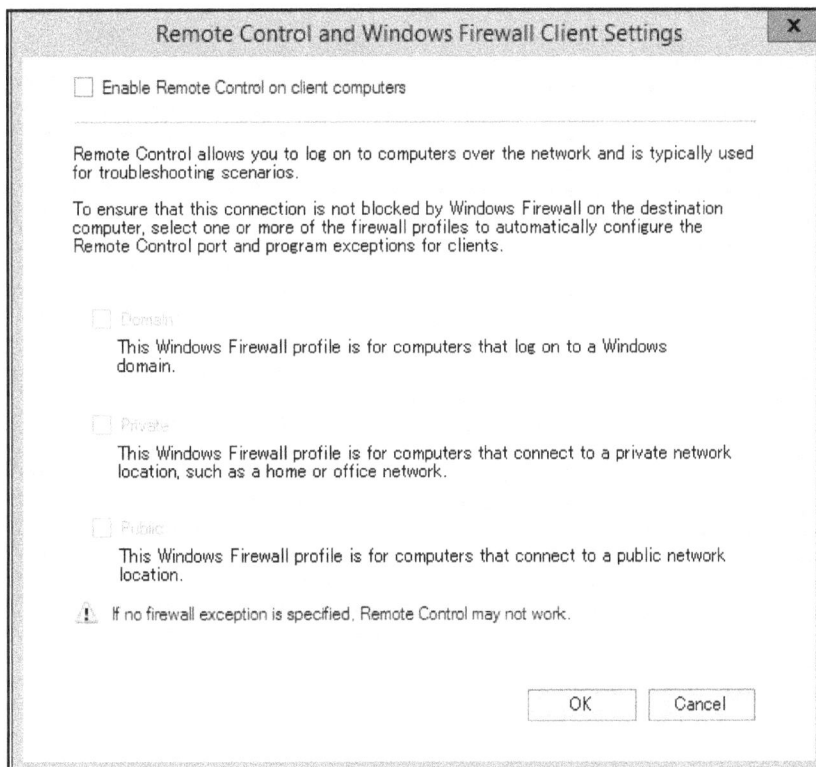

You have just created a policy that can be deployed as many times, to as many collections as you like. In this case, we want to target servers.

6. Right-click on the policy named **Disable Remote Tools** and select **Deploy**. Select **All Servers** then click on **OK**.

How it works...

The console will now show this policy is being deployed. If you target another collection, the count listed for **Deployments** will go up. Notice that this policy has a lower number than **Default Client Settings** which is **10,000**. The lower the number means that it has priority over the default.

If you were to later get a group who wanted remote tools on their servers, you would make a collection of their servers, create a new custom setting to enable it, target their servers, and then increment its priority to a lower number than the **Disable Remote Tools** policy.

There's more...

There are 20 custom device settings. Some are just on\off settings and others are so powerful that we have a dedicated chapter, Chapter 8, *Managing Inventory*. Let's also see some other useful settings available in the custom device settings.

Hiding all notifications

Let's say there is a line of business in your organization, which demands that their workstations never show CM notifications. A simple custom device setting can take care of their request.

1. From the CM admin console, navigate to **Administration | Client Settings** and click on **Create Custom Client Device Settings**.
2. For **Name** enter Hide All Notifications.
3. For **Description** enter CM popups must never appear.
4. For **Select the custom settings to be enforced on client devices**, check **Computer Agent**. This causes a new option called **Computer Agent** to appear in the left-side pane of the **Create Custom Client Device Settings** window; click on it.
5. Select **No** for **Show notifications for new deployments** in the right-side pane. Click on **General** in the left-side pane.
6. Check **Remote Tools** in the right-side pane. Click on **Remote Tools** in the left-side pane.
7. To change the settings, you first have to enable **Remote Tools**. Click on **Configure** in the right-hand pane and check the **Enable Remote Control on client computers** checkbox
8. Select **No** for **Show session notification icon on taskbar**. Select **No** for **Show session connection bar**, and select **No Sound** for **Play a sound on client**. Click on **OK**.

Deploy this new custom device setting to the line of business's workstation collection.

Deploying Endpoint Protection

Instead of using software distribution, a custom device setting can deploy **System Center Endpoint Protection** (**SCEP**). And keep it installed should someone remove it.

1. From the CM admin console, navigate to **Administration | Client Settings** and click on **Create Custom Client Device Settings**.
2. For **Name** enter `Install SCEP`.
3. For **Description** enter `Installs SCEP and Remove Existing AV`.
4. For **Select the custom settings to be enforced on client devices**, check **Endpoint Protection**. This causes a new option called **Endpoint Protection** to appear in the left pane of the **Create Custom Client Device Settings** window; click on it.
5. Select **Yes** for all options.

Deploy this policy to any and all collections where SCEP is to be installed. If you have previously set up Software Updates to sync definition files, clients will get the latest definitions upon installation.

> When you deploy SCEP by using this custom device setting, clients targeted by that policy will start installing the SCEP client. It's important to know that the SCEP client installation package is **already available** on every CM client in `C:\Windows\ccmsetup\SCEPInstall.exe`. When enabling SCEP using this policy, CM clients won't have to download anything except the latest definition from the SUP.

See also

- TechNet document on About Client Settings in Configuration Manager: `https://technet.microsoft.com/en-us/library/mt629384.aspx`

Enabling Device Health Attestation in Windows 10

Device Health Attestation (**DHA**) is a new Windows 10 feature that allows Windows 10 to do a health check to the cloud or to an on-premises server (requires Windows Server 2016) before gaining access to internal resources. It is a new health status that can be used as a rule in **Conditional Access** for Windows 10 devices.

The compliance policy using DHA status as a rule is only available for **Microsoft Intune** managed Windows 10 devices for now. If you are managing your Windows 10 devices through the CM client agent, DHA will only be used for **reporting**.

DHA lets the administrator ensure that client computers have the following trustworthy BIOS, TPM (1.2 or 2.0), and boot software configurations enabled:

- **Early launch anti-malware**: Early launch anti-malware (ELAM) protects your computer when it starts up and before third-party drivers initialize.
- **BitLocker**: Windows BitLocker Drive Encryption is the software that lets you encrypt all data stored on the Windows operating system volume.
- **Secure Boot**: Secure Boot is a security standard developed by members of the PC industry to help make sure that your PC boots using only software that is trusted by the PC manufacturer.
- **Code Integrity**: Code Integrity is a feature that improves the security of the operating system by validating the integrity of a driver or system file each time it is loaded into memory.

A Windows 10 device must be compliant to all of the preceding configurations to be reported as healthy by the Health Attestation Service.

Getting ready

To test **Device Health Attestation**, you need to prepare a device that has a **Trusted Module Platforma** (**TPM**) provisioned in a firmware (software) or discrete (hardware) format. For instance, Surface 3 integrates a software TPM in the firmware, whereas Surface Pro 4 integrates a discrete TPM.

Once **DHA** has been enabled by a CM policy, we will be able to see DHA compliance reports in a form of a dashboard within the CM console.

Most of the time, a virtual machine won't support DHA. If your virtualization solution offers a **virtual TPM** to your virtual machine, then DHA will work. For instance, Hyper-V in **Windows 10 1511** offers the virtual TPM feature. This feature will also be available in Windows Server 2016 once it will be made available.

How to do it...

The first thing to do is enabling **Device Health Attestation** on Windows 10 devices using **Client Settings**:

- In the CM admin console, navigate to **Administration | Client Settings** and double-click on **Default Client Settings** in the right-hand pane
- Under **Computer Agent**, select **Yes** for **Enable communication with Health Attestation Service**
- Click on **OK** to close the configuration windows

Wait for the policy to apply to your Windows 10 devices.

CM server will also connect to the cloud (`has.spserv.microsoft.com:443`) to collect the DHA reports from the Windows 10 devices it manages. These DHA statuses are visible from the CM console under **Monitoring | Security | Health Attestation**, as shown in the following screenshot:

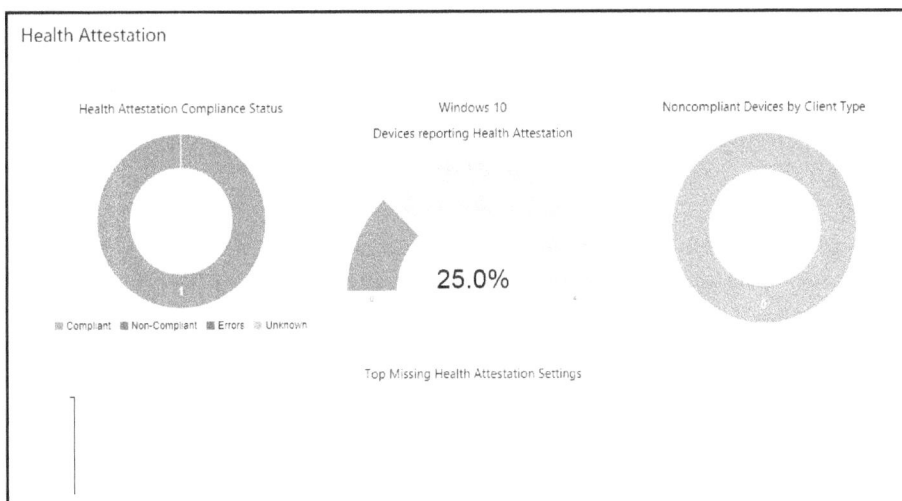

The information provided by this dashboard can be used to get an understanding of the impact of enabling conditional access based on the status reported by the **Health Attestation Service**.

How it works...

By default, Windows 10 devices will report DHA status to the cloud. In order to work, make sure to unblock communication between Configuration Manager client agent and `has.spserv.microsoft.com` (`port 443`) Health Attestation service. Later, when Windows Server 2016 will be available, it will be possible to make the CM client agent reports to an on-premises server instead of the cloud service.

If you manage your Windows 10 devices through Microsoft Intune, then it will automatically report to it.

There's more

The purpose of DHA is to use that compliance status in a compliance policy for **Conditional Access**. Again, be aware that the rule explained here can only be used in a compliance policy for **Windows 10 devices managed through MDM in an environment where Intune is integrated to CM**.

Let's create a compliance policy for Windows 10:

1. In the admin console, navigate to **Assets and Compliance | Compliance Settings | Compliance Policies** and click on **Create Compliance Policy** in the ribbon to launch the **Create Compliance Policy Wizard**.

2. Under **General**, enter `Company Compliance Policy for Windows 10` for **Name**. Select **Compliance rule for devices managed without Configuration Manager Clients** and select **Windows 8.1 and Windows 10**.

3. On the **Supported Platforms** page, select all versions of **Windows 10**.

4. Under **Rules**, you will get the different conditions that are available for Windows 10. Select **Reported as healthy by Health Attestation Service** and click on **OK**.

5. Continue the wizard to completion.

Deploy that new compliance policy to a collection containing Windows 10 devices. Starting now, only devices reporting as DHA compliant will get access to Office 365 services.

See also

- About Health Attestation in Windows 10 `https://technet.microsoft.com/itp ro/windows/keep-secure/protect-high-value-assets-by-controlling-the-health-of-windows-10-based-devices`
- Health attestation for Configuration Manager `https://technet.microsoft.com /en-us/library/mt651779.aspx`

Monitoring client installation and activity

Let's spend a little time talking about client installation, and new functionality with monitoring client activity. Also be sure to refer to the *Managing client health* recipe, for more information about the client health features in CM.

Getting ready

You should have a **Fallback Status Point** (**FSP**) enabled, and your client installation should specify the FSP, regardless of installation type (client push, software distribution, and so on). You should also have a **Reporting Services Point** (**RSP**).

How to do it…

1. From the CM admin console, navigate to **Monitoring** | **Reporting** | **Reports** | **Site – Client Information**, as shown in the following screenshot:

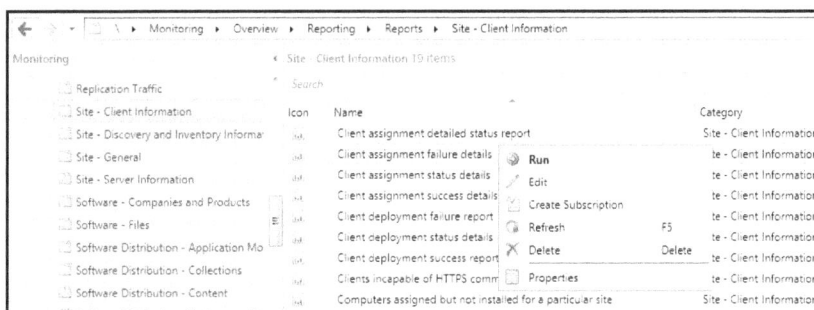

2. Run some of the following reports:
  - **Client assignment failure details**: Clients are unable to complete site assignment. Verify (using `hman.log`) that the site server is successfully publishing to Active Directory. Also, you can specify a **Management Point** (**SMSMP**) command line on the installation properties using the `SMSMP=servername.myfqdn.com` command line.
  - **Client deployment failure report**: Multiple issues can be included with this report – take a look at the **Description Parameter** field for additional information. For WMI and "unable to compile the MOF" issues, consider repairing WMI. For prerequisite installation issues, attempt to install the prerequisite component manually to view the error information.
  - **Problem details reported to the fallback status point for a specified collection**: Unfortunately, the error codes reported on this report are quite cryptic. Take some time to export the report, group similar error codes, and begin troubleshooting!

How it works...

Client installation can occur using several methods, but troubleshooting is basically the same. If you begin with client push installation, you will want to first look at `ccm.log` on the site server, to verify that the site server can copy installation files to the client, and initiate the installation.

Once the installation begins on the client, sasxgfxz `%windir%\ccmsetup\Logs` for all setup-specific logs. Here's a very brief description of the logs that may be found in this directory:

- `ccmsetup.log`: This is the installation log for `ccmsetup.exe`, which managed the client installation. This log will show you the complete installation command line, and provide details on additional required software installations (such as Microsoft Silverlight and Microsoft Policy Platform Setup).
- `client.msi.log`: This is the log for the actual CM client install. CCMsetup launches `client.msi` (never run `client.msi` directly). When troubleshooting client installation issues, search this log file for the phrase `return value 3`. This is a common Windows Installer phrase that occurs after an error is encountered.
- `dotNetFx4_Client_Setup.log`: This is the installation log for **.NET Framework 4.0 Client Installation** (if at least version 3.0 is not already installed). You probably won't see this log on most systems.

- `MicrosoftPolicyPlatformSetup.msi.log`: This is the installation log for **Policy Platform.**
- `WindowsFirewallConfigurationProvider.log`: This is the installation log for Firewall configuration provider.
- `ccmsetup-ccmeval.log`: This log is used as part of the daily client health evaluation. So it is normal to see it updated every day. Review this log to see the specific checks made for client installation and prerequisite information on a daily basis.

Not all logs will appear in the `%windir%\ccmsetup\Logs` directory, as many clients will already have some of the required prerequisites installed.

There's more...

View additional client health check SRS reports in the `Client Status` folder to review client status and activity.

- **Clients with Failed Client Check Details**: This detailed report groups failed checks by the type of check that failed, which allows you to easily focus on specific parts of the installation process to troubleshoot.
- **Inactive Clients Details**: This report displays the last time the client checked in, the last time the device password was updated, as well as the last client health check time and result.

By default, client activity is based on a combination of client policy requests, heartbeat discovery, hardware, and software inventory (if enabled), and status messages. **Seven days** is the magic number. You can modify those settings by highlighting the **Client Status** node under **Monitoring**, and then select **Client Status Settings** from the ribbon. Depending on how frequent your devices are offline, you may want to consider increasing the default setting of 7 to an acceptable number for your environment.

See also

- The *Managing client health* recipe for more information.

Making use of user-centric improvements

The **user-centric** model introduced in CM12 enables you to target users and devices better than ever. Note that it is still perfectly acceptable to deploy to systems (such as software updates, for example), but in a world where users work with several devices, user-centric model became even more important by offering software to users through Software Center or a web catalog instead of targeting only a specific device.

If you are currently using CM12, you might think "sounds like there's nothing new about that user-centric model". I won't tell you that everything has changed but you will be happy to hear that the user experience has been greatly improved in CM Current Branch. For instance, thanks to the new **Software Center** (SC), device targeted and user targeted applications both appear in the same SC. In CM12 in comparison, only device targeted applications appeared in SC; user targeted ones were only visible on the web application catalog. Because of this, two different portals were given to users and it became confusing.

In this section, we will discuss opportunities in CM to improve the end user experience. This recipe will describe how to be more efficient when deploying software to devices and/or users.

Getting ready

Prior to a required deployment, take advantage of the **simulate deployment** action to validate that **deployment types** work as expected.

How to do it...

The primary focus of this recipe is to create smarter application installations by leveraging the new application model to deploy the software. Here are the primary application model features that will improve your end user experience:

- Create precise deployment types.
- Use one application and multiple deployment types to deliver the right software to the right system. Carefully think of the multiple deployment types you may need (such as based on architecture, organizational unit, Active Directory site, or custom global conditions. Give the first priority to the most popular deployment type, to reduce evaluation times for installation and validation.

- Leverage the **Uninstall program** option to enable nonadmin users to uninstall nonmandatory applications through the **Software Center**.
- Leverage dependencies to ensure the required applications exist on a device prior to the application installation.
- Leverage supersedence to update or replace an installation.
- Populate the **Application Catalog** tab to provide the end user with as much information as possible.

How it works...

Deployment types allow you to be more generic on the collection level. For example, let's say you want to deploy 7-Zip to only users in the AcmeAustin **Active Directory** (**AD**) site. In CM07, you would create a collection of all systems in the AcmeAustin AD site and target the application to the new collection. In CM, simply add a **requirement** rule on the deployment type to require the system be in the AcmeAustin AD site, and then deploy to your All Systems or some other simple subset collection for the applications.

When the deployment arrives at the system, it will be evaluated to determine if the application is applicable to the system, and then make the software available or perform a required installation as defined.

The application model allows us to target a large number of systems, even if only a small number of systems are actually applicable. We can also deploy this application to a user or user group, and specify to install only if the device is associated to the end user of a primary machine.

There's more...

As you can see, **deployment types** give us the ability to easily target users and devices, and know with certainty that the installation will only proceed if the requirements are met.

Associating users to devices

Right-click on **User Collections** and select **Import User Device Affinity** to import a list of computer associations to users. You can also right-click on a device and select **Edit Primary Users** to modify primary users for one device.

Enable the new Software Center

To enable the new Software Center for all CM clients, we need to configure it in **Client Settings**:

- In the CM admin console, navigate to **Administration | Client Settings** and double-click on **Default Client Settings** in the right-hand pane
- Under **Computer Agent**, select **Yes** for **Use new Software Center**
- Click on **OK** to close the configuration windows

Before enabling the new Software Center, a user will have to access **Software Center** for applications deployed to his device and the web **Application Catalog** for applications deployed to users:

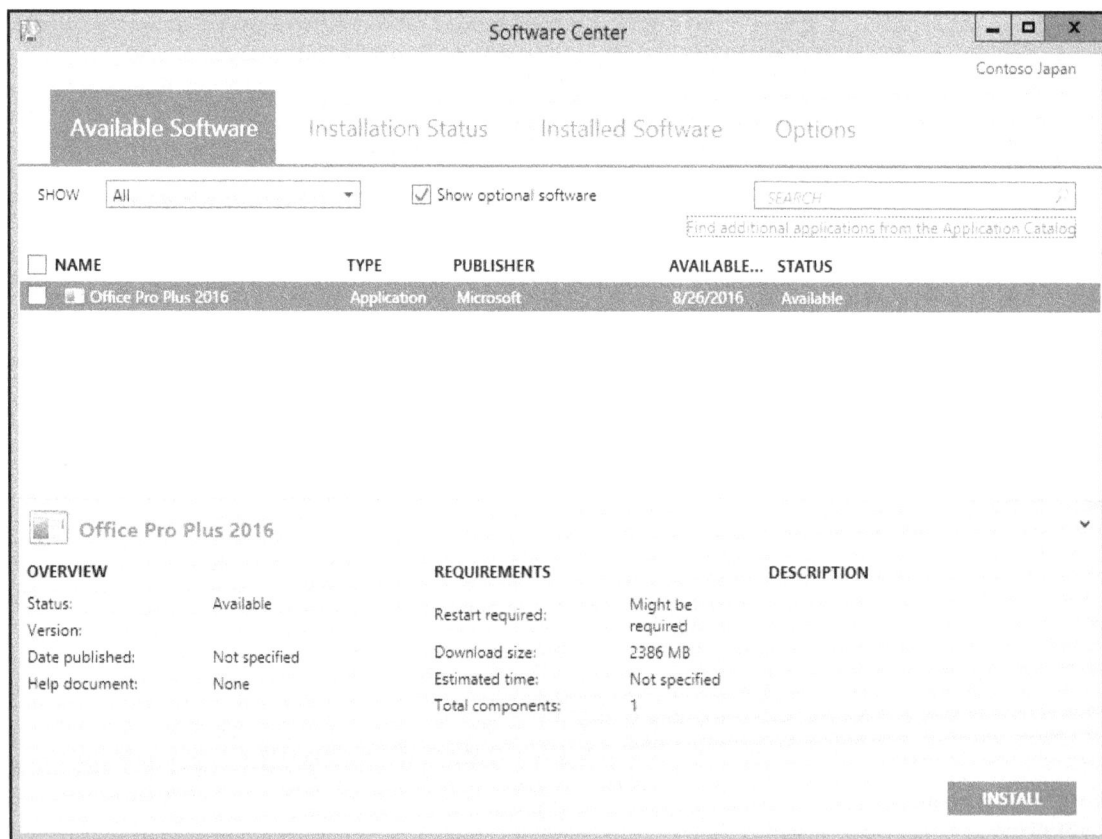

By clicking on **Find additional applications from the Application Catalog**, you can access the portal where user targeted applications are displayed:

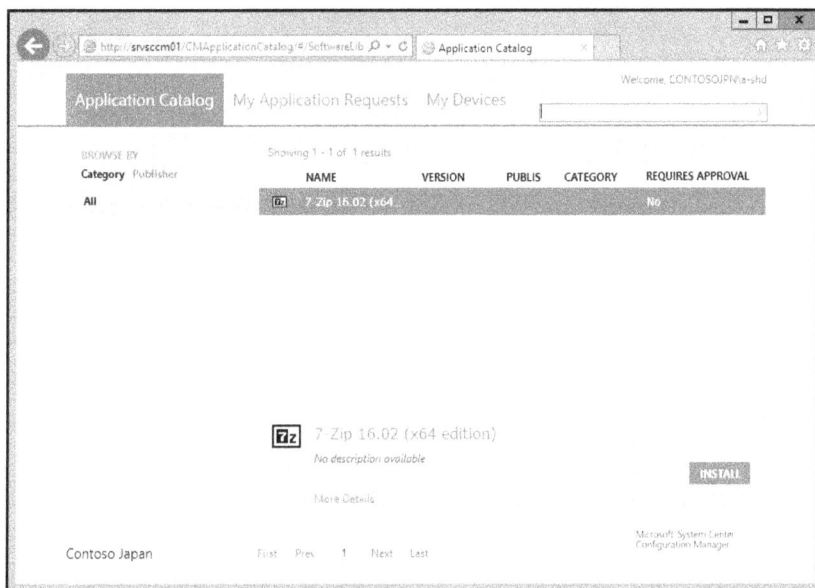

In comparison, the new **Software Center** offers both type of application deployments in the same portal:

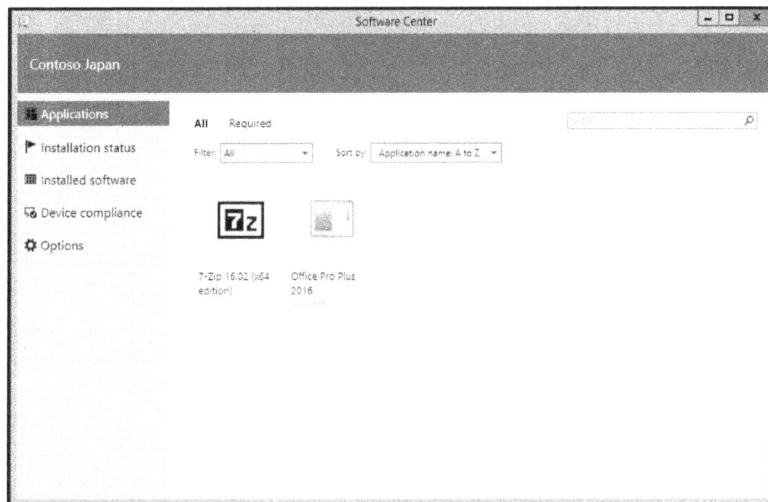

Since the Application Catalog is not needed anymore with the new Software Center, a Silverlight-enabled browser is no longer required.

See also

- Refer to the following link for more information on TechNet about User Device Affinity: `https://technet.microsoft.com/en-us/library/mt629338.aspx`
- Also, refer to the OS Deployment blog on TechNet for deployment tips with User Device affinity (article on CM12 but still valid in CM CB): `http://blogs.technet.com/b/inside_osd/archive/2011/06/20/configuration-manager-2012-user-device-affinity-and-os-deployment.aspx`

Configuring power management

Power management is a very popular (and necessary) topic in our world today. Use CM to manage and monitor power on client systems. Power management in CM gives you the ability to configure the power plans for peak and nonpeak hours, as well as specify a daily wakeup for desktop computers.

Check with your power company about discounts for power management. Some power companies provide a credit if you are able to show that you are actively managing power on your computers.

Getting ready

Power Management settings are enforced on a collection. Be sure to create a test collection of representative computer models to begin testing. Ensure that **Client Settings** for the **Power Management** setting is configured to **Allow power management of devices**. Our first example will be how to specify peak and nonpeak plans, and enable wakeup time for a selected collection.

How to do it...

1. From the CM admin console, navigate to **Assets and Compliance | Overview | Device Collections** and click on the desired collection.

2. Click on **Properties** from the ribbon and select the **Power Management** tab:

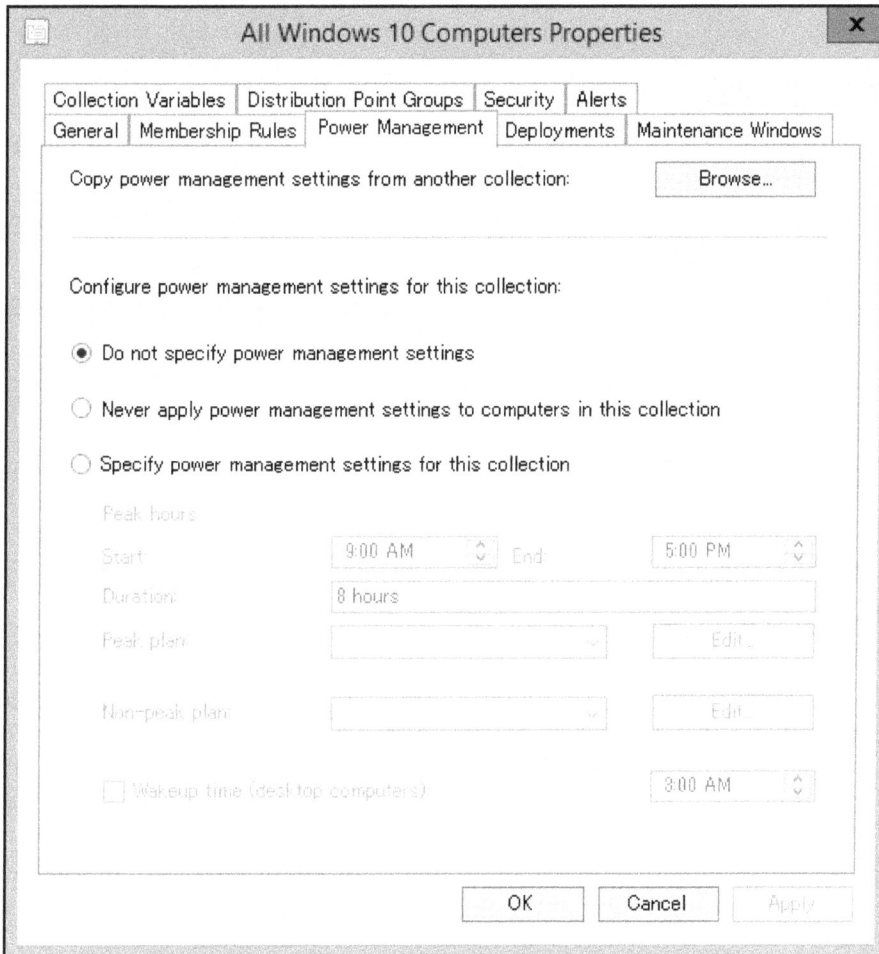

3. Select **Specify power management settings for this collection**, and specify the start and end times for **Peak hours**. Also, specify a preconfigured plan for both peak and nonpeak, or select**Customized Peak (ConfigMgr)** option and then configure the appropriate settings.

4. Enable the checkbox to wake up desktop computers daily at a specified time.

5. Click on **OK** to close the collection properties page.

How it works...

The CM client receives the power management settings as policy from the **Management Point** (**MP**), and configures the native Windows power management settings on targeted clients. The Wake Timer will also be configured on desktop clients, if configured. Review `Pwrmgmt.log` on client systems for more information.

> Power management reporting information relies on hardware inventory.

As you know, any given device will likely be a member of multiple collections, which means that multiple power configurations may be applied to a given device. As such, it's important to understand the available settings in more detail. The **Power Management** tab has three types of configurations:

- **Do not specify power management settings**: This is the default configuration – no power settings are applied to this collection.
- **Never apply power management settings to computers in this collection**: Use this option to ensure that no systems in this collection will receive power management settings from CM. This setting takes precedence over all other configurations, regardless of any other collection in which the system is a member.
- **Specify power management settings for this collection**: As described in the example, use this setting to configure power management for the collection.

When you specify a **Wakeup time** for a given collection, all desktop systems will wake up from sleep or hibernation at the specified time each day, and remain on for at least ten minutes, and then the current power plan will be followed. The wakeup time is randomized and computers will be woken over a one hour period from the specified wakeup time.

If a system is part of more than one collection with **Power Management** settings enabled, the following apply:

- **Power plan**: Here, the least restrictive power management settings are used
- **Wakeup time**: Here, the time closest to midnight is used

The power plan name chosen (or created custom) for a collection will appear in the **Power Options** properties in the **Control Panel**. For example, if you select a peak plan of **Balanced (ConfigMgr)**, the name of the power plan in the **Control Panel** will appear as **Balanced (ConfigMgr)**.

Power management settings only apply to Windows computer systems (not mobile devices.)

There's more...

Refer to the following sections for additional configuration information.

Copying power management settings from another computer

From the **Power Management** tab, you can browse to another device collection to import the Power Management settings to the current collection.

Enabling users to opt out of power management

In CM, you can enable an additional power management setting under **Client Settings** (Refer to the *Managing client settings* recipe discussed earlier in this chapter) to allow a user to opt out power management for the desired system. Once the client setting has been applied to a collection to allow the user launch **Software Center** from the device, under **Options**, expand **Power management**. Enable the **Do not apply power settings from my IT department to this computer** checkbox:

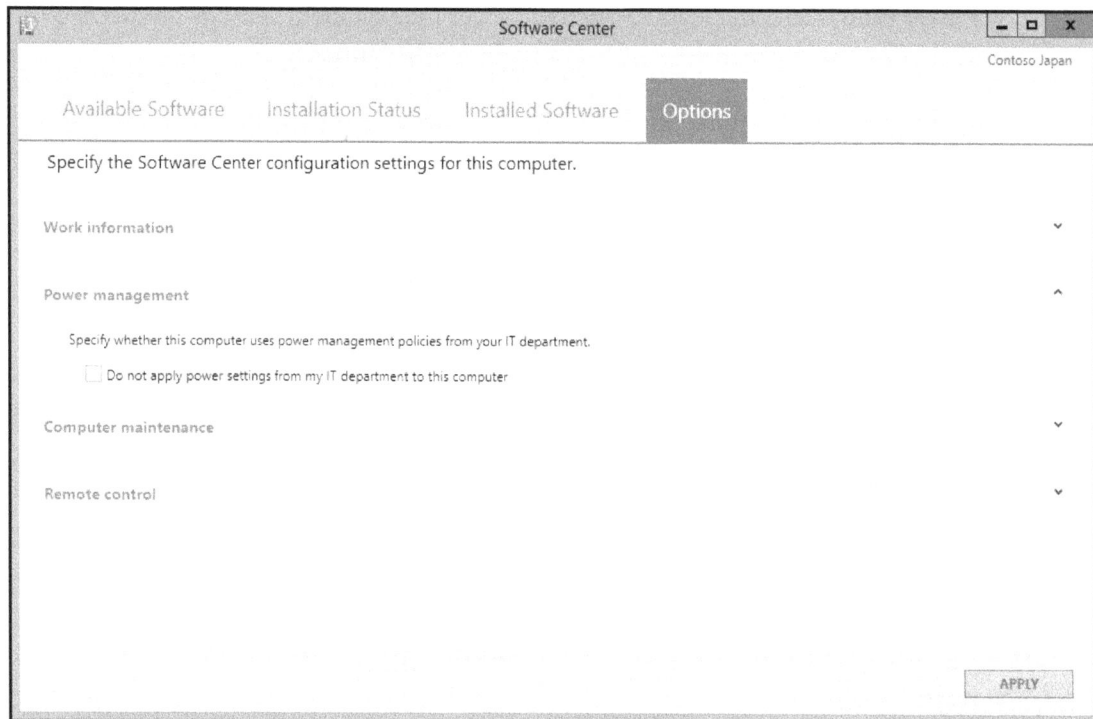

Creating an "always on" collection

Normally when we think of power management, we think of reducing power consumption. Hopefully that is the majority of any power management that you do. However, you may also have critical systems that must always remain powered on. You can create custom power plans, and peak and nonpeak hours to ensure targeted systems remain powered on.

Configure wakeup time, but no other settings

To only configure the wakeup time, create a custom peak and nonpeak power plan and disable all options except **Enable Windows wake up timer for desktop computers**.

Monitoring Power Management with Reporting

Reporting will be your friend – CM ships with nearly 20 reports dedicated to power management that allow you to compute energy cost, CO_2 emissions, power capabilities of systems, **insomnia** (systems that can't go to sleep, and processes that prevent sleep), and more. You can also run reports to identify computers with multiple power plans.

See also

- Before you enable Power Management, consider a monitoring-only phase to get a good look at the current power usage.
- Refer to the Microsoft TechNet documentation for Power Management with CM at `https://technet.microsoft.com/en-us/library/mt629343.aspx`.

8
Managing Inventory

In this chapter, we will cover the following recipes:

- Managing hardware inventory
- Managing software inventory
- Managing software metering
- Monitoring inventory data flow
- Integrating Asset Intelligence

Introduction

Inventory is central to most of what CM can do. It's needed for asset reports, targeting deployments, compliance, and more. How inventory is managed can affect workstation performance, network traffic, the overall size of the database, and more. Because of this, we're dedicating an entire chapter to the subject.

Managing hardware inventory

Most CM admins soon learn that hardware inventory is actually mostly made up of non-hardware related items. It probably should be called **WMI** inventory instead because data residing in WMI comes back to CM via the hardware inventory.

CM also offers the ability to target collections with distinct inventory requests instead of the entire site (and now hierarchy) at one time. Additionally, the old `sms_def.mof` has been replaced with a new UI, which we will use to gather some specific data off machines.

We will start with clearing off unneeded default inventory items, and then selectively targeting inventory to show you how to keep unneeded items from bloating your database. Then we'll show how to look for items that CM doesn't even know about.

Getting ready

Preferably before enabling inventory and adding lots of clients, you should remove unneeded inventory classes and class properties. If you've inherited a site from someone else, you should go right in and look to see that the former admin has cleaned out some of the defaults.

In the CM admin console, navigate to **Administration** | **Client Settings**. Select **Default Client Settings** in the right-hand pane and click on **Properties** in the ribbon. Select **Hardware Inventory** in the left-hand pane and click on **Set Classes** in the right-hand pane. The **Hardware Inventory Classes** window opens. Deselect every class you know you will never care about, such as CDROM Drive or PCMCIA Controller. Click on **OK** once when done, but leave the **Default Settings** window open.

You still do not need to enable hardware inventory yet. You can continue to refine the default settings as well as add new settings before ever flipping the switch.

> Use caution when cleaning older sites as it is possible that some class you are removing was used to create a collection where software was looking for that information. Additionally, try not to schedule inventory to run too often as it may generate unneeded traffic. Use the site maintenance task to delete aged inventory to as short an interval as you can live with. (Do you really need that data for three months?)

Next we'll show how to refine things at the next level by moving some inventory items out of the default settings and into new or existing custom agent settings.

How to do it...

1. While still in the **Default Settings** window with **Hardware Inventory** selected in the left-hand pane, click on **Set Classes** in the right-hand pane. Under **Disk Drives (Win32_DiskDrive)** deselect the four SCSI class properties. We will assume that this information is useful to you only for servers.
2. Under **Services (Win32_Service)** uncheck the entire class (again, we'll assume this is only vital for servers). Click on **OK** twice to return to the console.

3. If you do not have a custom client device setting for servers yet (perhaps you created it the earlier `Chapter 4`, *Managing Compliance Settings*), create one right away by clicking on **Create Custom Client Device Settings** and name it `Server Settings`. Deploy this policy to a collection of servers, if it isn't already (or feel free to pilot to a collection with just one server first if you wish).

4. Double-click on the **Server settings** policy to edit it. Select **Hardware Inventory** in the left-hand pane and **Set Classes** in the right-hand pane.

5. Under **Disk Drives (Win32_DiskDrive)**, select the four SCSI class properties.

6. Under **Services (Win32_Service)** check the following class properties: **Name**, **Display Name**, **Path Name**, **Service Type**, **Start Mode**, **Start Name**, and **Status**. Click on **OK** twice to return to the console:

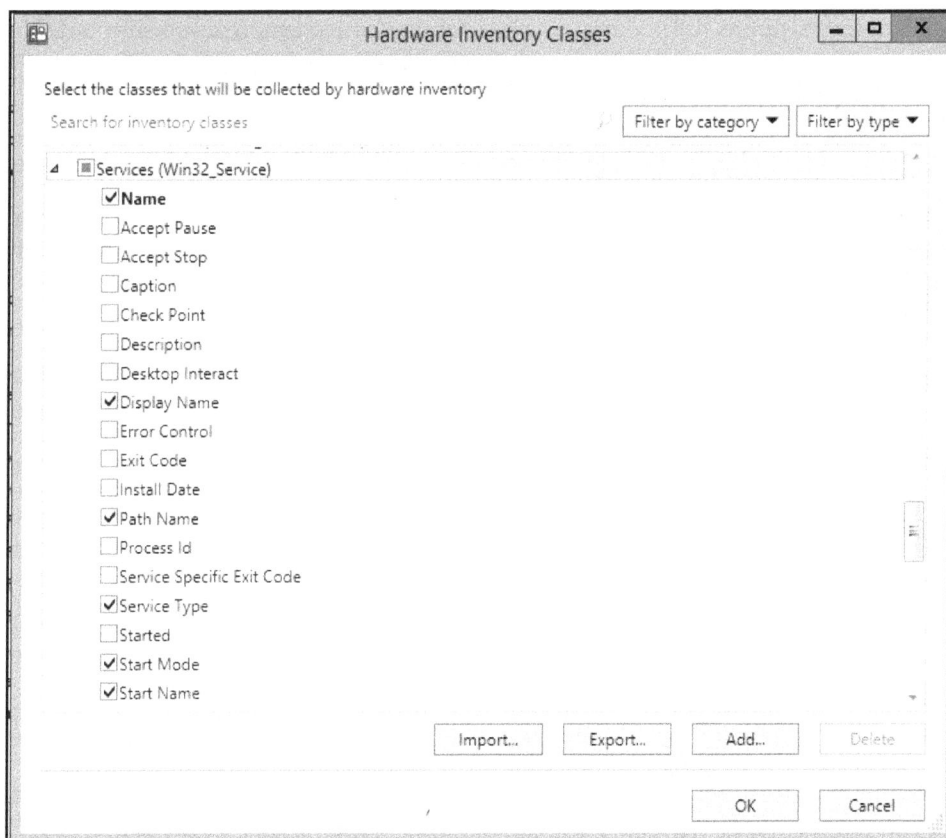

How it works...

What you've just done is to prevent workstations from returning data to inventory about the services they run or any SCSI disk drive data. The services data adds considerable bloat to your database that eats up drive space and prolongs maintenance tasks. Because only servers will now return this inventory, bloat is kept to a minimum. You should be able to consider many more classes which can be disabled site-wide through the **Default Client Settings**, but enabled in new **Custom Client Device Settings**.

There's more...

Selecting inventory items you need in the **Hardware Inventory Classes** window is obvious enough. But what happens if the data you are looking for isn't there to be selected with a check?

Extending hardware inventory

You've been charged with finding any workstations still using fans instead of heat pipes. Because this class doesn't exist, you must tell CM how to get it. This has to be done on the default settings level, even if you intend to target certain machines only via a custom setting. To do this perform the following steps:

1. In the CM admin console, navigate to **Administration** | **Client Settings**. Select **Default Client Settings** in the right-hand pane and click on **Properties** in the ribbon. Select **Hardware Inventory** in the left-hand pane and then click on **Set Classes** in the right-hand pane.

2. Click on **Add** in the **Hardware Inventory Classes** window. Click on **Connect**, check the **Recursive** checkbox, and then click on **Connect**. In the **Inventory classes** textbox, type `fan`, but be careful not to hit Enter. Select **Win32_Fan** and click on **OK**.

> Note that if **Win32_Fan** is already there, you can choose another class where **Exists** equals **No** for the purposes of this exercise.

3. Deselect the **Fan (Win32_Fan)** class (as we will wish to target only workstations with this instead of the entire hierarchy). Click on **OK** twice.

4. If you do not have a custom client device setting for workstations yet (perhaps you created one in `Chapter 4`, *Managing Compliance Settings*), create one by clicking on **Create Custom Client Device Settings** and name it `Workstation Settings`. Deploy this policy to a collection of workstations if it isn't already.

5. Double-click on the **Workstation settings policy** to edit it. Select **Hardware Inventory** in the left-hand pane and then select **Set Classes** in the right-hand pane.

6. Under **Fan (Win32_Fan)** select the following class properties: **DeviceID**, **Availability**, and **Status**. Click on **OK** twice.

If the workstation policy isn't deployed to a collection of workstations yet, do so now (right-click and deploy). Allow clients the time to pick up the new policy and report it back according to their schedule.

You can test a single machine if you don't want to wait by forcing a machine policy refresh cycle in the control panel applet of the test machine. Wait a minute and then force a hardware inventory. Within a few minutes, the site server should have the data and it should be viewable in **Resource Explorer** (assuming your test client has a fan).

Using RegKeytoMof

At the time of this writing, CM's hardware inventory UI can only browse to WMI, but it still cannot browse to registry keys like Compliance Settings can. While we wait for Microsoft to fill this gap, there is a great utility called RegKeytoMof, which is available free of charge at `https://gallery.technet.microsoft.com/RegKeyToMof-28e84c28`.

> Note that because Compliance Settings does have a registry browser, it makes sense to extend hardware inventory only when you also need to collect all the possible values of a key. If all you need is to verify whether a key is missing or similar, you can probably create a configuration item for it instead and keep your database lean.

Let's say that your company has a registry key, which shows the build version of your image in `HKLM\SOFTWARE\MyCompany`. You want to retrieve this company-specific data and get that version for all machines (not a good fit for Compliance Settings).

Before proceeding, use the**RegistryEditor** to create the **MyCompany** key. Select it and create a new **DWORD** value named **Build**. Modify **Build** to give it a value of **4**. The following screenshot shows **Registry Editor**:

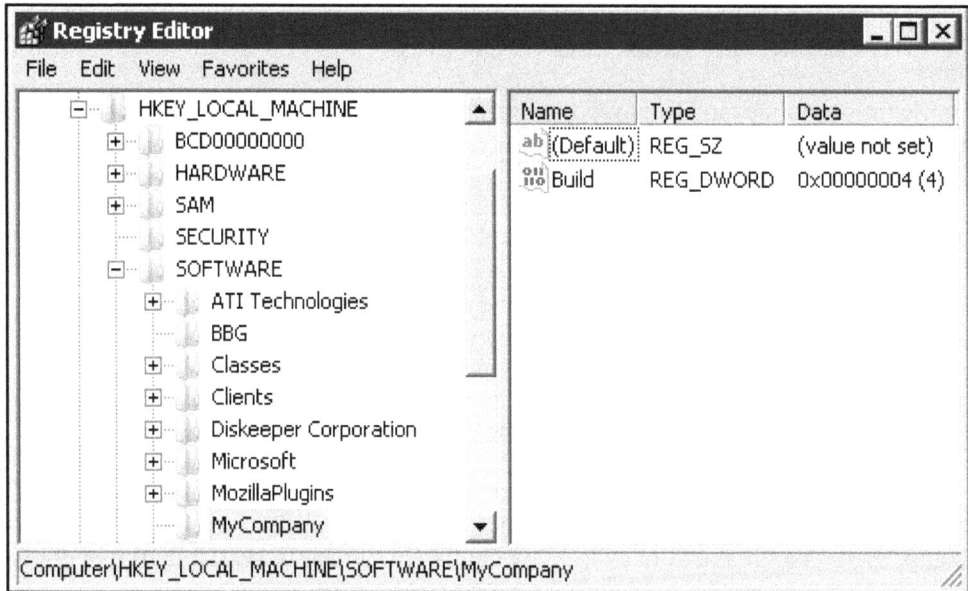

We'll use `RegKeytoMof` to import this key by performing the following steps:

1. From the same computer, open **RegKeytoMof**. In the left-hand pane, expand **SOFTWARE** and select **MyCompany** but unselect both checks in the right panel.

2. In the bottom pane, select the **ConfMgr12** tab (it will also work for **CM Current Branch**) and copy all the contents of the **configuration.mof** tab. Paste the contents into the `configuration.mof` file on the server (`inboxes\clifiles.src\hinv`) in the `Added extensions` section. Monitor `logs\dataldr.log` for any possible errors:

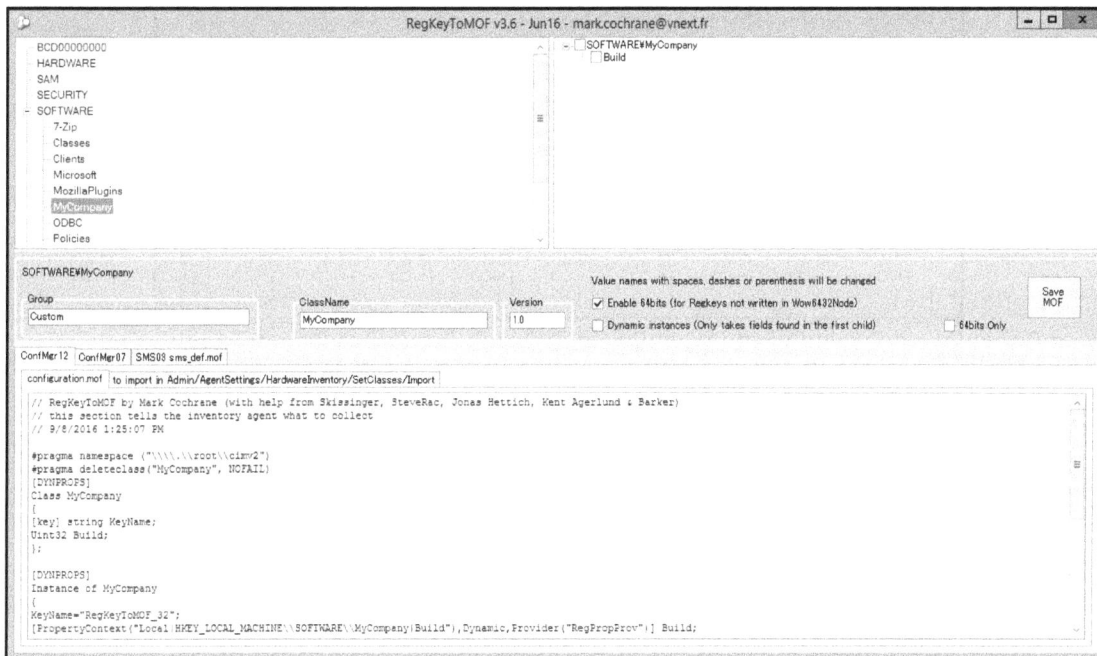

3. In the bottom pane of **RegKeytoMof**, select the tabnamed **to import in Admin/AgentSettings/HardwareInventory/SetClasses/Import**. Select all the text in it and copy it. Save it to a file called `MyCompany.mof`.

4. Return to the CM console and double-click on the **Default Client Settings** policy to edit it. Select **Hardware Inventory** in the left-hand pane and then select **Set Classes** in the right-hand pane.

5. Click on **Import** and browse to the `MyCompany.mof` file. You should see a green icon stating that the **MyCompany** and **MyCompany64** classes will be imported. Click on **Import**:

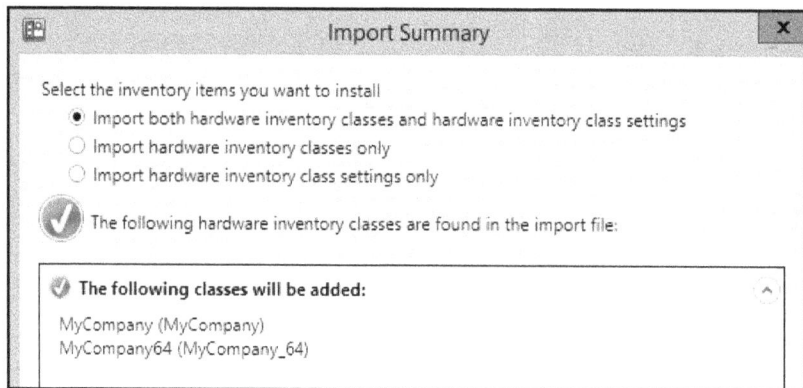

The new classes are checked, but could be unchecked here and checked on another custom settings policy, for example, a workstation policy to track builds there itself.

> If you have manually changed the `Configuration.mof` file to add custom inventory classes, these changes will be overwritten when you update to the 1602 release. To keep using custom classes after you update, you must add these to the *Added extensions* section of the `Configuration.mof` file after you update to 1602. A backup of your custom `Configuration.mof` can be found in: `<CM Install dir>\data\hinvarchive\`

Backing up your classes

CM offers in the UI a simple button to generate a backup file for you. Just open the **Default Client Settings** policy, navigate to **Hardware Inventory** | **Set Classes** and click on **Export**. This is also an excellent way to test first in the lab and easily bring the modifications to production with the **Import** button.

See also

- RegKeyToMof 3.6: `https://gallery.technet.microsoft.com/RegKeyToMof-28e84c28`
- RegKeyToMof 3.3 article on how to use the tool: `http://www.enhansoft.com/blog/how-to-use-regkeytomof`
- Microsoft TechNet: `https://technet.microsoft.com/en-us/library/mt488791.aspx`

Managing software inventory

If `Add/Remove Programs` and `Programs and Features` data is collected in hardware inventory, what is the use of software inventory? Software inventory is actually just a very old carry over from the early days of SMS. It scans the hard drive for executable files (installed or not) and reads their header data, and then sends all that data back to CM.

The key most CM admins have learned here is that you often are asked to find a file on computers that isn't always related to a program. For example, you may be asked to report all machines with `.mp3` files on them. Hardware inventory can't do that natively.

Because software inventory can slow a computer while scanning, admins like to run it as little as possible. They also like to tell CM exactly where to look for a file rather than scanning the entire drive, as that speeds up scanning.

Once upon a time, software inventory was enabled by default and scanned the entire hard drive for all `.exe` files. Now it's not even enabled by default.

Getting ready

First off, ask yourself if you really need software inventory run at all. If you ever need to, go hunt down specific files and know things about them (date, size, and so on), then perhaps you can save your hard drives a lot of wear and tear.

Secondly, even if you decide to enable it, ask yourself if you can enable it on just workstations or just certain workstations. If so, you can enable it with a custom policy targeting them instead of a hierarchy-wide policy from the `Default Client Settings` policy.

Assuming you do need to enable software inventory, we recommend that before even touching it, you open Microsoft OneNote (or Excel) and dedicate a tab to monitoring what you want inventoried.

You should track the following:

- The date you are adding something to the defaults
- The name of the file(s) added
- The date you can stop looking for the file(s), so you can remove the entry
- The contact of who requested the change

It's common for files to be added over time and they just build up to where nobody knows if anyone even needs the data anymore. Set yourself an Outlook reminder to check this list quarterly.

By the way, this list can be used for hardware inventory as well. Disabling classes you no longer need data on, helps to keep your database lean.

Now that we've got all that out of the way, let's create the two most commonly used rules and then show you how to add a couple of items.

How to do it...

We will scan the program files and folders for all executables to catch what hardware inventory might miss (for both x86 and x64 systems). Open OneNote and make an entry for .exe files and that two new rules have no ending date:

1. From the CM admin console, navigate to **Administration | Client Settings** and double-click on the **Default Client Settings** policy. Select **Software Inventory** in the left-hand pane. If **Enable software inventory on clients** is set to **False**, change it to **True**. (this is hierarchy wide, so it's possible to enable this inside the custom policies instead).
2. Do not adjust the schedule to anything sooner than the weekly default unless you know you have no choice. For most people, weekly is just fine.
3. Click on **Set Types** in the right-hand pane. The **Configure Client Setting** window opens.
4. Click on the yellow starburst and enter *.exe in the text pane.

5. Click on **Set** and check the radio button **Variable or path name**.

6. Type `%programfiles%` in the text pane. Click on **OK**.

7. Repeat step 6 for `%programfiles(x86)%`. Click on **OK** twice.

For those of you who have inherited the site, you may see many more entries listed. Try to track down who requested them and if they're still needed.

Leave the **Configure Client Setting** window open.

How it works...

You enable software inventory on the CAS (if you have one), which tells the primary about it, which in turn tells the MPs about it, and is then picked up by clients on their next refresh cycle. At that moment, they enable it, scan in the places for the files you asked, and then send that data back to the MP.

> All clients doing that at roughly the same time can cause lots of traffic as these are full-sized inventory files going up (delta afterwards). You might consider enabling inventory via Custom Client Settings to a collection whose membership you can increase over time, or perhaps just enable it late on a Friday.

There's more...

Let's add a couple of items to inventory and then look at the other features software inventory brings.

Adding new software inventory rules

Let's say your company has an internally developed application that leaves a file on the system drive in a folder called `MyCompany`. You need to report on any files in that folder that end with an `.img` extension.

Because this application runs company wide, we'll add it to the default client setting policy.

1. Open OneNote and make an entry for the `*.img` file, and that it will have no end date.

2. While still in the **Configure Client Setting** window, click on the yellow starburst and enter `*.img` into the text pane.

3. Click on **Set** and check the radio button **Variable or path name**.
4. Type %systemdrive%\MyCompany in the text pane and click on **OK** twice.

It's that easy. Just remember to review added entries quarterly and remove them if possible.

Creating a software inventory rule with a custom client policy

Perform the following steps to create a software inventory rule with a custom client policy:

1. Open OneNote and make an entry for a file called msi.dll, which will have no end date, will be used to track Windows Installer versions, and its location will be %windir%\system32.
2. Double-click on the **Workstation Settings** policy in the right-hand pane. If it isn't there, refer to the *Managing hardware inventory* recipe to create it.
3. Click on **General** in the left-hand pane, then **Software Inventory** in the right-hand pane.
4. Click on **Software Inventory** in the left-hand pane, then **Set Types** in the right-hand pane.
5. Click on the yellow starburst and enter msi.dll in the text pane.
6. Click on **Set** and check the radio button **Variable or path name**.
7. Type %windir%\system32 in the text pane and click on **OK** twice.

The take away here is that we're not scanning the entire drive, but a specific folder, which eases the load to the clients. And that we're as specific as possible on the title, this time giving the exact name of the file instead of asking for all .dll files.

Ignoring other options

Software inventory offers the option to collect files from computers. While it makes for a good joke about collecting MP3 files to build yourself a nice jukebox, it's really just a good way to beat on your network and kill drive space on your server. It's extremely rare for anyone to make use of this feature, so proceed with utmost caution.

Software inventory also attempts to let you try to normalize your data by making use of the **Set Names** button. The idea is to turn Macromedia into Adobe and so on. But the reality is that most people abandon the process in the hope that syncing Asset Intelligence will normalize the data for them. But even Microsoft can't seem to keep up and we see most people turning to third-party vendors.

See also

- Microsoft TechNet – How to configure software inventory in Configuration Manager : `https://technet.microsoft.com/en-us/library/mt488904.aspx`
- Software inventory tips for ConfigMgr by Sherry Kissinger: `http://myitforum.com/myitforumwp/2011/10/04/software-inventory-tips-for-configmgr/`

Managing software metering

Use **software metering** to monitor and collect software usage data on CM clients. Software metering reports can help you identify targets for removal of excess software, which helps you re-allocate software to required users, and reduce costs.

We're going to walk through the process to get you up and running with software metering.

Getting ready

Before we configure any software metering rules, we should ensure that metering is enabled. With CM, we can enable metering on all systems by using the **Default Client Settings** or as a **Custom Client Device Setting** targeted to one or more collection of systems. For example, with a custom setting, you could enable metering on a workstation collection so that server systems do not run software metering. Refer to `Chapter 7`, *Managing Clients* for more information about managing **Client Settings**.

There are only two options for software metering:

- Enable software metering on clients (True or False)
- Schedule data collection

The default data collection schedule is every seven days, which is usually sufficient. We recommend using the **Simple schedule** so that clients summarize on a random interval of every seven days, instead of all clients summarizing at the same time. You must enable metering before proceeding.

> If you enable software metering on a terminal server (or remote desktop services server), be advised that the metering data may be very large for the site server to process. Keep an eye on the inbox folder `inboxes\swmproc.box` as well as the log `swmproc.log` on each primary site server.

How to do it...

Follow these steps to enable software metering for the core Microsoft Office products:

1. From the CM admin console, navigate to **Assets and Compliance** | **Software Metering** and click on **Create Software Metering Rule** in the ribbon.
2. For **Name** enter `Outlook`.
3. For **File Name** enter `Outlook.exe`.

> You can browse to `Outlook.exe` on any system to automatically import **File name**, **Original file name**, **Version**, and **Language**. Just keep in mind that you will only meter for that specific version of Outlook.exe instead of all versions.

4. Leave **Original file name** blank.
5. Leave * for **Version**.
6. Set the **Language** property to **-Any-**.
7. Select **All clients in the hierarchy** for **Apply this software metering rule to the following clients**.
8. Complete the **Create Software Metering Rule Wizard**.

Repeat the same steps for `Winword.exe`, `MSAccess.exe`, `Excel.exe`, and `PowerPoint.exe`.

How it works...

You have just created a software metering rule. No deployment is required. The new rule works from enabling metering via Client Settings and by targeting the rule to the hierarchy in the wizard when you selected**All clients in the hierarchy**. All clients that have software metering enabled, and are targeted by the configuration in the rule will receive policy on their next polling interval (the default is 60 minutes) to begin metering for `Outlook.exe`. The information will be reported back to the site server on the next metering summarization schedule (the default is every seven days).

Verify that the CM site maintenance tasks are configured to software metering summarization. Navigate to **Administrator** | **Site Configuration** | **Site**. Right-click on the desired site and select **Site Maintenance**. Review the following tasks, ensure that they're enabled and are configured to the desired interval:

- **Delete Aged Software Metering Data:** This deletes all summarized data older than the number of days specified (the default is five).
- **Delete Aged Software Metering Summary Data:** This deletes all summarized software metering data older than the number of days specified (the default is 270).
- **Summarize Software Metering File Usage Data:** This summarizes the number of distinct user/computer combinations to approximate the number of concurrent users.
- **Summarize Software Metering Monthly Usage Data:** This summarizes all software metering data into a general record. This task is used to compress and optimize the amount of stored data in the CM12 database.

> Some applications spawn additional executable files. For example, `CMTrace.exe` contains both an x86 and x64 version. When run on an x64 system, you will see that `CMTrace.exe` does not actually continue running, but starts a file with a random filename, with the extension of `.tmp`, for example, `TRA105A.tmp`. For `CMTrace.exe`, you would want to meter based on the original filename, `Trace32_amd64.exe`.

There's more...

We have another method to enable software metering rules as well as an alternative to software metering. We'll also discuss reporting on this information.

Automatically create metering rules based on recent usage data

By default CM will automatically create software metering rules for your environment. Navigate to **Assets and Compliance** | **Software Metering**, and from the ribbon select **Software Metering Properties**. From this tab, you will see that, by default, metering rules will be automatically created for any program that has more than 10 percent of computers installed, up to 100 rules.

Automatically-created rules are disabled by default. Simply right-click on any desired rule and select **Enable**. Also note that the metering rule property is probably very specific to the version and language, so you may need to modify the rule to have fewer constraints, depending on your environment.

Reviewing metering reports

Take time to review software metering reports from SQL Reporting Services. The reports will help you identify installed software that has not been run on a system, as well as concurrent usage analysis.

There are more than a dozen built-in metering reports, which are viewable via the console. Just navigate to **Monitoring** | **Reporting** | **Reports** and search for **Metering** as a category.

Automating uninstall processes to remove unused software

CM does not have a feature to automatically uninstall unused applications, but it does provide you with enough data to create your own. The following are the basic steps we need to perform:

1. Ensure you don't have a required installation to targeted systems for the desired software to uninstall (if both install and uninstall application deployments are targeted, install always wins).
2. You must have a proper uninstall process. You can use either a built-in application uninstall, or a package/program uninstall. You can also use a task sequence if desired.

3. Create a new query-based collection. The following example is a complex query rule where WQL depends on software inventory, software metering, and metering summarization from the site server:

```
SELECT DISTINCT SMS_R_System.* FROM SMS_R_System INNER JOIN
SMS_G_System_SoftwareFile ON
SMS_G_System_SoftwareFile.ResourceID = SMS_R_System.ResourceID
INNER JOIN SMS_MeteredFiles ON SMS_G_System_SoftwareFile.FileID
= SMS_MeteredFiles.MeteredFileID INNER JOIN
SMS_MeteredProductRule ON SMS_MeteredProductRule.RuleID =
SMS_MeteredFiles.RuleID WHERE SMS_MeteredFiles.RuleID = 34 AND
DateDiff(day, SMS_G_System_SoftwareFile.ModifiedDate,
GetDate()) > 30 AND DateDiff(day,
SMS_MeteredProductRule.LastUpdateTime, GetDate()) > 30 AND
SMS_R_System.OperatingSystemNameAndVersion LIKE '%Workstation%'
AND SMS_G_System_SoftwareFile.ResourceID NOT IN (SELECT
DISTINCT SMS_MonthlyUsageSummary.ResourceID FROM
SMS_MonthlyUsageSummary INNER JOIN SMS_MeteredFiles ON
SMS_MonthlyUsageSummary.FileID = SMS_MeteredFile.MeteredFileID
WHERE DateDiff(day, SMS_MonthlyUsageSummary.LastUsage,
GetDate()) < 90 AND SMS_MeteredFiles.RuleID = 34)
```

> Safety measures in this query are added to prevent us from uninstalling the application on a system that recently installed it.

4. Find the software metering internal rule ID, which can be viewed by unhiding the column in the software metering details pane. In our sample WQL, 34 is the internal rule ID for `Excel.exe`. On your server, that number will be different. Replace 34 in the query with your number for Excel. Some conditions which can be true for Excel are:

- `Excel.exe` is installed on the system (according to software inventory).
- `Excel.exe` has existed on the system for at least 30 days (based on the software inventory modified date).
- The metering rule for `Excel.exe` is at least 30 days old from the last modification.
- The last time `Excel.exe` was launched was more than 30 days ago (or has never been launched).

5. Configure the collection to update once per week; preferably, the day after the software metering summarization occurs.

6. Deploy a mandatory package or program, or an application uninstall to this collection to force the software to uninstall.

> This example uses the modified date of the executable file. Be advised that the modified date may not be the first day the user had access to the software. The modified date can reflect when the software was installed, or when a hotfix or service pack was installed. Depending on the application you care to manage, you may be able to leverage more reliable data such as install date from the registry, if it exists.

Leveraging CCM_RecentlyUsedApps

Creating software metering rules require several weeks for metering data to be actionable (because systems should be metered for a while before you proceed to uninstall software). You can leverage `CCM_RecentlyUsedApps` to determine application utilization for some scenarios. Recently used applications data is populated from the CM client and collected via hardware inventory. Ensure that `CCM_RecentlyUsedApps` is enabled in hardware inventory.

> Hardware inventory on terminal servers (or remote desktop services) may exceed the default maximum inventory size of 50 MB.
>
> You may need to consider deploying custom inventory settings for multiuser systems. Keep an eye on `logs\dataldr.log` for rejected inventory files due to size.
>
> The proper way to go about excluding servers would be to create a Custom Client Setting with RecentlyUsedApps disabled. Target these servers with the setting, and then give it a higher priority than the setting enabling RecentlyUsedApps.

You can view this information for a specific computer with `Resource Explorer`. You will also find several built-in web reports in the `Asset Intelligence` category of CM reporting.

The following is an SQL example of how to identify all systems that have launched Microsoft Visio in the past, but have not launched it in the past 90 days:

```
SELECT DISTINCT Datediff(DAY, rua.lastusedtime0, Getdate())
        AS
        [Days Since Last Used],
        sysvalid.netbios_name0
```

```
            AS [Computer Name],
            rua.productname0
            AS APPLICATION,
            rua.filedescription0
            AS [File Description],
            rua.explorerfilename0
            AS [File Name],
            rua.fileversion0
            AS [File Version],
            rua.companyname0
            AS publisher,
            CASE
             WHEN ( Isnull(rua.productcode0, N'') = N''
                ) THEN 'N'
             ELSE 'Y'
            END
            AS [Associated with an Installer],
            rua.lastusedtime0
            AS [Time Last Used(GMT)],
            rua.lastusername0
            AS [Last Used By]
    FROM  v_gs_ccm_recently_used_apps AS rua
        INNER JOIN v_r_system_valid AS sysvalid
         ON rua.resourceid = sysvalid.resourceid
    WHERE ( rua.explorerfilename0 = N'visio.exe' )
        AND ( Datediff(DAY, rua.lastusedtime0, Getdate()) >
           90 )
    ORDER BY [Days Since Last Used] DESC
```

As you can see from the SQL query, we depend on the SQL views
v_gs_ccm_recently_used_apps and v_r_system_valid. This will only show results for
systems that have actually run Visio. If you wanted to identify "All systems that have Visio
installed, but have not run it within the last 90 days (including systems that have never run
it)", you will need to leverage software inventory or add/remove programs information
from hardware inventory.

Now that we have seen this information in SRS, the next logical step is to make it actionable.
You should have enough information from SRS to contact users, as well as report
information to your procurement department. But wouldn't it be great if we could target
these systems to remove Visio? Depending on your environment, this might be a great idea,
but be sure to confirm with your chain of command first. The following is an example WQL
that you can use to create a collection of systems that have not used Visio in the past 90
days:

```
select SMS_R_SYSTEM.ResourceID, SMS_R_SYSTEM.ResourceType,
SMS_R_SYSTEM.Name, SMS_R_SYSTEM.SMSUniqueIdentifier,
```

```
SMS_R_SYSTEM.ResourceDomainORWorkgroup, SMS_R_SYSTEM.Client
from SMS_R_System inner join SMS_G_System_CCM_RECENTLY_USED_APPS on
SMS_G_System_CCM_RECENTLY_USED_APPS.ResourceID = SMS_R_System.ResourceId
inner join SMS_G_System_CH_ClientSummary on
SMS_G_System_CH_ClientSummary.ResourceID = SMS_R_System.ResourceId
where SMS_G_System_CCM_RECENTLY_USED_APPS.ExplorerFileName = "visio.exe"
and SMS_G_System_CH_ClientSummary.ClientActiveStatus = 1 and (DateDiff(day,
SMS_G_System_CCM_RECENTLY_USED_APPS.LastUsedTime , Getdate()) > 90)
```

You can now deploy a package or application to this collection to remove software.

Monitoring inventory data flow

Troubleshooting inventory can be a challenge even for a seasoned CM administrator, so we felt it best to walk through the process in this recipe. This process will help you with other client troubleshooting issues, as well as help you understand the communication flow.

Getting ready

To walk through this flow, use a test environment to easily see the information in log files. Use CMTrace.exe to view CM client and server logs. As with any process, there are some variables based on the complexity of your hierarchy. We will walk through the steps in a basic scenario, and then discuss the variations for more complex environments.

How to do it...

The following is a list from where we can monitor the inventory data flow:

- Client
- Management Point
- Site

Client

1. From a CM client, launch the**Configuration Manager** applet from the **Control Panel**.
2. From the **Actions** tab select **Hardware Inventory Cycle**, and click on **Run Now**.

3. Open `InventoryAgent.log` with `CMTrace.exe` (the default location is `%windir%\ccm\logs\InventoryAgent.log`).

4. Use the **Date/Time** column to find the beginning of the action you just ran. You can confirm the hardware inventory by searching for this text: **Inventory: Action=Hardware ReportType=Delta**. You may see **ReportType=Full** if this is the first inventory for the system, or a resynchronization. You can then scroll down the log file and see inventory classes. You will probably see some failures that say that the class or namespace doesn't exist. This is normal, as all systems may not have all the classes and namespaces that CM tries to inventory. Near the end of the log, you will see a line that reads similar to **Inventory: Successfully sent report. Destination:mp:MP_HinvEndpoint**. This means that the client forwarded the inventory record to the Management Point. A few lines prior to this entry, you will see the location of the temporary `.xml` file. This is the file that is sent to the MP. Depending on the Asset Intelligence classes you have enabled, you may also see activity in the `AssetAdvisor.log` file. This action collects the AI info, and populates WMI so that hardware inventory can consume it.

Management Point

1. Since the MP depends on IIS, we should first check the IIS log to confirm the inventory was received from the client. By default, IIS logs are in `C:\inetpub\logs\LogFiles\W3SVC1`. Open the most recent log with `CMTrace.exe`, and use the **Filter** feature (under the **Tools** link). Filter for when a line of text contains the IP address of the client. You will see a few entries for a BITS session (new, upload, and close). Once that's confirmed, close the IIS logs and proceed to the next step.

2. Open `MP_Hinv.log`. This log will be in the CM12 client agent log directory, which is normally `%windir%\ccm\logs`. If the MP was installed before the client, the logs will be in the `\SMS_CCM\Logs` directory. From this log, you will see an entry similar to **Delta report from client COMPUTER1, action description = Hardware**, followed by **Hinv Task: Translate report attachment...**. This will tell you where the `.mif` file (the MP has already converted the `.xml` file to a `.mif`) will be moved to. If the MP is on the site server, it will be moved directly to the `inboxes\auth\dataldr.box` on the site server.

Site

On the site server, open `Logs\dataldr.log`. You will see a line that reads `Moving MIF File ...\inboxes\auth\dataldr.box\%Filename%.MIF to ...\inboxes\auth\dataldr.box\process\%Filename%.MIF`. Files are moved into the `process` folder, and then committed to the database, look for **Begin transaction** and **Commit transaction**, and finally **Done**, which will also mention how many stored procedures were run. If you have a very busy site, you may want to filter `dataldr.log` by **Thread**.

How it works...

Clients obtain inventory policy from their MPs, and commit requests to WMI where inventory generates an `.xml` file, which is sent to the MP, and then to the inbox of the primary where it is finally committed to the site database.

As you can see, there are a few steps involved with updating hardware inventory. If you tried to follow along and look at files in the directories mentioned earlier, you may have missed them, as CM is constantly watching the inboxes, and processing files when they appear. Should you want to slow this process down, you can stop services (SMS Agent Host for MPs, and SMS_Executive for primary sites) to see files through the process.
There's more... As you can see, there are a few steps involved with updating hardware inventory. If you tried to follow along and look at files in the directories mentioned earlier, you may have missed them, as CM is constantly watching the inboxes, and processing files when they appear. Should you want to slow this process down, you can stop services (SMS Agent Host for MPs, and SMS_Executive for primary sites) to see files through the process. Note that if you have a CAS, much of this inbox activity is replaced by the primary site sending that data via SQL replication.

The flow described in this recipe is for a simple site, assuming the following:

- The client sends data to the site Management Point (no secondary site)
- The Management Point is on the same server as the primary site (not offloaded)

Let's discuss how the flow mentioned earlier would be different for more complex scenarios:

- The Management Point for the primary site is on a separate server. The change would be in step 2 of the *Management Point* section. You can see in `MP_Hinv.log` that the MIF is moved to the MPs installation directory here: `mp\outboxes\hinv.box\`. You can then see in `logs\mpfdm.log` that the MIF is moved from `\hinv.box\` to `\\%SiteServer%\SMS_LAB\inboxes\auth\dataldr.box\` (where `LAB` is the site code for the primary site – this is a UNC path).

- The client is in the boundary of a secondary site with a **Proxy Management Point** (**PMP**). In this scenario, steps 1 and 2 of the *Management Point* section occur at the PMP. At the end of step 2, the secondary site will forward the MIF file to its parent site, as logged in `invproc.log`. Scheduler and sender then handle the process to compress and move the file to the primary site. In the primary site, you will see in `despool.log` that the inventory is copied to the `inboxes\auth\dataldr.box\` inbox, where processing occurs as described in step 1 of the *Site* section.

Integrating Asset Intelligence

Asset Intelligence (**AI**) provides enhanced collection of data from client systems, adding value in the following three areas:

- **Hardware Information**: This collects additional information such as primary computer user (mostly the logged-in user), shared computers, detailed USB device information
- **Software Information**: This collects additional information such as Internet browser helper objects (Adobe, Java, and more), autostart software, categorized software information to improve software and license management
- **Licensing Information**: This identifies Windows operating systems that are near expiration, verifies the **Key Management Services** (**KMS**) server, Microsoft volume licensing reconciliation report

Getting ready

In order to fully leverage AI and obtain updates from Microsoft about software information, you must create an AI synchronization point at your CAS or primary. This role requires Internet access. You can specify an Internet proxy and credentials, if required. Monitor `logs\AIUpdateSvc.log` for more information about synchronization. The remainder of this recipe will walk you through the process of enabling AI in your environment (assuming the AI synchronization point is installed).

How to do it...

Follow these steps to configure Asset Intelligence:

1. Verify that the required AI reporting classes are enabled. From the CM site server admin console, navigate to **Assets and Compliance | Asset Intelligence** and click on **Edit Inventory Classes** from the ribbon. Notice that you have two options, **Enable all Asset Intelligence reporting classes** or **Enable only the selected Asset Intelligence reporting classes**. Any configuration that appears on the **Edit Inventory Classes** dialog will be applied to the Default Client Settings. Choose the desired setting and click on **OK**.

2. Verify that `AI synchronization point` installed successfully. From the CM site system that contains the AI synchronization point, navigate to `SMS\Logs\` and open `AIUpdateSvc.log` (AI will install to the drive with the most space). Check for errors.

> Note that the default AI synchronization runs once per week, so review at least the past 7 days for successful synchronization.

3. Enable auditing of successful logon events. In order to obtain system console user data, enable this setting via local policy or group policy.

4. Select the **Asset Intelligence** node and view summary information. This landing page will display information regarding the last synchronization, items pending online identification, and any recent updates.

How it works…

As you can see, there are multiple features within Asset Intelligence. Depending on how you intend to use AI, you may not need to enable all features. For example, you don't need an AI synchronization point to capture system console user data, KMS server information, and other hardware-specific information. If you want to rationalize your application inventory, then you will need the AI synchronization point.

There's more…

Depending on your environment, you may want to selectively choose which inventory classes to enable, as well as whether you want to enable on all devices, or only a specific group of systems. If you know you want these settings enabled on all CM clients, enable the checkboxes described in the *How to do it…* section of this recipe. If not, consider deploying custom hardware inventory configuration to desired collections using Client Settings, as discussed in `Chapter 7`, *Managing Clients:*

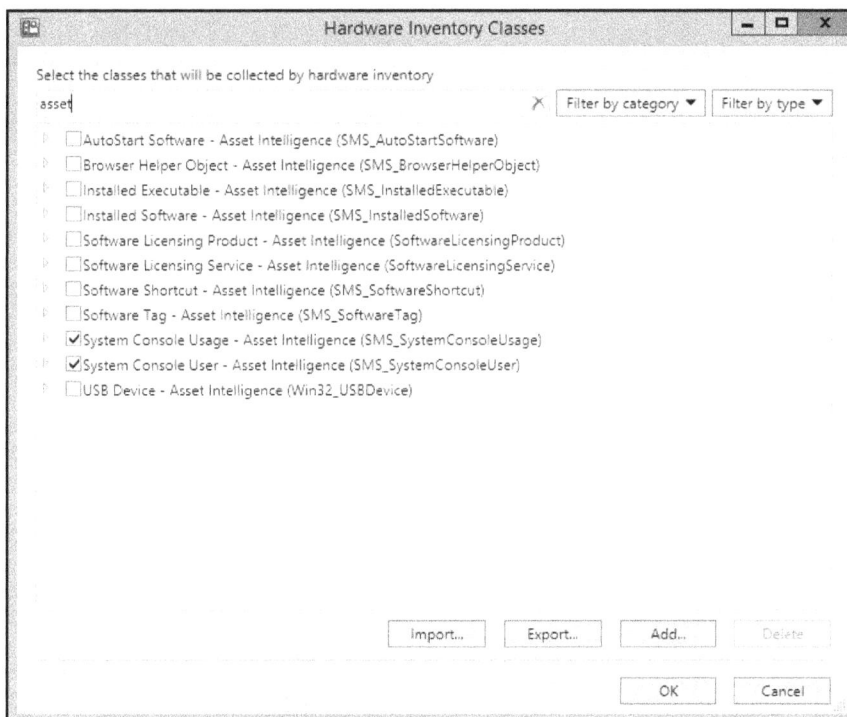

To find the hardware inventory classes, just enter `asset` into the filter, and all hardware inventory classes related to Asset Intelligence will appear. The following is a brief description of each class:

- **AutoStart Software:** This lists all software that starts at system boot or user login. This is equivalent to the system information utility (`msinfo32.exe`), under **Software Environment | Startup Programs**. Service desk and on-site teams tend to appreciate having this information handy.
- **Browser Helper Object:** This lists all browser helper objects, such as Lync 2012, Adobe PDF helper, and Java SE.
- **Installed Executable:** This identifies executable files associated with an installed application (uses Windows Installer data).
- **Installed Software:** This merges installed software information from multiple sources to provide categorization information.
- **Software Licensing Product:** This identifies the Windows license used on the target system (pro, enterprise, KMS, and so on).
- **Software Licensing Service:** This identifies the KMS server, as well as activation and renewal info.
- **Software Shortcut:** This provides information about the shortcuts such as path, product name, version, and target executable.
- **Software Tag:** This provides information about software that contains a software identification tag that is compliant with ISO/IEC 19770-2.
- **System Console Usage:** This defines usage data about devices, based on the security event log. This class will tell you the most logged in user for a device, total security log time (in minutes), and total console time (in minutes).
- **System Console User:** This defines usage data about users, based on the security event log. This class will tell you the number of console logins per user, as well as total user console minutes.
- **USB Device:** This tracks devices connected to USB ports. This includes keyboards, mice, and other USB peripherals, such as printers, flash drives, and so on.

> Asset Intelligence reports require Asset Intelligence reporting classes to be enabled. Review the CM online documentation to determine which AI classes are required for each AI report that you need.

Submitting applications to Microsoft for categorization

When you browse to **Asset Intelligence**, and review **Inventoried Software**, you will probably see several applications with a **Category** of **Unidentified** and a **State** of **Uncategorized**. This means that AI does not have information for this software. You can submit the application to Microsoft for categorization by selecting the application and then selecting **Request Catalog Update** from the ribbon. You can also select and multiple items submit up to 100 at a time.

In an ideal world, Microsoft would categorize the application, and the metadata would appear at your next AI synchronization. Unfortunately, there are a lot of variables, and it would be nearly impossible to categorize every application. So the AI team has a method to prioritize application rationalization, and the first step is to prioritize the applications that many companies are requesting first. If you have custom in-house or very rare (or extinct) applications, you may want to avoid submitting them, as they will probably not be categorized. For this type of application, you can specify your own custom labels and category.

See also

- More information on configuring Asset Intelligence on Microsoft TechNet at: `htt ps://technet.microsoft.com/en-us/library/mt488912.aspx`

9

Managing Reports and Queries

In this chapter, we will cover the following recipes:

- Installing SQL Server Reporting Services – SSRS
- Configuring reporting services
- Sharing your reports with others
- Configuring report subscription
- Building queries
- Editing and creating reports

Introduction

CM gathers a vast amount of data from your clients, but in order to use that data to make useful asset reports, you will need to install **SQL Server Reporting Services** (**SSRS**) so that you can install a **Reporting Services Point** (**RSP**).

In order to edit the default reports that come with an RSP or to help locate and target certain systems or users with a deployment, you need to know how to create and edit queries (both, SQL and WQL queries).

> **SQL versus WQL – What's the difference?**
> **Structured Query Language** (**SQL**) is used to query SQL database, such as the Microsoft SQL database used with CM. **WMI Query Language** (**WQL**) is used to query **Windows Management Instrumentation** (**WMI**). CM relies heavily on WMI. You can watch smsprov.log on any primary or CAS and learn a lot about WQL and SQL, including how to convert between the two. In CM, we use SQL to build reports, and WQL to create collections and queries.

Installing SQL Server Reporting Services - SSRS

An RSP is the sole means of reporting in CM. For most admins, installing this role directly on the single primary in their hierarchy will be rather common simply out of simplicity and financial constraints.

Larger companies that have a **Central Administrative Site** (**CAS**) are also likely to install the RSP on the CAS for the simple reason that buying more RAM to get by is cheaper than managing another server for reporting.

Should you wish to offload this role to another server, the major requirements are x64 OS and SQL (IIS not needed). Review the CM supported configuration documents at `https://technet.microsoft.com/en-us/library/mt589499.aspx` for up-to-date information for required OS and SQL versions. The performance will be directly tied to the speed of disk and amount of memory. A simple VM with 2 GB RAM is not a good candidate.

We will start with installing SSRS on the CAS or primary, and then later show what to do if you want SQL on another server.

Getting ready

In the unlikely situation that you have not even installed SQL or CM yet and you wish to keep the RSP on the CAS or primary site, you can go to the SQL chapter in this book and using the answer file from the appendix, change SQLREPORTING to True. And then you can skip ahead to the next section on building queries.

Whether you intend to install SSRS off box or on, you are going to have to provide the SQL installation media. Have that share, folder, or disc ready.

How to do it...

From the CAS or primary server, follow these steps:

1. Click on the *Windows start button* and enter SQL Server Installation Center (64 bit) in the search box and hit *Enter*.

> **TIP**
> If you have previously run an upgrade, you might see two versions having the same name `show`. Hover over each to determine the newest which is what you want to select.

2. Click on **Installation** in the left-side pane of the SQL Server Installation Center and then click on the right-side pane on New SQL Server standalone installation or add-on features to an existing installation.
3. You are prompted for the source location of your SQL installation files. Click on **Run** when prompted and then click on **OK** on the Setup Support Rules page.

> **TIP**
> When adding a feature, you cannot point the following to your installed location of SQL: Other editions (STD versus ENT), a Cumulative Update source, or a version with a service pack different from the one that is currently installed.

4. Under **Installation Type**, select **Add features to an existing instance** (not new installation).
5. Continue through the SQL Server Setup wizard until you get to **Feature Selection**. Once you are there, check the `Reporting Services` checkbox and continue through the wizard until you reach `Instance Configuration`.
6. You may now choose a new Named Instance, but on this same CM server, we recommend just using the Default Instance.
7. From here you can simply complete the wizard selecting all of the defaults.
8. If you had previously run a Cumulative Update over SQL, you will want to run it again now because you introduced old files into SQL. If you have never run a Cumulative Update, now is a good time to do so.

How it works...

Now, this server is ready for the RSP role to be installed. Before doing so, if running on a local disk, you might want to consider moving the SSRS database file and transaction logs to another free volume (if available). Increasing RAM will also help performance.

You can always move this role off to another server. You can always bring up another RSP while leaving this one in place. Larger companies will want to weigh the cost of RAM rather than adding another server to the hierarchy.

Run reports off this server yourself before making it available to the company so you are confident it can keep up.

There's more…

Now let's consider SSRS off box.

Remote SSRS – remote RSP

Selecting a properly-sized server is more important than the setup itself! Anyone can muddle through the install, but the selection is critical. Take the following into account when making that selection.

If reports are slow or timed out, managers will be likely to conclude that all of CM is slow, not just reporting. Reports are where you expose CM to the company. If it looks bad, you might look bad. Here are a few considerations for your RSP:

- The more memory and disk you can give your RSP, the better it will perform.
- A server on a slow link across the country will show serious latency if you try to make it the RSP for your site. Pick a server in the same rack, if possible.
- If you offloaded SQL from your primary already, that same SQL server is likely to be a good candidate for your RSP.
- You can have multiple RSPs. One scenario might be that someone never wants data from a European primary site, but only wants data from the US. In such a scenario with two primary (and one CAS), it might make sense to place a RSP on the US primary.

Installation of SSRS is similar to the preceding directions for adding to an existing primary site:

1. Click on **setup** in the SQL setup source files to open the SQL Server Installation Center (64 bit).
2. Click on **Installation** in the left-side pane of SQL Server Installation Center and then in the right-side pane click on **New SQL Server stand-alone** installation or add on features to an existing installation.
3. Under **Installation Type**, select **Add features** to an existing instance (not new installation).

4. Under **Feature Selection**, select **Database Engine Services** and **Reporting Services**.
   - You may optionally select **Management Tools: Basic and Complete**, but these could just as easily be installed to your desktop instead.
   - For Shared feature directory, just like installing SQL for CM, if you can dedicate a disk volume here instead of the default C drive, do so. The same applies to the (x86) folder.Under **Server Configuration** click on `Use` the same account for all SQL Server services, select `NT AUTHORITY\SYSTEM`, and click on **OK** and then on **Next**.

5. Continue through the SQL Server Setup wizard until you get to**Feature Selection**. Once there, check the **Reporting Services** checkbox and continue through the wizard until you reach **Instance Configuration**.

6. Under **Database Engine Configuration**, click on **Add** and enter your team's AD group account so that you and your team have permissions to the database.
   - Also add the machine account of your primary or CAS so that it has permissions to the database when you install the RSP.
   - Under the **Data Directories** tab, if you have other volumes to ease the load of SSRS on the server, specify them here.

7. From here you can simply complete the wizard selecting all of the defaults.

Install the latest supported service pack and cumulative update for SQL once complete.

Copying installation files local to the system
You might run into an error trying to run a cumulative updtae across the network on SQL Server, so we advise you to copy the files locally, and then tun them.

If you missed the step to grant your primary or CAS permissions to this SSRS server, you must grant the machine account of the primary or CAS sysadmin on the remote SSRS server. Follow these steps:

1. In **Microsoft SQL Server Management Studio** (**SSMS**), connect to the SSRS server and navigate to **Security | Logins**.
2. Add the machine account of the primary or CAS here as a sysadmin so that when you run the RSP setup, it can create the database.
3. Open port `1433` on the firewall to allow remote access from the CAS or primary.

It's worth noting that you can create an empty SSRS database in advance and then install the RSP role. The benefit is that you can put the files on the correct drives, set the default size (expected size so it doesn't have to slowly grow), growth rates, and so on.

See also

- Configuring Reporting in CM: `https://technet.microsoft.com/en-us/library/mt488921.aspx`
- SSRS Predefined Roles: `http://msdn.microsoft.com/en-us/library/ms157363.aspx`
- Install SQL Server: `http://msdn.microsoft.com/en-us/library/ms143219.aspx`
- Microsoft MSDN SSRS: `https://msdn.microsoft.com/en-us/library/ms159106.aspx`
- Hardware requirements for SSRS: `http://technet.microsoft.com/en-us/library/ms143506.aspx`

Configuring reporting services

Before you can make the SSRS server an RSP, you need to configure it. This recipe will walk through the process of configuring reporting services and installing the CM Reporting Services Point (RSP). You will also learn how to cache reports to eliminate multiple SQL queries against your CM database for the same report.

Getting ready

In order to configure SSRS, you must first install it. Review the previous recipe, *Installing SQL Server Reporting Services – SSRS* for installation information.

How to do it...

From the SSRS box, follow these steps:

1. Click on the *Windows start button* and enter `Reporting Services Configuration Manager` in the search box and hit *Enter*. Click on **Connect**.

2. Under **Web Service URL**, enter `SRSReports for the Virtual Directory` and click on **Apply**.

3. Under **Database**, click on **Change Database**. Click on **Next** to create a new report server database.

4. Under **Database Server**, click on **Test Connection**. If you don't have permissions, you missed the preceding step 3. Continue to click on **Next** until you complete the wizard and then click on **Finish** to exit.

5. Under **Report Manager URL**, enter `CMReports for the Virtual Directory` and click on **Apply**.

6. If you have access to an SMTP Server, click on **E-mail Settings** and enter an e-mail address for Sender Address: (This e-mail address will appear as sender, when report subscribers gets e-mail reports). For SMTP Server, enter the FQDN of your SMTP server.

> Report viewers cannot subscribe to reports until the SMTP server is set. This can be skipped for now, but it is well worth the effort to work with your Exchange admin to get access to do this.

7. Click on **Exit**.

SSRS is now ready to become an RSP.

Making the SSRS server an RSP

Now you can create the RSP role which will make all of the built-in CM reports available to you. From the CM admin console:

1. Create a domain user account that has permissions to nothing else (simple domain user) in Active Directory. This account will be used for SSRS to connect to the CAS or primary when no user initiates a report (such as a cached report or subscription).

2. Navigate to **Administration** | **Site Configuration**, right-click on **Servers and Site System Roles** and select **Create Site System Server**.

3. Under **General**, click on **Browse** to locate and select your SSRS server (if local, just enter the name of the CAS or Primary). For Site code, select the CAS (or Primary if it's only site). Click on **Next**.

4. Under **System Role Selection**, check the Reporting services point checkbox and click on **Next**.

5. Under **Folder name**, enter CM_Reports.

6. Under **Reporting Services Point**, click on **Verify**. Click on **Set** to browse to the domain user account created in step **1**. Enter the password twice and then click on **Next** twice.

Within a few minutes, you should be able to run any of the reports in the reporting node of the console or from a web browser via http://mysrsserver/CMReports where mysrsserver is the name of your SSRS server.

Installation of the RSP automatically adds users defined in the CM console (whether individual accounts or AD groups) to a new SSRS role called **ConfigMgr Report Users**. Then add all admins in CM (users with Site Modify permissions) to a new SSRS role called **ConfigMgr Report Administrators**.

Don't manually modify SSRS report security

ConfigMgr will verify rights are properly configured for the reporting point every 10 minutes. Modifying SSRS report security on an RSP will only cause you pain, as you try to determine why your custom rights keep disappearing. Refer to srsrp.log as well as the next recipe for more information.

Saving resources of your CAS or Primary – cache reports

SSRS queries your CAS or primary to report findings to users. So what happens when a user hits refresh every 10 seconds to watch client count during a rollout? Your poor server will spend more time trying to answer that query than processing the new data coming up. SSRS can be told to cache that report for an hour so that no matter how many times the user hits refresh, the CAS and primary will not be asked for new data until that hour is up.

This is how you can do that:

1. From a web browser, navigate to `http://mysrsserver/CMReports` where `mysrsserver` is the name of your SSRS server.

2. In the search box, enter the count of clients and hit *Enter*. Click on the drop-down arrow to the right of Count of clients assigned and installed for each site and select **Manage**.

3. In the left pane, click on **Processing Options**. Select the radio button to Cache a temporary copy of the report. Enter `60` for Expire copy of the report after a number of minutes. Click on **Apply**.

From now on, anyone trying to refresh that report will get nothing more than a cached copy for an hour. You can do this for any other reports you know might strain your CAS or primary.

> Caching relies on the SQL Server Agent service to be running, so be sure to set that service to run automatically.

Less effective, but no less needed is cloning reports for specific users or teams. Caching their results may not match those of another team's report. In such scenarios, you will also have to make use of the `Parameters` and `Data Sources` tabs to tie in the specific results for each team.

See also

- Configuring Reporting in CM: `http://technet.microsoft.com/en-us/library/gg712698.aspx`
- SSRS Predefined Roles: `http://msdn.microsoft.com/en-us/library/ms157363.aspx`
- Install SQL Server: `http://msdn.microsoft.com/en-us/library/ms143219.aspx`
- Microsoft MSDN SSRS: `https://msdn.microsoft.com/en-us/library/ms159106.aspx`
- Hardware requirements for SSRS: `http://technet.microsoft.com/en-us/library/ms143506.aspx`

Sharing your reports with others

RBAC in CM makes security a breeze. But the one area you'll find that you cannot create a role for is reporting. That's because SSRS has its own RBAC. CM will add CM Full Administrators the SSRS RBAC role of ConfigMgr Report Administrators. It will add the remaining admins you have configured with the SSRS RBAC role of ConfigMgr Report Users.

Getting ready

You must have SSRS and the RSP role configured before you can share reports within your company.

How to do it...

Here is how you could let everyone in your company view the reports:

1. Navigate to **Administration** | **Security** | **Security Roles** and copy the Read-only Analyst role. Name the new role Report Users. Click on **OK**.
2. Right-click on **Administrative Users** and create a Add User or Group. Click on **Browse** and enter `Domain Users`. Click on **OK**.
3. Click on **Add** and check the checkbox for the Report Users role.
4. Check the radio button for **All instances of the objects that are related to the assigned security roles**.

At this point, anyone with a login ID should be able to run reports off your RSP.

> Depending on your security requirements, you may need to ease off such a broad setting. Note that as you drill down to any report, you can set permissions on groups of reports or individual reports, granting you the granularity to meet any security requirement.

It would make sense to show you how to edit Reports here, but first we should be sure you know how to create queries so that you don't bring your CAS or primary site to its knees by running a report such as `select * from v_Add_Remove_Programs` against a large site.

Configuring report subscription

Report subscriptions in SQL Server Reporting Services provides the automatic delivery of specified reports by e-mail or to a file share at scheduled intervals. Use the Create Subscription Wizard in CM to configure report subscriptions.

Getting ready

Prepare a `share` folder (`\\server\share\folder`) for the report subscriptions, and allow write permissions to the subscription account for the share.

Prepare notification settings for sending e-mail subscription reports using the following three steps:

1. Enable e-mail notification for alerts.
2. Configure E-Mail Settings of Reporting Services Configuration Manager.
3. Configure SQL Server Agent Service.

Step 1: Enable e-mail notification for alerts

1. Navigate to **Administration** | **Site Configuration** | **Sites**.
2. In the Ribbon, click on **Configure Site Components** and select **E-mail Notification**.

3. On the **General** tab, check **Enable email notification for alerts**, and specify the smtp server amd the sender's address. Click on **OK**:

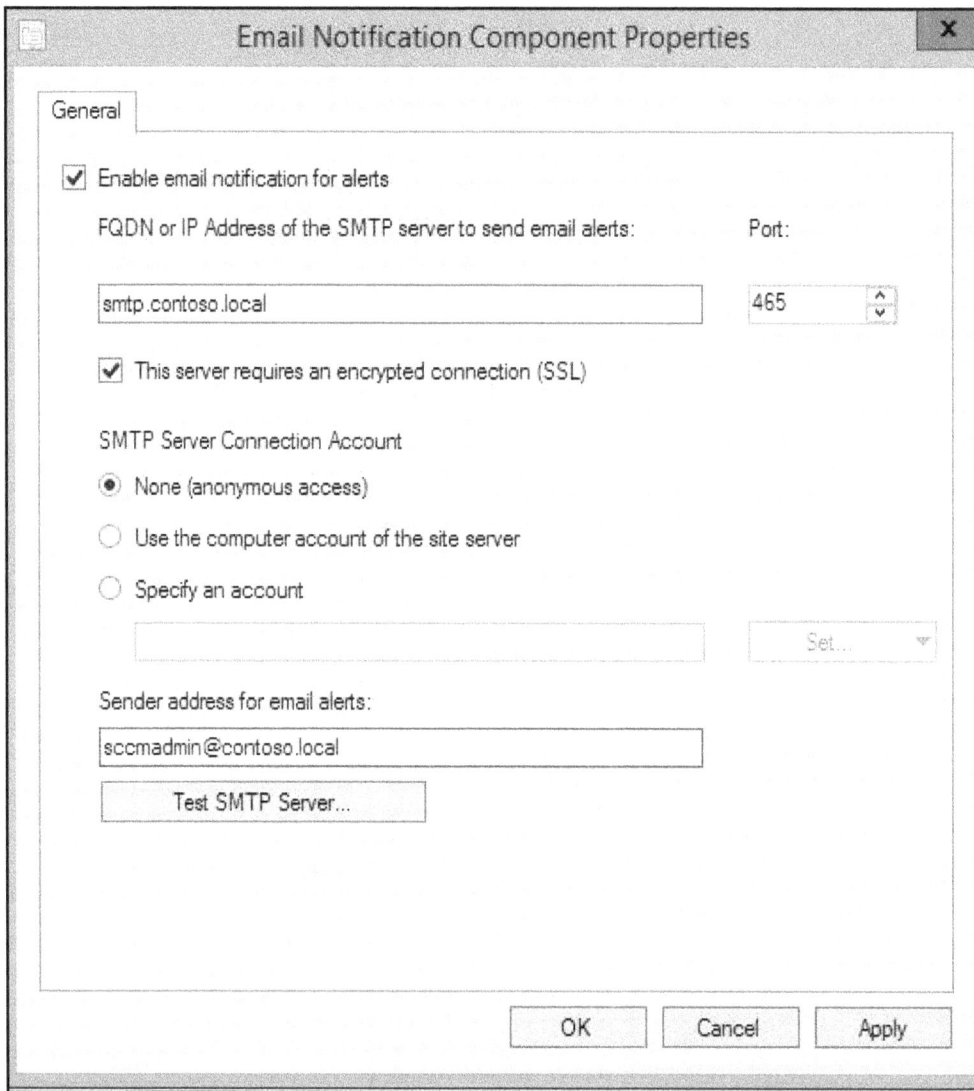

Step 2: Configure E-Mail Settings of Reporting Services Configuration Manager

1. Open SQL **Reporting Services Configuration Manager**.
2. Click on **E-Mail Settings**, and specify the smtp server, the sender's address, and then click on **Apply** and **Exit:**

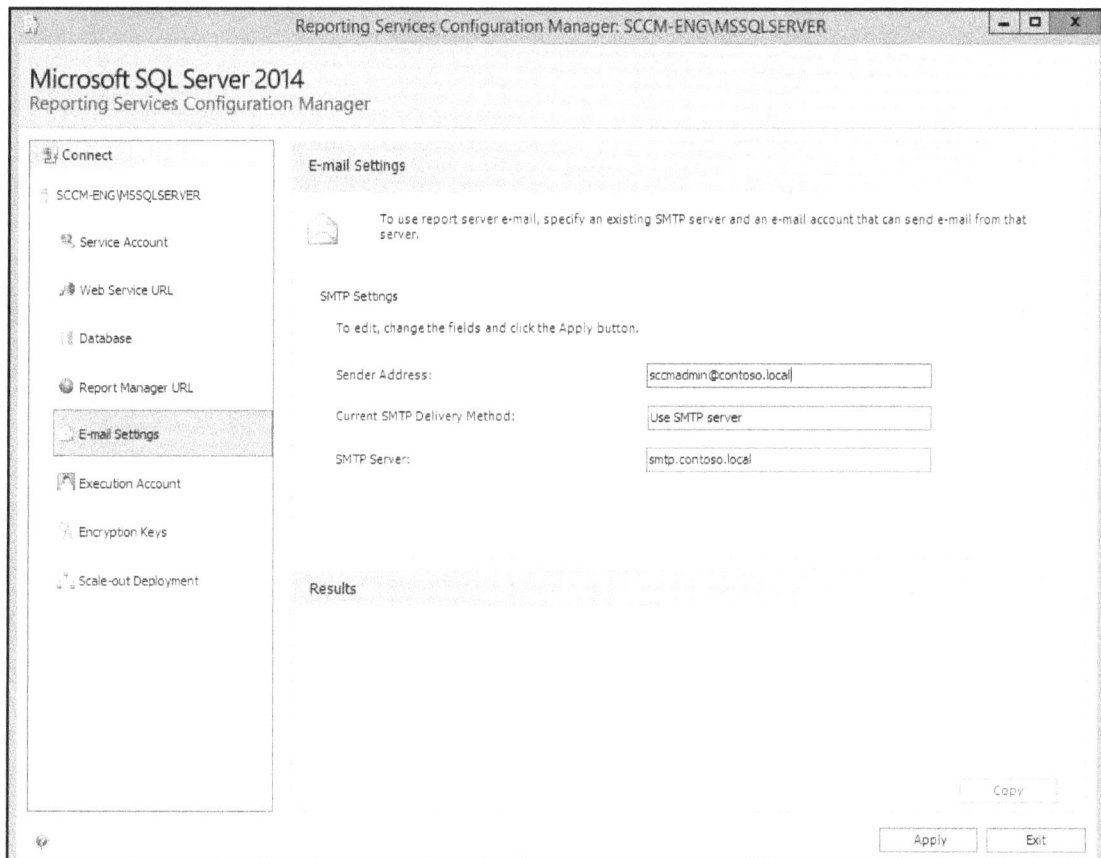

Step 3: Configure SQL Server Agent Service

1. **SQL Server Agent** service must be running.
2. Open `Services` and set the service to started and `Startup` to `Automatic`:

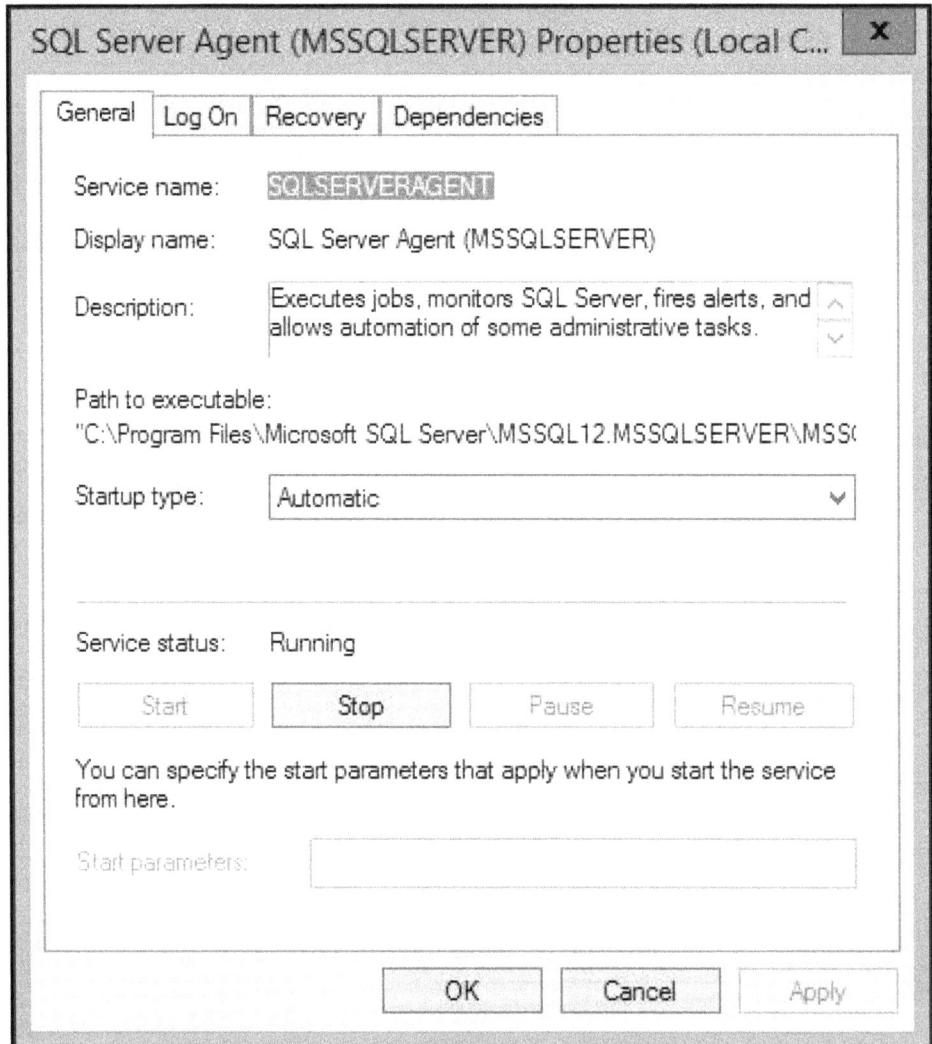

You can review more information on how to configure e-mail notifications at `https://tech net.microsoft.com/en-us/library/ms159155(v=sql.100).aspx` and `https://technet.microsoft.com/en-us/library/ms345234(v=sql.100).aspx`.

How to do it...

To create a file-based report subscription:

1. Navigate to **Monitoring** | **Reporting** | **Reports**, and select the target report of a subscription.
2. Under the **Home** | **Report Group**, click on **Create Subscription**.
3. On the **Subscription Delivery**, configure the following:
   - **Report delivered by**: Select `Windows File Share`.
   - **File Name**: Specify the filename for the report.
   - **Path**: Specify a UNC path to where you want to save.
   - **Render Format**: Select one of the formats (XML, CSV, TIFF, PDF, HTML 4.0, MHTML, RPL, Excel, or Word).
   - **User Name**: Specify a Windows user account with write permissions to the share.
   - **Password**: Specify the password for the Windows user account.
   - **Overwrite option**: Select one of the following options: Overwrite an existing file with a newer version, Do not overwrite an existing file, or Increment filenames as newer versions are added:

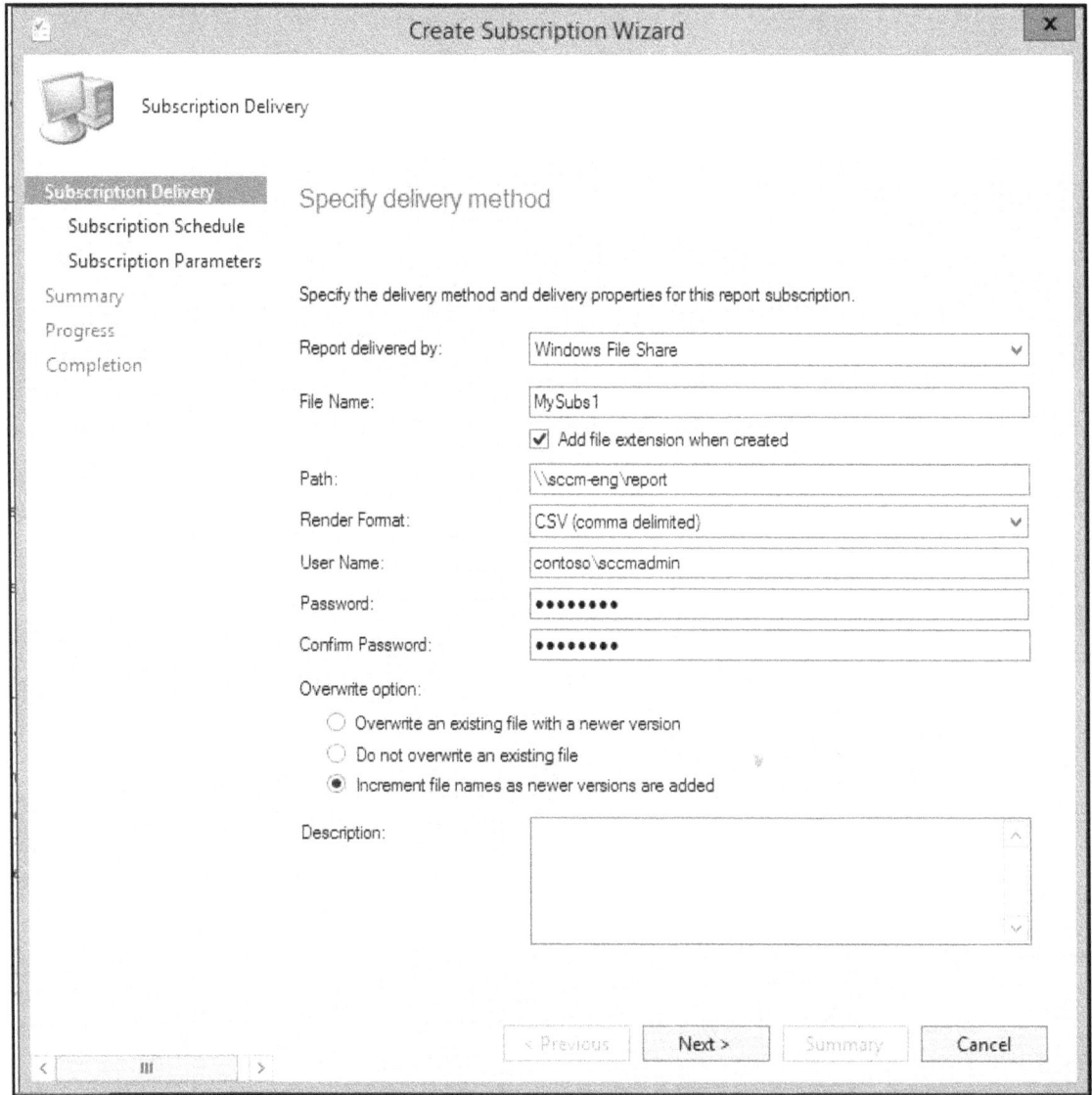

4. Click on **Next**.

5. On the **Subscription Schedule**, select one of the following delivery schedule options:
    - **Use shared schedule**: Use a previously defined schedule that can be used by other report subscriptions.
    - **Create new schedule**: Configure the schedule on which this report runs.
6. On the **Subscription Parameters**, specify the parameters for this report.
7. On the **Summary**, click on **Next**.
8. On the **Completion**, click on **Close**.

To create a email-based report subscription:

1. Navigate to **Monitoring | Reporting | Reports**, and select the target report of a subscription.
2. Under **Home | Report Group**, click on **Create Subscription**.
3. On the Subscription Delivery, configure the following:
    - **Report delivered by**: Select E-mail
    - **To**: Specify e-mail addresses to send this report to by separating a semicolon
    - **Cc**: Optionally, specify an e-mail address
    - **Bcc**: Optionally, specify an e-mail address
    - **Reply To**: Specify the reply address when the recipient replies
    - **Subject**: Specify a subject line for the subscription e-mail message
    - **Priority**: Select the priority flag for this e-mail message. Select Low, Normal, or High
    - **Comment**: Specify the body of the subscription e-mail message
    - **Include Link**: This includes a URL to the subscribed report in the e-mail message
    - **Include Report**: Specify that the report is attached to the e-mail message
    - **Render Format**: Select one of the formats (XML, CSV, TIFF, PDF, HTML 4.0, MHTML, RPL, Excel, or Word), as shown in the following screenshot:

Managing Reports and Queries

Create Subscription Wizard ✕

Subscription Delivery

Subscription Delivery	**Specify delivery method**
Subscription Schedule	
Subscription Parameters	
Summary	Specify the delivery method and delivery properties for this report subscription.
Progress	
Completion	

Report delivered by: E-mail ⌄

To: sccm-users@contoso.local

Cc:

Bcc:

Reply-To: sccmadmin@contoso.local

Subject: Weekly Alert Check Report

Priority: Normal ⌄

Comment: Please check the latest alerts that were generated during last week.

Description:

☑ Include Link

☑ Include Report

Render Format: Excel ⌄

‹ Previous   Next ›   Summary   Cancel

4. Click on **Next**.

5. On the **Subscription Schedule**, select one of the following delivery schedule options:

- **Use shared schedule**: Use a previously defined schedule that can be used by other report subscriptions.
- **Create new schedule**: Configure the schedule on which this report runs.

6. On the **Subscription Parameters**, specify the parameters for this report.
7. On the **Summary**, click on **Next**.
8. On the **Completion**, click on **Close**.

There's more...

You can manage report subscriptions under **Monitoring** | **Reporting** | **Subscriptions**.

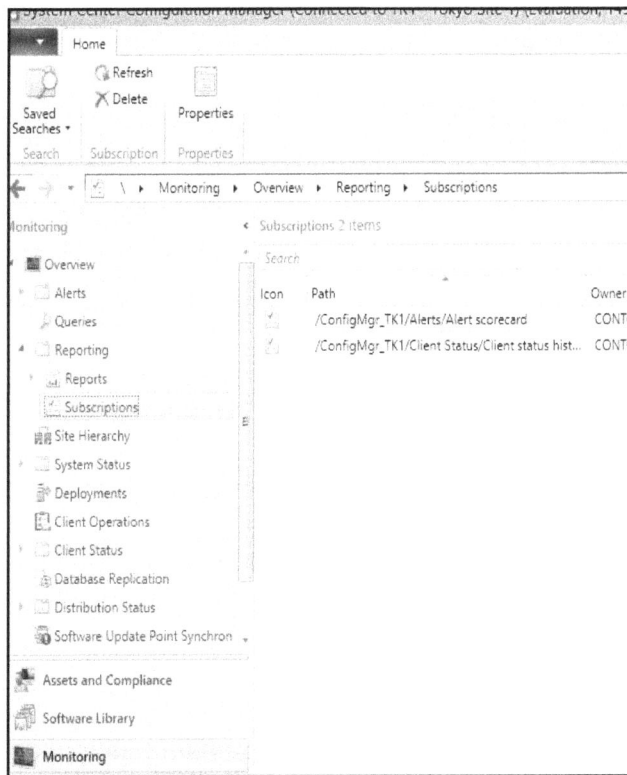

See also

- Review Microsoft's document at `https://technet.microsoft.com/en-us/libr` `ary/mt488915.aspx#BKMK_ManageReportSubscriptions`

Building queries

Seasoned CM admins should already understand the difference between SQL and WMI queries and how to write a subselect query. If you do, you should be able to skip ahead with just this one reminder-with CM's ability to use exclude or include in a collection query, you won't have to make subselect queries as often.

Now for all of the rest of you, we're going to show you how to make a query to show all machines which have Office installed. Then we'll show how to find all machines which don't have Office 2010 installed (and for that we need a subselect). We'll do this first in SQL and then again in WMI. SQL is for reports where WMI is more commonly used for CM console queries and collections.

Getting ready

You will need access to any machine with Microsoft SQL Server Management Studio (SSMS) installed. You will need SQL access to your primary site or CAS.

We're going to make a query to find all machines with Office 2010 installed.

How to do it...

1. Open SSMS, enter the name of your CAS or primary server when prompted and click on **Connect**.
2. In the left pane (Object Explorer) expand the **Databases** node.
3. Right-click on your CM database (CM_CAS, for example) and select **New Query**.
4. Enter the following query in the right pane and click on **Execute**:

```
select * from v_R_System SYS where SYS.Netbios_Name0 = 'myprimary'
```

(Replace `myprimary` with the name of your CAS or primary server). This query simply shows the basic client information of the server in the bottom pane. So what does that query mean? How do you read it?

- We're just asking SQL to show us all (that's the asterisk) rows in the table that maintains the DDR data that have this server name.
- `SYS` is just an alias so we don't have to enter `v_R_System` a bunch of times.
- `v_ part` is actually a view which is usually one or more CM tables joined appropriately. We never query tables directly because CM can't update them if we have them open.
- We pick `Netbios_Name0` instead of `Name0` as the former is indexed and easier for SQL to find.

5. We're not going to want to see all that data from the DDR, so revise this to return just the server name:

```
select SYS.Netbios_Name0 from v_R_System SYS
where SYS.Netbios_Name0 = 'myprimary'
```

6. Because we'll want to just see any machine, not just this server, remove the where clause:

```
select SYS.Netbios_Name0 from v_R_System SYS
```

7. We're no longer interested in a certain name; we're trying to find all machines with Office installed. So we'll join this query to the Add/Remove View where Office data is stored.

8. Highlight the preceding query in SSRS, right-click on the text and select **Design Query in Editor** which opens **Query Designer**.

9. In any open space in the top pane of **Query Editor**, right-click and select **Add Table:**

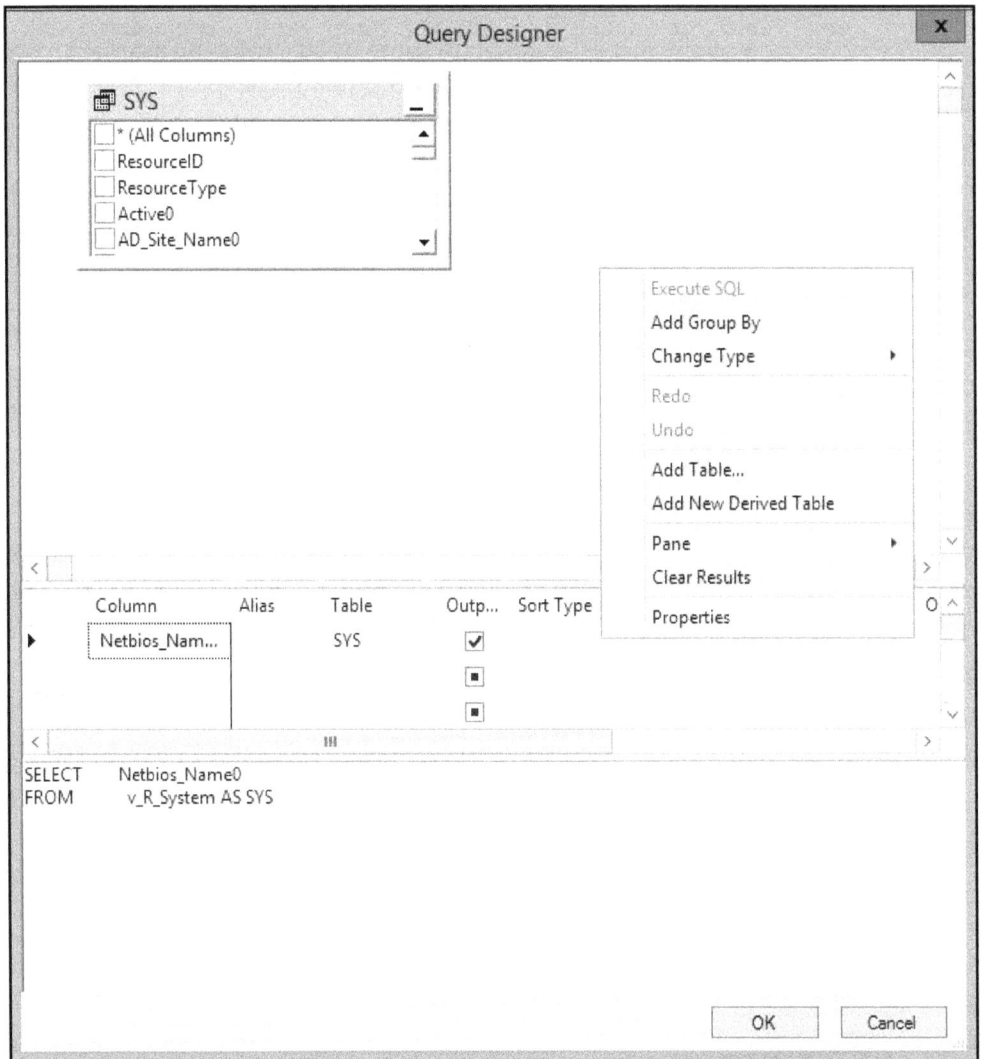

10. Click on **Views** (remember, we never query tables, only views) and select `v_Add_Remove_Programs`. Click on **Add** and then on **Close**.

11. Click on `ResourceID` in the `v_Add_Remove_Programs` table (not the checkbox itself, but anywhere on the word), hold the mouse down and drag-and-drop to `ResourceID` in the `SYS` table.

12. In the bottom pane of the **Query Designer**, enter ARP before the word ON. This alias will help us read the query easier. Make sure it has a *space* before and after ARP. Click anywhere in the top pane of the designer and you'll notice the table has been renamed to ARP.

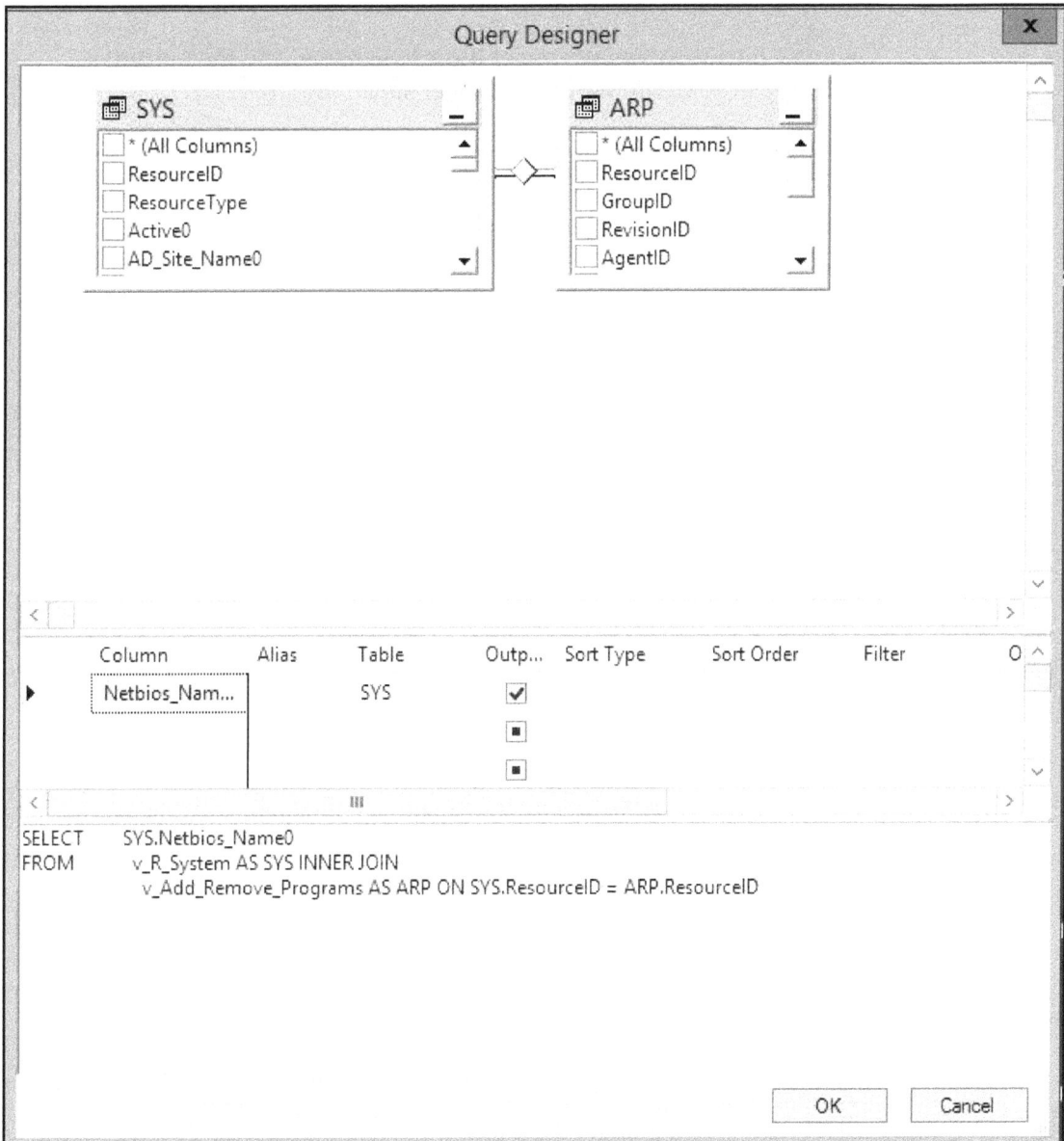

Query Designer								x

SYS
- * (All Columns)
- ResourceID
- ResourceType
- Active0
- AD_Site_Name0

ARP
- * (All Columns)
- ResourceID
- GroupID
- RevisionID
- AgentID

Column	Alias	Table	Outp...	Sort Type	Sort Order	Filter	O
► Netbios_Nam...		SYS	✔				
			■				
			■				

```
SELECT   SYS.Netbios_Name0
FROM     v_R_System AS SYS INNER JOIN
         v_Add_Remove_Programs AS ARP ON SYS.ResourceID = ARP.ResourceID
```

OK   Cancel

13. In the ARP table, check the checkbox for `DisplayName0` which tells SQL to show us that name when it returns the results.

14. We're just interested in Office, so let's filter for it by entering it in the Filter field:

    - In the middle window of the Query Designer, to the right of `DisplayName0` under the column named Filter, enter `LIKE 'Microsoft Office 2010%'`

    - `LIKE` means we're not sure of the whole name, and the percent is telling SQL where we are no longer sure:

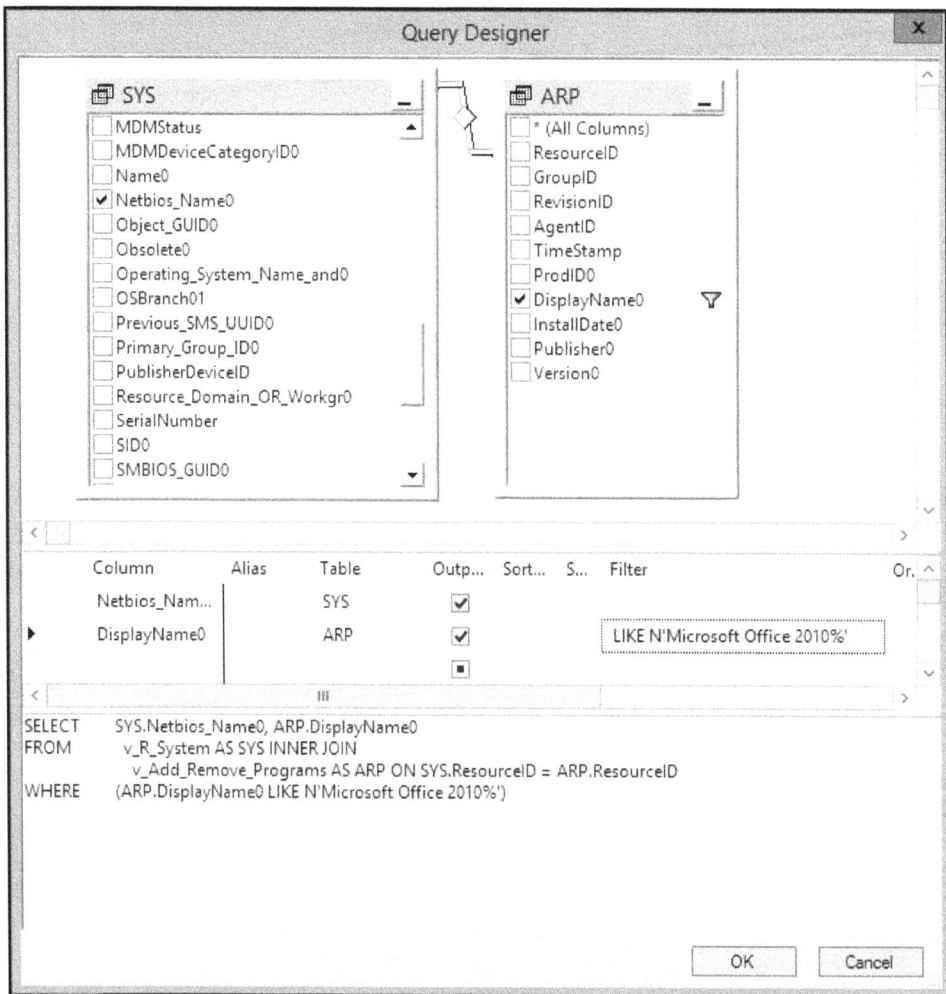

15. Click on **OK**. Click on **Execute** to see the results. If you have no Office 2010, you can try Office 2007 instead. You should see a list of names of machines in the bottom pane with Office 2010. If you show more than one entry per machine, it's because there are probably various entries for each application such as Word, Excel, and Outlook that can be removed by adding a DISTINCT statement:

```
SELECT DISTINCT SYS.Netbios_Name0, ARP.DisplayName0
FROM v_R_System AS SYS INNER JOIN
v_Add_Remove_Programs AS ARP ON SYS.ResourceID = ARP.ResourceID
WHERE (ARP.DisplayName0 LIKE 'Microsoft Office 2010%')
```

16. Make sure your query matches the preceding query and execute it.

> **TIP**
>
> Paste into Notepad when copying SQL queries from other sources. Then copy that text and paste into the SQL editor. It's a good way to force Office smart quotes to straight quotes. SQL hates anything but straight quotes. It's also advisable to disable smart quotes in your Office editor.

You now have a report that could be used for SSRS. Next we'll find all machines that don't have Office 2010 in the Creating subselect queries in T-SQL section.

How it works...

You have just written a query in T-SQL, Microsoft's language to talk to the database. Queries are quite sensitive to case and syntax. Make a typo and you're likely to generate an error.

It's best to practice in a lab if you can. If not possible, you still have to learn this to be an effective CM admin, so just be more careful as you can cause stress to your production server if you make a mistake. Use the stop button if your query is running too long.

There's more...

Now that we've found all machines with Office 2010, let's find all the machines that don't have it. To do that, we will use a subselect query.

Creating subselect queries in T-SQL

Mostly admins tend to write the following code:

```
SELECT SYS.Netbios_Name0, ARP.DisplayName0
FROM v_R_System AS SYS INNER JOIN
v_Add_Remove_Programs AS ARP ON SYS.ResourceID = ARP.ResourceID
WHERE (ARP.DisplayName0 NOT LIKE 'Microsoft Office 2010%')
```

Adding NOT before LIKE might seem like the easy way to find machines without Office, but what that really does is ask SQL to find all machines with any program that isn't Office. A machine with Office 2010 will have many other programs too that are not Office and will still show up in your query. This is where a subselect query comes into play.

A subselect query finds all the machines with Office 2010 first and then asks SQL to show all machines except that bunch. So you're asking SQL to do two queries. But that's what it takes. To get started, we'll refine this query to make things easier on SQL as we're pushing it harder:

```
SELECT SYS.ResourceID
FROM v_R_System AS SYS INNER JOIN
v_Add_Remove_Programs AS ARP ON SYS.ResourceID = ARP.ResourceID
WHERE (ARP.DisplayName0 like 'Microsoft Office 2010 Service Pack 1 (SP1)')
```

We change LIKE to = and give a full name of the product so that SQL can more quickly find what it's looking for. This step isn't necessary, but it helps. You could use OR and add another exact name as well.

This query isn't as pretty, but it will mean the same thing when we exclude anything it finds. So the next step is to tell SQL to return the names of all the machines not in this group:

```
SELECT SYS.Netbios_Name0
FROM v_R_System SYS
WHERE SYS.ResourceID NOT IN (SELECT SYS.ResourceID
FROM v_R_System AS SYS INNER JOIN
v_Add_Remove_Programs AS ARP ON SYS.ResourceID = ARP.ResourceID
WHERE (ARP.DisplayName0 = 'Microsoft Office 2010 Service Pack 1 (SP1)'))
```

In simple words it means, show all NetBIOS names from the system view which are not in the group of machines that have Office 2010 installed.

This query is something that could be placed into an SSRS report. We'll show how to do that soon. And of course, it's pretty clear any application could be used here instead. The concept of the subselect is what's important.

Before going into report creation and editing, we'll show the equivalent in WMI.

Creating a WMI query

A WMI query can be written either in the query node of the console (**Monitoring** | **Queries**) or directly into a query-based collection on the fly. The former can be saved for use in multiple collections, so if you plan to write a query that will be used often, the query node is the best bet.

We're going to recreate the Office 2010 query using the query node so it can be saved for future use and to use later to make a collection of machines based on this query.

From the CM admin console:

1. Navigate to **Monitoring** | **Queries** and select **Create Query** to open the **Create Query** Wizard.
2. For **Name**, enter `All Office 2010 SP1 Systems`.
3. Click on **Edit Query Statement** and then select the **Criteria** tab. Click on the yellow starburst to open the **Criterion Properties** window. This window is roughly the WMI equivalent of the SQL Query Designer.
4. Click on **Select** and for the **Attribute** class, select **Add/Remove Programs**.
5. For **Attribute**, select **Display Name**. Click on **OK**.
6. For **Value**, enter `Microsoft Office 2010 Service Pack 1 (SP1)`. Click on **OK** and then on **Next** as needed to exit the wizard.

This query can be run from here, but we are going to use it now to make a collection.

Creating a WMI-based query collection

Using our new Office 2010 query, we create a query-based collection. From the CM admin console:

1. Navigate to **Assets and Compliance | Device Collections**. If you have a folder created that you would like to create this collection in use that. If not, right-click on **Device Collections**, navigate **Folder | Create Folder** and create a folder named **Test**.

2. Right-click on the **Test** folder or your folder of choice and select **Create Device Collection** to open the **Create Device Collection** Wizard.

3. For **Name**, enter `All Office 2010 Systems`.

4. Click on **Browse** to select **All Desktop and Server Clients**. Click on **OK** and then on **Next**.

5. Click on **Add Rule** and select **Query Rule**.

6. For **Name** enter `Office 2010`.

7. Click on **Import Query Statement** and select **All Office 2010 Systems**. Click on **OK**.

8. Click on **OK** and then on **Next** as needed to exit the wizard.

To view the members of this collection, simply click it in the console and select **Show Members** from the ribbon. If you see an hourglass on the collection, CM is still working on the query. Be patient, especially on a CAS. Next, we'll make a collection of all systems which do not have Office 2010 installed.

Creating subselect queries in WMI

From the CM admin console:

1. Right-click on your test folder and select **Create Device Collection** to open the **Create Device Collection** Wizard.

2. For **Name**, enter `All non-Office 2010 Systems`.

3. Click on **Browse** to select All Desktop and Server Clients. Click on **OK** and then on **Next**.

4. Click on **Add Rule** and select **Query Rule**.

5. For **Name** enter `No Office 2010`. Click on **Edit Query Statement** and then click on the **Criteria** tab. Click on the yellow starburst to open the **Criterion Properties** window.

6. Click on **Select** and this time, select **SubSelected** values for the **Criterion Type**.

7. Click on **Select** and select **System Resource** for the Attribute Class and
   `ResourceID` for the Attribute. Click on **OK**.

8. Select `not in` for Operator.

9. Click on **Browse** and select **All Office 2010 Systems**. Edit the text in the subselect
   box to replace the asterisk with `SMS_R_SYSTEM.ResourceID`. The subselect
   query will look like this:

```
SELECT *
FROM    SMS_R_System
WHERE   SMS_R_System.ResourceId NOT IN (SELECT
SMS_R_SYTEM.ResourceID
FROM    SMS_R_System
INNER JOIN SMS_G_System_ADD_REMOVE_PROGRAMS
ON SMS_G_System_ADD_REMOVE_PROGRAMS.ResourceId =
SMS_R_System.ResourceId
WHERE   SMS_G_System_ADD_REMOVE_PROGRAMS.DisplayName =
"Microsoft Office
2010 Service Pack 1 (SP1)")
```

10. Click on **OK** and then on **Next** as needed to exit the wizard.

A key takeaway here is that the query for the `NOT IN` section targets `ResourceID` only.

That was a little more work than you should have to do. One great thing about CM is that
we can use include and exclude as collection rules. So in this case, you could also have
simply added an exclude rule for All Office 2010 Systems and an include rule for All
Desktop and Server Clients and you would have the same results. Much faster to set up!

See also

- SQL intro on TechNet: `http://msdn.microsoft.com/en-us/library/bb
  264565(v=sql.90).aspx`

Editing and creating reports

With a functional RSP and the knowledge of how to make some basic queries, you should
now be prepared to create new reports or edit existing reports. This can be done straight
from the CM admin console, straight from your RSP, or using Microsoft SQL Management
Studio.

Getting ready

To upgrade your admin console to leverage Report Builder 3.0, follow the steps listed here at `http://technet.microsoft.com/en-us/library/gg712698.aspx`. The steps that follow are for the more common version-Report Builder 3.0. We're going to start by editing one of the built-in reports.

Additionally, it's rather common to edit reports from workstations and servers other than the SRS server itself. If that's true for you, you'll need to export the SQL certificate off the SRS server and import into your local Trusted People store. The export/import process is well explained in the document, To transfer a copy of self-signed certificate from the site server to another computer, at
`http://technet.microsoft.com/en-us/library/gg712698.aspx`.

How to do it…

First of all, it is best practice to not edit a built-in report directly. It's best to save a copy (and optionally hide the original) and then edit the copy to upload. The main reason for this is in case you make a mistake and need to revert (or perhaps you were not aware others were looking at the original).

Now say someone complains virtual machines are cluttering the report that shows memory changing on systems. The report called Computers, where physical memory has changed compares new inventory against old inventory for memory. As Hyper-V systems may be changing memory used often, you need to hide them from this report.

We first start by saving a copy of the existing report.

1. From a web browser, navigate to `http://mysrsserver/Reports` where `mysrsserver` is the name of your SSRS server.
2. Use the search box to find the report Computers where physical memory has changed.
3. Use the drop-down arrow to the right of the report to select Download. Save the report to your documents' folder. (Feel free to start an organized file/folder system for these).
4. Return to the home page of Report Manager by clicking on the Home link in the upper-right corner.
5. Click on **Report Builder** to open Report Builder 3.0.
6. Go to **Open** | **My Documents**, select the report you just saved and click on **Open**.
7. Expand **Data Sources** and delete the autogenerated dataset.

8. Right-click on **Data Sources** and click on **Add Data Source**. Click on **Browse**. Double-click on `ConfigMgr_<SITE>` (or whatever you've named your root folder to). Select `{5C6358F2-4BB6-4a1b-A16E-8D96795D8602}`.

9. Click on **Test Connection** to make sure you can now query the database. Click on **OK**.

10. Expand **Datasets** in the left pane, right-click on **DataSet0**, and select **Dataset Properties**, as shown in the following screenshot:

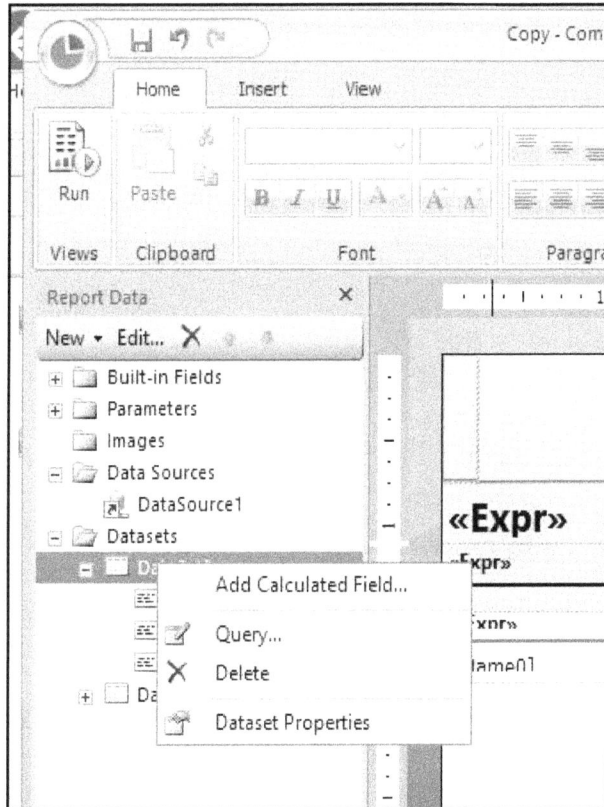

11. Copy all the text from Query (which is the SQL query we need to change):

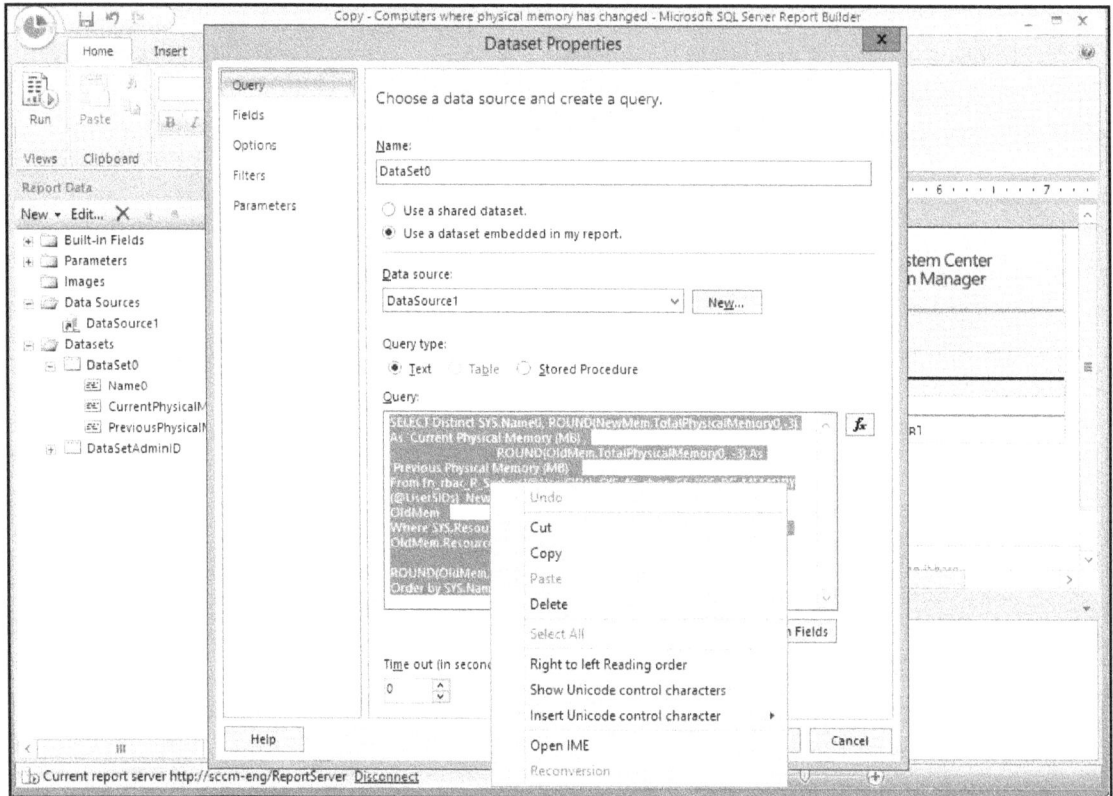

12. Open SSMS and connect to your primary or CAS.
13. Right-click on your CM database and select **New Query**.
14. Paste the query you copied from **Report Builder** into the right-side pane.
15. Highlight the query, right-click and select **Design Query** in **Editor**.
16. In the SYS table, check the Is_Virtual_Machine0 checkbox. This filters out any virtual machines from the report.
17. In the middle pane, enter 0 under **Is_Virtual_Machine0\Filter**.
18. In the SYS table, uncheck the Is_Virtual_Machine0 checkbox. Click on **OK**.
19. Copy this new query back over the old text in the query window of Report Builder's Dataset Properties. Click on **OK**.

20. If prompted for credentials, select **Use the current Windows** user and click on **OK**.
21. Save this report (which also serves as a backup) and exit from Report Builder.
22. Return to Report Manager and click on **ConfigMgr_<SITE>**. Click on **Hardware – Memory** and then click on **Upload File**.

> We pick this folder location to stay organized, but you can start creating new folders and organize how you see fit.

23. Click on **Browse** to locate the saved file that will be uploaded to SSRS. Give this report a new name such as Non VMs where memory has changed and click on **OK**.
24. Verify the new report is using the default data source by clicking on the drop-down arrow next to the report and choosing Manage. Select Data Sources. If the shared data source is {5C6358F2-4BB6-4a1b-A16E-8D96795D8602}, browse to it and select it. Click on **Apply**.

Test the report by clicking on it to run it.

How it works...

Clicking on the Report Builder button from Report Manager actually runs a light ClickOnce version of Report Builder. You can also download a local MSI-based version.

Report Builder is capable of adding graphs, changing the layout, and saving reports as backups should you have to revert for any reason.

There's more...

Reports can be edited directly from Report Manager using Report Builder. But new reports can also be created and uploaded to your RSP. We'll show how next.

Creating a new report with Report Builder 3.0

Using the SQL queries we made earlier for machines without office, we'll use Report Builder to add them to the RSP. (Two queries can go into one report as you will soon see.) Follow these steps to get started:

1. From a web browser, navigate to `http://mysrsserver/Reports` where `mysrsserver` is the name of your SSRS server.

2. Double-click on**ConfigMgr_<SITE>** and then **Software – Companies and Products**. This is where it will make sense to upload our new report so it's a good starting point.

3. Click on **Report Builder**. The left-side pane already has New Report highlighted so in the right pane choose **Table** or **Matrix Wizard**.

4. Click on **Next** to create a dataset.

5. Click on **Browse**, double-click on **ConfigMgr_<SITE>** (or whatever you've named your root folder to). Select `{5C6358F2-4BB6-4a1b-A16E-8D96795D8602}`. Optionally, click on **Test Connection**. Click on **Next**.

6. At the prompt, you can select **Use the current Windows user** and then click on **OK**.

7. In the New Table or Matrix window, click on **Edit as Text**.

8. Paste the first SQL query we wrote:

   ```
   SELECT DISTINCT SYS.Netbios_Name0, ARP.DisplayName0
   FROM v_R_System AS SYS INNER JOIN
   v_Add_Remove_Programs AS ARP ON SYS.ResourceID = ARP.ResourceID
   WHERE (ARP.DisplayName0 LIKE 'Microsoft Office 2010%')
   ```

9. Because we don't need to show the name Office 2010 in a report about Office 2010, remove the comma after **Netbios_Name0** and remove `ARP.DisplayName0` by highlighting that text and hitting *Delete*.

10. Optionally, click on the exclamation mark to test results.

11. Click on Next. Drag `Netbios_Name0` to the Values pane. Click on **Next**, **Next**, **Finish**.

12. Expand the shown box for room for long computer names.

13. Change the title text to `All Systems with Office 2010`.

14. Change Netbios Name0 over the blue to Computer Name.

15. Click on **Run** to test, and then click on **Design** to return to the editor.

16. Now we add the second query of all machines without Office 2010.

17. Select the **Insert** tab the click on Text Box.

18. Under `Netbios_Name0` draw a textbox that matches the width of the top textbox. Set the font to Verdana 20 (same as the top text box) and enter All Systems without Office 2010.

19. Right-click on Datasets and select **Add Dataset**. Select Use a dataset embedded in my report. For Data Source, use the drop-down box to select the available dataset.

20. Paste the second SQL query we wrote in the query pane:

```
SELECT SYS.Netbios_Name0
FROM v_R_System SYS
WHERE SYS.ResourceID NOT IN (SELECT SYS.ResourceID
FROM v_R_System AS SYS INNER JOIN
v_Add_Remove_Programs AS ARP ON SYS.ResourceID = ARP.ResourceID
WHERE (ARP.DisplayName0 = 'Microsoft Office 2010 Service Pack 1
(SP1)'))
```

21. Click on **OK**. Select the **Insert** tab and click on **Table** and select **Table Wizard**.

22. Select `DataSet2` in the New Table or `Matrix` window. Click on **Next**.

23. Drag `Netbios_Name0` to the `Values` pane. Click on Next. In the next window, again click on **Next** and then on **Finish**.

24. Move the newly create box below the second title and expand its width to match the top table's width.

25. Change `Netbios_Name0` in this second table to `Computer Name`.

26. Click on **Run** to test and then click on **Design** to return to the editor.

This report could be uploaded right now to the RSP, but let's add some bling first.

Incorporating readability aids in your report

To incorporate readability aids in your report, follow these steps:

1. Under Computer Name at the top, click on `Netbios_Name0`.

2. Right-click on the box to the left of `Netbios_Name0` and select **Row Visibility**.

3. Click on the **Hide** radio button. Check the bottom checkbox and select **Textbox2**. Click on **OK**.

4. Right-click on the box to the left of **Netbios_Name0** and select **Tablix Properties**.

5. In the **Tablix Properties** window, click on **Sorting** in the left-side pane and **Add** in the right pane. For Sort by, select [Netbios_Name0]. Click on OK.
6. Under Computer Name at bottom, click on Netbios_Name0.
7. Right-click on the box to the left of Netbios_Name0 and select **Row Visibility**.
8. Click on the **Hide** radio button. Check the bottom checkbox and select Textbox6. Click on **OK**.
9. Right-click on the box to the left of Netbios_Name0 and select **Tablix Properties**.
10. In the **Tablix Properties** window, click on **Sorting** in the left pane and **Add** in the right pane. For Sort by, select [Netbios_Name0]. Click on **OK**.
11. Click on **Run** to test then **Design** to return to the editor.
12. Select the **Insert** tab and click on **Header** and select **Add Header**.
13. Click on **Text Box** and in the new header space of the report drag out a box to a size of your choice. Enter **My Company** in the box.
14. Click on **Run** to test the **Design** to return to the editor.

Notice the machine names are now hidden by default until expanded. And they are sorted by name. Now the report is ready to be uploaded to the RSP. Click on the System Center logo in the upper-left corner of Report Builder and save this report to your documents folder as Office 2010 Systems.

Uploading reports to the RSP

Return to Report Builder. We left off on the Software – Companies and Products page. If not there, return to that space now as this is where a software report like we just made belongs.

Click on **Upload File**. Click on **Browse** to browse to your documents folder and select **Office 2010 Systems**. Click on **Open** and then click on **OK**.

Test your new report by clicking on Office 2010 Systems.

See also

- TechNet CM Reporting:
  `http://technet.microsoft.com/en-us/library/gg699377.aspx`
- TechNet Report Builder: `http://technet.microsoft.com/en-us/library/dd 220460.aspx`
- A document on To transfer a copy of self-signed certificate from the site server to another computer: `http://technet.microsoft.com/en-us/library/gg712698. aspx`

Index

www.ingramcontent.com/pod-product-compliance
Lightning Source LLC
Chambersburg PA
CBHW080909220326
41598CB00034B/5521